Gateway

2nd Edition

Student's Book

David Spencer

B1+

macmillan
education

Contents

Listening	Speaking	Writing	✓ Exam success
▶ **Personality test** What is self-esteem? Asking for and giving personal information	▶ **Asking for and giving personal information** Talking about talents Describing people	▶ **An informal email describing people** A positive-thinking list	Reading: True/false activities Listening: Matching the speaker and information
▶ **Travelling around the world** Responsible tourism Asking for information	▶ **Asking for information** Talking about travel Discussing life in the past	▶ **A blog post** A presentation about responsible tourism	Speaking: Exchanging information Writing: Checking your work
▶ **A podcast** Explaining statistics Describing photos – 1	▶ **Describing photos – 1** Talking about megacities Giving explanations	▶ **An informal email describing a place** Statistics for a city	Reading: Missing sentence activities Use of English: Multiple-choice cloze activities
▶ **Food in the future** Teen chef competition Negotiating	▶ **Negotiating** World food problems Future predictions	▶ **Replying to informal invitations** A recipe	Speaking: Negotiating Writing: Transactional tasks
▶ **Extracurricular activities** How to use web sources A presentation	▶ **A presentation** Talking about school projects Asking about conditions	▶ **A formal letter of application** An information text	Speaking: Giving a presentation Writing: Thinking about the reader

1 Personal best

Vocabulary

Appearance

1 Work with a partner. Put these words in the correct column.

attractive • bald • blonde • curly • cute • dark
fair • good-looking • long • medium-height
medium-length • overweight • pretty • short
spiky • straight • strong • tall • thin • wavy
well-built

Build	Height	Hair	General
thin	short	short	attractive

2 ▶ 01 **Listen, check and repeat.**

3 SPEAKING **Work with a partner. Take it in turns to describe the people in the photos.**

Personality

4 Match the personality adjectives with their opposites.

1	serious	a	untidy
2	lazy	b	unfriendly
3	tidy	c	talkative
4	quiet	d	cheerful, funny
5	patient	e	hard-working
6	friendly	f	impatient
7	calm	g	nervous

5 Match these personality adjectives with their definitions.

arrogant • bossy • clever • confident • nice
reliable • selfish • shy

1 When people can depend on you or count on you to do something. ....

2 When you only think about yourself and you don't care about other people. ....

3 Good, friendly, kind. ....

4 Good at learning and understanding things.
....

5 When you are not very confident or comfortable with other people. ....

6 When you think you are better or more important than other people. ....

7 When you are always telling other people what to do. ....

8 When you believe in your own abilities and don't feel nervous or frightened. ....

6 LISTENING ▶ 02 **Listen to four teenagers talking about themselves. What adjective of personality best describes each person?**

1 Rose ....   3 Jessica ....

2 William ....   4 Brandon ....

7a SPEAKING **Choose five adjectives of personality from 4 and 5 which describe you. Tell your partner your adjectives and say why you chose them.**

> *I'm quite shy because I feel a bit nervous when I meet new people.*

7b Now tell the class about your partner.

1 Work with a partner. Look at the photos in the article and describe what you can see. Why do you think these two people are so special?

2 READING Read the article and check your ideas in **1**.

SPECIAL PEOPLE!

The human mind and body are capable of amazing things, especially when you train them hard. Meet two people who, thanks to their natural talent and to their effort, seem almost superhuman!

Tom Sietas

When people first see Tom Sietas, they don't usually notice anything special. He's not very tall, and he's not particularly
5 well-built. But those factors help Tom to do something incredible. Tom has the world record for 'static apnea'. In other words, Tom can hold his breath
10 underwater, without moving, for just over 22 minutes! He only discovered his ability by accident when he went diving in Jamaica at the age of 18.
15 Because he isn't very big it means that he doesn't need to get a lot of oxygen to his muscles. And it helps that his lungs are 20% larger than is usual for his height and build. But it isn't only a question of his body. His personality plays a big part in his success, too. Thought processes
20 use a lot of oxygen. So it's important that Tom is calm and patient. Luckily, he rarely gets nervous in the water. In fact, Tom is so calm that he occasionally falls asleep underwater! Obviously he always trains very carefully to prepare for a new record because what he does is highly
25 dangerous. We're waiting this year to see what he does next. Are we expecting another record attempt? Definitely!

Judit Polgár

'People are always saying that geniuses are born, not made. I want to prove that it is not true!' This was the obsession of a Hungarian teacher called László Polgár. To prove that he could
30 make someone a genius, he took his three daughters out of school and started to teach them a specialist subject – chess. One of the three, Judit, is now the greatest female chess player of all time and the only woman so far to be in the world top 10! László himself wasn't a great chess player, but he was a
35 clever teacher. At first, Judit's sisters were better than her, but she gradually became more serious about playing. At first, she played just ten minutes a day. When she was 12, it had increased to ten hours. At 15 she was the youngest grandmaster ever. To win at chess, you need to be confident, hard-working
40 and a little bit selfish. Judit's wins include victories against 10 male world champions, including Kasparov and Karpov. Thanks to Judit, little by little,
45 people are starting to pay more attention to women chess players. She now has children of her own but she isn't teaching them in the same way as her
50 father. Her children don't play chess for hours every day. They only play for fun.

✔ **EXAM SUCCESS**

You are going to do a True/False reading exercise. What do you think is a good procedure for doing this type of exercise?

➤ EXAM SUCCESS page 144

3 Read the text again. Are the statements True (T) or False (F)? Write the number(s) of the line(s) where you found the answer.

1 For what Tom does, it is important to be big and strong. T / F ....

2 Tom can swim underwater for over twenty minutes without breathing. T / F ....

3 Tom always knew about his natural talent for staying underwater. T / F ....

4 Mental qualities are also important to be good at static apnea. T / F ....

5 László Polgár had a theory and he proved that it was true. T / F ....

6 Judit's chess ability was easy to see right from the beginning. T / F ....

7 From the start, she played for hours and hours every day. T / F ....

8 After her experience, Judit doesn't want to teach her children chess. T / F ....

4 ⚙ CRITICAL THINKING

Think! Then compare ideas with your class.

■ 'Geniuses are born, not made.' Does the writer of the text appear to agree with this statement? Why/Why not? Do you agree with it?

5 What do the underlined words in the text mean? Guess and then check in your dictionary.

6 SPEAKING **What about _you_?**

1 How good are you at water sports and/or chess?

2 What special talents and abilities do you have, or would you like to have?

Grammar in context

Present simple and present continuous

1a Read the sentences (a–g) and match them with the rules (1–7).

a Little by little, people are starting to pay more attention.

b Thought processes use a lot of oxygen.

c Her children don't play chess for hours every day.

d People are always saying that geniuses are born, not made.

e I'm not sure what she's doing right now.

f Athletes train hard.

g This year we're waiting to see what he does next.

We use the present simple for

1 routines and habits. ....

2 things that are always or generally true. ....

3 scientific facts. ....

We use the present continuous for

4 actions that are happening now or near the moment of speaking. ....

5 actions that are temporary or not a normal routine. ....

6 actions that happen very often and annoy the speaker. ....

7 changing situations. ....

1b Look at the article on page 7. Find a negative sentence and a question in the present continuous.

GRAMMAR REFERENCE ➤ PAGE 16

2 Choose the correct alternative.

1 Right now my brother *plays/is playing* chess.

2 I *play/am playing* tennis every Friday.

3 This new online game *becomes/is becoming* really successful.

4 You *need/are needing* money to buy things.

5 My cousin *studies/is studying* in the US for a month.

6 Water *changes/is changing* into ice at 0°C.

7 Police officers *wear/are wearing* uniforms.

Adverbs of frequency

3 Read the sentences. The words in blue are all adverbs of frequency. Choose the correct alternative to complete the rules in 1–4.

a They don't **usually** notice anything special about him.

b He **occasionally** falls asleep underwater.

c She's **always** taking our things without asking.

d Tom **always** trains hard.

e They **never** play competitively.

f He's **rarely** nervous.

g She **often** beats the best players.

h She **sometimes** plays for fun.

1 Adverbs of frequency usually go *after/before* the verb **to be**.

2 Adverbs of frequency usually go *after/before* main verbs.

3 Adverbs of frequency usually go with the *present continuous/present simple.*

4 The adverb of frequency *always/sometimes* goes with the *present continuous/present simple* to talk about frequent actions that annoy the person who is speaking.

GRAMMAR REFERENCE ➤ PAGE 16

4 Complete the text with the present simple or continuous forms of the verbs given and the adverbs.

I'm really angry with my brother at the moment because he (a) .... (always use) the computer when I want to use it. He (b) .... (not usually play) computer games, but he (c) .... (become) more and more interested in online games at the moment. Right now he (d) .... (make) a new avatar for his favourite game. It's funny because my brother (e) .... (not usually wear) anything apart from jeans and T-shirts, but his avatar (f) .... (have got) really spectacular clothes. People (g) .... (often say) that boys (h) .... (play) more computer games than girls, but I think that (i) .... (change). The only reason that I (j) .... (not often play) is because when it's my turn to use the computer I (k) .... (always do) my homework on it first. Oh, good! My brother (l) .... (finish) now. It's 5 pm and he (m) .... (usually play) football with his friends at this time. My turn to use the computer at last!

5a Write two true sentences, one in the present simple and one in the present continuous, using the expressions below. Write negative sentences if necessary.

> do homework • eat fast food
> go to school • play computer games
> read • send text messages
> study English • use a tablet • watch TV
> wear jeans

My mum never wears jeans. I'm not wearing jeans at the moment because we can't wear them at our school.

5b Read your sentences to your partner. How many of your sentences are the same?

6 **SPEAKING** Interview your partner using these questions.

1 What are the first two things you do when you get to school?
2 What are the first two things you do when you get home after school?
3 What are people in your class doing right now?
4 In what ways are you, or people in your family, changing?
5 What do you usually do at the weekend?
6 What are members of your family doing now?
7 How do you usually spend your summer holidays?
8 Is anybody always doing things that annoy you? Who and what?

> *What are the first two things you do when you get to school in the morning?*

> *I take my coat off and I say hello to my friends.*

7 Write at least three more questions like the ones in 6. Use them to continue interviewing your partner.

> *What subjects are you studying this year?*

> *What sports do you do after school?*

Synonyms and partial synonyms

1 Look at these words. Do they have similar meanings? If there is a difference between the words, what is the difference?

> attractive • beautiful • cute • good-looking
> handsome • pretty

2 Match these words with their synonyms or partial synonyms. Some words can have more than one.

> bright • cheerful • clever • difficult • elderly
> friendly • glad • happy • hard • intelligent • old
> outgoing • slim • sociable • thin

bright – clever – intelligent

3a **PRONUNCIATION** Work with a partner. Say the words in 1 and 2 aloud. Which words have three syllables?

3b ▶ 03 Listen and check your answers. Write each word in the correct column.

Ooo (e.g. *talkative*)	oOo (e.g. *impatient*)

3c Practise saying the words with the correct stress.

4 Choose the best alternative. If there is no difference, choose both.

1 Don't call your grandmother *old/elderly*! It's more polite to call her *old/elderly*.
2 That new actor is really *attractive/good-looking*.
3 My cousin is always smiling. She's a really *glad/cheerful* type of person.
4 Your cat needs to eat more. It looks a bit *slim/thin* to me.
5 This question is really *hard/difficult*.
6 I'm *clever/bright* enough to do this exercise!

5 Prepare a description of a famous person. You can use words from 1 and 2 and from page 6.

6 **SPEAKING** Work with a partner. Describe the person you chose in 5. Can your partner guess who it is?

> *He's a politician. He's got short, dark hair. He's very intelligent. He's not very old. I think he's tall and slim.*

> *Is it Barack Obama?*

> *Yes, it is.*

Building your confidence

LIFE SKILLS OBJECTIVES	KEY CONCEPTS
▪ To think about the importance of self-esteem. ▪ To learn about different ways to build your confidence. ▪ To think positively about yourself.	**self-esteem [n]:** *My self-esteem is quite high because I have a good opinion of myself.* **objective/goal [n]:** *My objective/goal is to pass all my exams with a high mark this year.* **(un)realistic [adj]:** *It's unrealistic to think that anybody is perfect.* **proud (of) [adj]:** *I was very proud of my school results last year.* **achievement [n]:** *Getting 10 out of 10 in every subject is a great achievement.*

1a Look at the glass of orange juice. Is it half empty or half full?

1b Work with a partner. Compare your answers in 1a.

1c In your opinion, do you generally think positively or not? Try to give examples to justify your answer.

2 `READING` **Read the article below. Does it say that these things are good (✓) or bad (✗)?**

1 Liking yourself
2 Making mistakes
3 Celebrating when you do things well
4 Trying to be perfect
5 Making slow progress

3a Choose the three pieces of advice that you think are the best and decide why.

3b `SPEAKING` **Work with a partner. Compare and justify your answers in 3a. Do you have similar opinions?**

3c Talk about which of the ideas in the text you already do.

WHAT IS SELF-ESTEEM?

Self-esteem means you really like yourself, both inside and out. It's important because positive self-esteem gives you the courage to be confident, to be yourself, and not just do what others do, or tell you to do. Believing in yourself means you will have the freedom to be the person that you want to be and make decisions that are right for you.

How can you improve your self-esteem?

1 Think positively. Think about all the great things about being you. Concentrate on how you feel when you pass an exam at school, or make your friends laugh. Focus on the positive aspects and see the glass as half full, not half empty.

2 Remember that perfect doesn't exist. Everyone has things they would like to improve, even people who seem 'perfect'. The most important things to focus on are what you're good at and what you enjoy … and go for it!

3 Try new things. Experiment with different activities, for example sports, crafts, or music that will help you to discover your talents.

4 Take exercise. It helps to reduce stress and to be healthier and happier.

5 Have realistic goals. If there's something about yourself that you want to improve, go step by step and do it gradually. Be patient. And keep thinking of the progress that you're making, even if it's small.

6 Celebrate your achievements. Be proud of the things that you are good at and allow family and friends to celebrate the things you are good at, too.

7 Relax. Enjoy spending time with the people you care about and doing things that make you feel good.

8 Be confident in your own opinions, ideas and feelings. Don't be afraid to express them. Your friends may put pressure on you to agree with their ideas, but you can make your own decisions.

9 Make mistakes. Everyone makes mistakes. You might feel bad if you miss a goal or get an answer wrong, but making mistakes is part of being human. The good news is that mistakes are a valuable part of learning.

10 Make a contribution. Help a classmate who is having trouble. Give your parents a hand at home. Making a difference to others is great for your self-esteem.

4 Work with a partner. Use the ideas in the text in 2 to help you give advice to these people.

1

I feel bad because I missed a penalty in my last football match.

2

I'm nervous because it's my turn to give a presentation in class next week.

3

My friends want me to go ice-skating next week. I'm not sure about going with them because I've never skated before.

4

I love taking photos and I'm quite good at it. There's a photography competition at school, but I don't think it's worth entering because other people are probably better than me.

5a LISTENING ▶ 04 Watch or listen to four teenagers talking about something they are good at. Write down what each speaker is good at.

Callum: ....

Naomi: ....

Rachel: ....

Toby: ....

5b ▶ 04 Watch or listen again. Are these sentences True (T) or False (F)? Correct the false sentences.

1 Callum prefers simple, easy games. **T / F**

2 He thinks you need to be clever to do what he does. **T / F**

3 Naomi thinks she is good at listening because of her personal characteristics. **T / F**

4 She listens and doesn't tell anyone what she hears. **T / F**

5 Rachel only realised her skill when she was older. **T / F**

6 She doesn't usually show her work to other people. **T / F**

7 Toby's friends play football. **T / F**

8 His dad coaches him and helps him to improve. **T / F**

6 SPEAKING Discuss with a partner. Which person do you think is the most confident? And the least? Why?

LIFE TASK

Do this positive-thinking activity individually:

1a *Write down a list of your strong points. Think about:*

- *things that you are good at*
- *things you have achieved*
- *any other abilities, talents or skills you have*
- *things you do or have done for other people*
- *your personality*

1b *Now exchange lists with your partner. What could you add to the list that your partner hasn't mentioned?*

2 *Keep your list with you and look at it on days when you have a problem or when you are nervous about something like an exam!*

1 Copy this picture onto a piece of paper. You have three minutes to draw something on it.

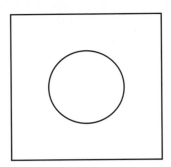

2 LISTENING ▶ 05 The activity in 1 is from a psychology magazine. The magazine gives a personality analysis for the most common things that people draw. Listen to five people explaining if they agree with the magazine's analysis. What did each one draw?

Speaker 1 ....

Speaker 2 ....

Speaker 3 ....

Speaker 4 ....

Speaker 5 ....

✓ EXAM SUCCESS

In the next task you match the speakers with the correct information. What should you do <u>before</u> you do the task?

➤ EXAM SUCCESS page 144

3 ▶ 05 Listen again and identify the speaker.

Which speaker …

		1	2	3	4	5
a	likes drawing?					
b	thinks the analysis of their personality is totally wrong?					
c	spends a long time on their favourite hobby?					
d	didn't draw what they immediately thought of?					
e	doesn't want a parent to see their picture?					
f	thinks they look attractive?					
g	understands the analysis of their personality, but doesn't agree with it?					
h	got the idea for their picture thanks to a place?					

4 What about *you*?

Look at your drawing in 1.
1 Is it one of the things in 2? Do you agree with the personality analysis in the magazine?
2 If you drew something else, what do you think the personality analysis could be?

State and action verbs

1a Read these sentences. Do the verbs in blue describe states and situations or do they describe actions?

1 I **have** a big garden.
2 I **love** warm weather.
3 I **like** sitting out there.
4 My picture **looks** like me.
5 The flowers **smell** good.
6 I **don't believe** that's true.
7 I **know** why I drew a flower.
8 I **think** I'm the opposite.

1b Read the sentences again. Are they in the present simple or present continuous? Why?

1c Put the verbs from 1a in the correct lists.

1 verbs of feeling and liking: ....,
.........................., hate, want, prefer, need

2 verbs of thinking: ....,
.........................., ...,
remember, mean

3 verbs of the senses: ....,
.........................., hear, see, taste, sound, feel,
seem

4 verbs of possession: ...., own,
belong

GRAMMAR REFERENCE ➤ PAGE 16

2 Decide if each verb describes a state or an action. Then choose the correct alternative.

1 I *look/am looking* for my ball. *Do you know/Are you knowing* where it is?
2 Isn't he attractive? He *looks/is looking* like a film star.
3 My sister *has got/is having* a new pet.
4 Jack can't speak to you at the moment. He *has/is having* a shower.
5 *Do you know/Are you knowing* the answer now?
6 I *don't understand/am not understanding* a word you're saying.
7 OK, OK, don't get angry. I *believe/am believing* you.
8 I *don't like/am not liking* this film. I *want/am wanting* to leave now.

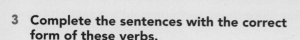
3 Complete the sentences with the correct form of these verbs.

> feel • look • seem • smell • sound • taste

1 I love this song. I think it .... great.

2 Mmmm! What are you cooking? It .... delicious. I want to try it.

3 What's the matter? You don't .... very cheerful today.

4 Emma .... like her sister. Their personalities are very different but their appearance is almost identical.

5 There's too much sugar in this coffee. It .... too sweet.

6 Your hand is cold. It .... like ice!

4a Write sentences about the items in the photos. Use one of the verbs and at least one of the adjectives in each sentence.

Verbs:

> feel • look • smell • sound • taste

Adjectives:

> cold • colourful • delicious • frightening
> hard • horrible • loud • lovely • soft
> warm • wet

4b SPEAKING Work with a partner. Read your sentences but don't give the name of the items you are describing. Can your partner identify them?

> I think it feels cold and wet, but I'm not sure. It looks frightening.

> Is it a snake?

> Yes, it is!

5 Complete the dialogue with the present simple or present continuous form of the verbs given.

Ryan: Hi, Molly. How are you? You (a) .... (sound) really happy.

Molly: I am. I (b) .... (have) a great time.

Ryan: Where are you?

Molly: I (c) .... (stay) at my cousin Lily's house.

Ryan: Lily? Ah, yes. Now I (d) .... (remember). She's the one who (e) .... (have) a house near the coast.

Molly: That's right. Well, in fact, the house (f) .... (belong) to a good friend of my cousin. She always (g) .... (let) her stay when she (h) .... (want).

Ryan: And what exactly (i) .... you .... (do) now?

Molly: I (j) .... (get) the table ready for dinner. Lily (k) .... (cook) really well. She (l) .... (make) something special for tonight. It (m) .... (smell) great.

Ryan: Stop! You (n) .... (make) me hungry. Anyway, I (o) .... (need) to go now. Somebody (p) .... (call) me. I'll phone again soon.

Molly: OK.

6 SPEAKING Complete these sentences about yourself and then predict your partner's answers. Compare predictions. How well do you know your partner?

You

1 I think .... sounds great.

2 I think .... looks really attractive.

3 I usually feel .... on Monday morning.

4 I think coffee tastes ....

5 I don't need .... to be happy.

6 I believe that ....

7 At the weekend, I like ....

Your partner

1 My partner thinks .... sounds great.

2 My partner thinks .... looks really attractive.

3 My partner usually feels .... on Monday morning.

4 My partner thinks coffee tastes ....

5 My partner doesn't need .... to be happy.

6 My partner believes that ....

7 At the weekend, my partner likes ....

Developing speaking

Asking for and giving personal information

1 `LISTENING` ▶ **06 Listen to a conversation between two teenagers called Megan and Ellie on the first day of school. What are each person's hobbies?**

Megan: ....

Ellie: ....

2 ▶ **06 Complete the dialogue. Listen again if necessary.**

Megan: Hi. You're Lucy's cousin, aren't you?

Ellie: Yes, that's right. My name's Ellie.

Megan: I'm Megan. This is your **(a)** .... year at this school, isn't it?

Ellie: That's right.

Megan: Hey, you don't play **(b)** ...., do you? We need new players for the team.

Ellie: I play a little, but I'm not mad about basketball.

Megan: Do you play any other sports?

Ellie: Yes, I really enjoy **(c)** ....

Megan: Great! What are your other hobbies?

Ellie: I love music.

Megan: Really? What kind of music?

Ellie: I like all sorts, but my favourite is **(d)** ....

Megan: Now I remember! You can play the **(e)** ...., can't you? Lucy told me once.

Ellie: Yeah, I'm in a band. We're really **(f)** ....

Megan: Do you know Josh, Josh Smith? He plays in a band, too. Come on. Let me introduce you to him …

3 `SPEAKING` **Work with a partner. Practise the completed dialogue in 2.**

4 **Look at the Speaking bank. We use question tags when we want somebody to confirm something. Choose the correct alternative.**

1 We use *nouns/subject pronouns* at the end of question tags.

2 We use *auxiliary verbs and 'to be'/main verbs* in question tags.

3 Usually the question tag in an affirmative sentence is *affirmative/negative* and the question tag in a negative sentence is *affirmative/negative*.

> 💬 **SPEAKING BANK**
>
> **Question tags**
> - You're Lucy's cousin, **aren't you**?
> - This is your first year at this school, **isn't it**?
> - You like rock music, **don't you**?
> - You don't play basketball, **do you**?
> - You can play an instrument, **can't you**?

5 **Complete these sentences with question tags.**

1 You've got a sister, ... ?

2 You can't play the piano, ... ?

3 That girl sings really well, ... ?

4 She's your best friend, ... ?

5 That boy isn't very tall, ... ?

6 Her dad doesn't like listening to that music, ... ?

7 Jamie and Becky can swim fast, ... ?

6 `SPEAKING` **Work with a partner. Read out the first part of the sentences. Your partner says the question tag.**

Student A: Turn to page 147.
Student B: Turn to page 148.

> She's American …

> … isn't she?

PRACTICE MAKES PERFECT

7a `SPEAKING` **Write down five things you think you know about your partner's free-time habits.**

7b **Ask your partner about their free-time habits. Use question tags for confirmation and to keep the dialogue going.**

> You like doing judo in your free time, don't you?

> Yes, I do. I've got a brown belt.

> It's difficult to get a brown belt, isn't it?

7c **Work with a new partner and do another dialogue.**

Developing writing

An informal email describing people

1 READING **Read Mia's email to her e-pal, Luke. Match the names to the people in the photo she attaches.**

a
b
c
d

To: Luke <ljackson@realmail.com>

Subject: Me and my friends

Attached: My Friends.JPG (354KB)

Hi Luke,

I'm sending you a photo of me and my friends. I took it this weekend. Do you know who everybody is?

Of course, you already know that I'm the girl with long blonde hair in the middle of the photo ;-) The boy is Brad. He looks a bit tired here. He's working hard at the moment because he has exams next week. But Brad's great. He's totally mad and always makes us laugh.

The girl with red hair is Rose. She looks like an American actress in this photo! Rose is extremely clever and helps us with our maths homework.

The other girl, the one with long dark hair, is Olivia. She looks really happy here, doesn't she? She's always cheerful. In the photo, we're very near her house. We often go there at the weekend.

When you send your next email, don't forget to send me a picture of you and your friends.

All the best,

Mia

1 attachment

2 **Read the email again and find out something about each person's personality.**

Brad: ....

Rose: ....

Olivia: ....

3 **Look again at Mia's email. Complete examples 1–3 in the Writing bank. Then, choose the correct alternative in 4–6.**

✏ WRITING BANK

Descriptive language

■ To describe somebody's appearance we often use the verb *look*. We can use:

1 *look* + adjective (e.g. *He looks* (a) ....)

2 *look like* + noun/pronoun (e.g. *She looks like* (b) ....)

3 *look like/as if* + noun/pronoun + verb (e.g. *It looks like* (c) ....)

■ We use modifying adverbs to make adjectives stronger or softer in order to give more accurate descriptions. For example, we use:

4 *very*, *extremely* and *really* to make 'normal'/'extreme' adjectives (*good, bad, clever*) stronger.

5 *totally, absolutely, really* and *completely* to make 'normal'/'extreme' adjectives (*fantastic, awful, mad*) stronger.

6 *quite, a bit,* and *rather* to make 'normal' adjectives a little softer/stronger.

4 **Complete these sentences to describe people in the photo.**

Pete
Lucy
Josh
Eliza

1 Lucy is really .... and has got quite ....

2 Josh looks .... and is totally ....

3 Eliza looks like a .... and she is extremely ....

4 Pete is a bit .... and he looks as if ....

PRACTICE MAKES PERFECT

5a **Find a photo of you with friends or family. Write an email describing the people in the photo. Use the email in 1 as a model and include expressions from the Writing bank.**

WRITING BANK ➤ PAGE 150

5b **Work with a partner. Take turns to show your photo and description. Can they identify the people in your photo correctly?**

Language checkpoint: Unit 1

Grammar reference

Present simple

FORM

Affirmative	I/You/We/They **run**. He/She/It **runs**.
Negative	I/You/We/They **don't** (do not) **run**. He/She/It **doesn't** (does not) **run**.
Question	**Do** I/you/we/they **run**? **Does** he/she/it **run**?
Short answers	Yes, I/you/we/they **do**. No, I/you/we/they **don't**. Yes, he/she/it **does**. No, he/she/it **doesn't**.

USE

We use the **present simple** to talk about:

1 regular habits and routines.
   I do sport on Wednesday and Sunday.
2 things that are always or generally true.
   A lot of people study English.
3 general and scientific facts.
   The Earth goes round the Sun.

Present continuous

FORM

Affirmative	We're reading.
Negative	She **isn't** reading.
Question	**Are** they reading?
Short answers	Yes, I **am**. No, they **aren't**.

USE

We use the **present continuous** with time expressions such as *now, at the moment, currently,* etc. to talk about:

1 actions that are happening now or near the moment of speaking.
   I can't talk now. I'm having a meeting with the head teacher.
2 temporary actions and situations.
   I'm staying with my uncle and aunt this week.
3 changing situations.
   I'm getting good at this computer game.
4 actions that happen very often and annoy the speaker.
   My little brother is always shouting.

Adverbs and expressions of frequency

USE

We often use **adverbs of frequency** with the present simple to talk about routines and habits. They usually go after the verb *to be* or just before main verbs.

*He's **always** cheerful.*

*They **rarely** eat out.*

*We don't **usually** play computer games.*

We can also use *always* with the present continuous to talk about actions that happen very often and annoy the speaker. See Present continuous 4.

We can use other **expressions of frequency** with the present simple to talk about routines and habits. These usually go at the end of the clause/sentence.

*I watch TV **once/twice/three times a day/week/month/year**.*

State and action verbs

Some verbs are not usually used in the present continuous because they describe **states** not **actions**. These are usually:

1 verbs of feeling and liking: *like, love, hate, want, prefer, need*
2 verbs of thinking: *know, understand, believe, remember, mean, think (= have an opinion), see (= understand)*
3 verbs of the senses: *look, seem, sound, hear, see, smell, feel, appear*
4 verbs of possession: *have, own, belong*

Be careful! Some verbs can describe a state <u>and</u> an action.

*I **have** two sisters. (state) I'm **having** a great time. (action)*

Vocabulary

Appearance Build: overweight • strong • thin • well-built **Height:** medium-height • short • tall **Hair:** bald blonde • curly • dark • fair • long • medium-length • short • spiky • straight • wavy **General:** attractive cute • good-looking • pretty

Personality arrogant • bossy • calm • cheerful • clever • confident • friendly • funny • hard-working impatient • lazy • nervous • nice • patient • quiet • reliable • selfish • serious • shy • talkative • tidy unfriendly • untidy

Synonyms and partial synonyms attractive • beautiful • bright • cheerful • clever • cute • difficult • elderly friendly • glad • good-looking • handsome • happy • hard • intelligent • old • outgoing • pretty • slim sociable • thin

Other words and phrases ➤ page 136

Grammar revision

Present simple and present continuous / 6 points

1 Complete the sentences with the correct form of the present simple or present continuous given.

A: Why (a) .... you .... (wear) a jacket and a tie? You (b) .... (not usually wear) smart clothes like that.

B: I (c) .... (go) for a job interview. I (d) .... (start) to get bored this summer.

A: My sister and I are bored too, but that's because we (e) .... (work) every summer. We (f) .... (save) up money to buy a new computer.

Adverbs of frequency / 6 points

2 Are these sentences correct or not? If not, correct them.

1 I'm not usually going to school by bus.
2 You're always interrupting me. I don't like it.
3 My friends and I play sometimes football after school.
4 Adam often is late.
5 Mia always does her homework before dinner.
6 My friend is a vegetarian. Never he eats meat.

State and action verbs / 8 points

3 Choose the correct alternative.

1 Can we stop at the bank? I _need/am needing_ some money.
2 _Do you know/Are you knowing_ the answer?
3 How are you? _Do you have/Are you having_ a good time?
4 He _owns/is owning_ three mansions.
5 You _don't seem/aren't seeming_ happy.
6 I _prefer/am preferring_ drinking juice to milk.
7 Hey! Why _do you look/are you looking_ out of the window?
8 I don't know who this cat _belongs/is belonging_ to.

Vocabulary revision

APPEARANCE / 7 points

1 Complete the words with vowels. Then write the correct category for each word (build/height/hair/general).

1 ... t t r ... c t ... v ...   .
2 w ... l l - b .... l t   ....
3 m ... d .... m - h .... g h t   ....
4 s t r .... g h t   ....
5 c .... t ....
6 ... v ... r w .... g h t   ....
7 b .... l d   ....

PERSONALITY / 7 points

2 What are the opposites of these words?

1 quiet ....
2 tidy ....
3 cheerful ....
4 stupid ....
5 friendly ....
6 hard-working ....
7 patient ....

SYNONYMS AND PARTIAL SYNONYMS / 6 points

3 Write a synonym for each _underlined_ word.

1 She's a very <u>bright</u> student. ....
2 Do you think he's <u>attractive</u>? ....
3 This question is really <u>difficult</u>. ....
4 She seems a very <u>happy</u> person. ....
5 My sister is very <u>outgoing.</u> ....
6 Can you see that <u>old</u> lady over there?
   ....

Total: / 40 points

2 Travelogue

Vocabulary

Transport and travel

1 Work with a partner. What types of transport can you see in the photos? Put them in the correct column.

Land transport	Air transport	Water transport
motorbike		

2 Work with a partner. Add these words to the columns and any others you can think of. Compare lists with another pair and add any new words.

> bike • coach • lorry • tram
> underground/subway • van • yacht

3 Complete the text with these words.

> arrivals • cancel • catch • delay • departures • fare
> luggage • miss • platform • return • single • ticket office

When you go to the station to (a) .... a train, if you don't already have a ticket, you go and buy one at the (b) .... You can buy a (c) .... (if you're only going one way) or a (d) .... (if you're coming back). The (e) .... is more expensive when you travel first-class because it's more comfortable and you have more space. There isn't an extra cost for (f) .... – you can take at least two or three big bags.

When you have your ticket, you need to find the (g) .... where your train is leaving from. If you arrive late, you may (h) .... your train. But sometimes there can be a (i) .... and your train doesn't arrive on time. And sometimes there's no train at all because they (j) .... it! It's important to keep looking at the information screens which show the (k) .... (the times that trains are coming into the station) and the (l) .... (the times that trains are leaving).

4 ▶ 07 **Listen and check your answers.**

Accommodation

5 Match the photos to these words. Sometimes there is more than one word for a photo.

> bed and breakfast • campsite • caravan
> hostel • hotel • motel • tent

6 SPEAKING Work with a partner. Explain the difference between these words.

1 hotel/motel
2 hotel/hostel
3 hotel/bed and breakfast
4 tent/caravan
5 tent/campsite

> *A motel is a type of hotel that's next to a big road. People usually stay there when they drive a long distance.*

7 LISTENING ▶ 08 **Listen to four recordings. Where are the people? Choose from these alternatives.**

> bed and breakfast • caravan • hostel • hotel
> motel • platform • tent • ticket office

1 .... 3 ....

2 .... 4 ....

8 SPEAKING Work in groups. Decide on the perfect weekend away and describe it to the rest of the class. Think about these things.

- how you travel
- where you go and where you stay
- how you get around while you are there

Reading

1 Look at the map of south-west England below. It is approximately 70 kilometres from Exeter to Plymouth. What types of public transport do you think are best for a trip like this?

2 READING **Bill Bryson is an American travel writer. Read this Bill Bryson extract and answer the questions.**

1 What types of transport does the writer mention?

2 Where does the writer go? Mark his route on the map.

3 Read the text again and choose the best answers.

1 The writer decided to catch a train to Barnstaple because …

  a he didn't want to wait for a long time at the station.

  b he really wanted to visit Barnstaple.

  c it was the only possible place to go from Exeter.

2 The man at the ticket office …

  a didn't want to give the writer a cheap fare.

  b didn't want to explain why the return fare was cheaper.

  c didn't know why the return fare was cheaper.

3 The writer suggests that British people …

  a need to confirm many times that they are catching the right train.

  b usually get on the wrong train.

  c always leave their bags and other things on trains.

4 The two women at the bus station …

  a didn't give the writer any information.

  b seemed surprised about where the writer wanted to go.

  c didn't know if there were any buses to Minehead.

5 In the end, the writer …

  a decided to stay the night at a hotel.

  b didn't get to where he wanted to be.

  c decided to go back to Exeter after a long meal at a hotel.

4 ⚙ CRITICAL THINKING

> **Think! Then compare ideas with your class.**
>
> ■ What do you think are the author's intentions in this text – to give us facts, to give us opinions, to make us laugh or to share experiences? Explain your answer.

5 **What do the underlined words in the text mean? Guess and then check in your dictionary.**

6 SPEAKING **What about you?**

1 Do you prefer to travel by train, bus or car? Why?

2 Are there any unusual customs for using public transport in your country?

Notes From a Small Island

When I had eaten my sandwich, I returned to the hotel, collected my luggage, and thought: Now what? I went back to Exeter train station and looked at the television screens. I thought about catching a train to Plymouth but the next one wasn't for a couple of hours. There was, however, a train to Barnstaple leaving soon. I decided to catch that train. From Barnstaple I could catch a bus to Minehead. It seemed a great idea.

I asked the man at the ticket office for a single to Barnstaple. He told me a single was £8.80, but I could buy a return for £4.40.

'Could you explain how the fare for a return is cheaper than for a single?' I asked. 'I'm sorry but I can't, sir,' he answered honestly.

I went to the correct platform and I sat down. The platform televisions weren't working and I couldn't understand the announcements. Every time there was a new arrival, I had to get up and ask which train it was. For the benefit of foreign readers, I should explain that there is a certain ritual at British train stations. Even though you have heard the conductor tell the person in front of you that this is the Barnstaple train, you still have to say: 'Excuse me, is this the Barnstaple train?'

When he tells you that the large object next to you is indeed the Barnstaple train, you have to point to it and say: 'This one?'

Then when you board the train you must additionally ask the people already there: 'Is this the Barnstaple train?'

Most people will say that they think it is, except for one man who will look worried and quickly pick up all his things and get off the train. Always take that person's seat as they may leave a bar of chocolate.

It took over an hour and a half to travel the thirty-eight miles to Barnstaple. When I arrived I went into the bus station. Two women were sitting in the ticket office. I asked them about buses to Minehead, approximately thirty miles east. They looked at me as if I'd asked for a ticket to Tierra del Fuego. After they had explained that there were no buses to Minehead that afternoon, I thanked them and left. I tried to think what to do next. I went to a hotel and ordered a tuna sandwich and a cup of coffee. While I was eating my sandwich, I took out my timetable and saw that I had twenty-three minutes to eat my sandwich, drink my coffee, and walk back to the railway station to catch a train to Exeter, where I could start again. That was exactly what I did.

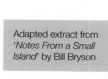

Adapted extract from *'Notes From a Small Island'* by Bill Bryson

Past simple, past continuous and past perfect

1a Read the sentences. Which tenses are the verbs in?

a When I **had eaten** my sandwich, I **returned** to the hotel.

b I **went** to the correct platform and I **sat** down.

c While I **was eating** my sandwich, I **took** out my timetable.

1b Complete the rules with *past simple, past continuous* or *past perfect*. Then match a–c with each rule.

1 We use the .... to talk about actions that happened before another action in the past. ....

2 We use the .... to describe finished actions or situations in the past, or to say that one thing happened after another. ....

3 We use the .... to talk about activities in progress at a moment in the past, to describe scenes in a story or description, or to talk about an activity in progress in the past that is interrupted by another action. ....

1c Rewrite these sentences, first in the negative form and then in the question form.

1 He sat down.

2 He was eating his sandwich.

3 He had eaten his sandwich.

GRAMMAR REFERENCE ➤ PAGE 28

2a Complete the sentences with the past simple or past continuous form of these verbs.

> buy • catch • hear • look • ride
> shine • snow • wait

1 When I left home this morning, the sun ....

2 I .... the bus at 8.45.

3 While I .... my bike to school this morning, I saw an accident.

4 When we arrived at the station, a lot of people .... to buy tickets.

5 She .... her ticket and got on the train.

6 Somebody stole his passport while he .... for something in his luggage.

7 There was a delay with the plane because it .... very hard.

8 As she was leaving the shop, she .... somebody call her name.

2b Look at the words *while* and *as* in sentences 3, 6, and 8. Do they usually go with the past simple or past continuous?

3 Choose the best alternative.

1 I fell asleep while I *watched/was watching* the film.

2 The teacher called me back as I *left/was leaving* the classroom.

3 The head teacher *came/was coming* in while we were doing the exam.

4 As we *drove/were driving* to the airport, I realised I didn't have my passport.

5 While you *shopped/were shopping*, three people called for you.

6 She *met/was meeting* one of her friends while she was taking the dog for a walk.

7 As we *talked/were talking*, I realised that I'd met her before.

8 They didn't speak while they *did/were doing* their homework.

4 Look at the example. Write explanations in the past perfect for each of the situations.

1 Why was she crying? **miss the plane**
   Because she had missed the plane.

2 Why couldn't he find his bike? **somebody steal it**
   ....

3 Why did they buy a new car? **have the old one for 15 years**
   ....

4 Why were you scared of flying? **never fly before**
   ....

5 Why was everything white in the morning? **snow the night before**
   ....

6 Why didn't she pass her exam? **not study much**
   ....

7 Why didn't he board the plane? **lose passport**
   ....

8 Why didn't Alex have any money? **spend it**
   ....

9 Why did she miss the bus? **not leave on time**
   ....

Developing vocabulary

Phrasal verbs connected with travel

1 **Look at these sentences. Match the phrasal verbs in red with the definitions below.**

1 We **got on** the first train that came but we **got off** when we realised it was the wrong one.

2 When all passengers are in their seats, the plane can **take off**.

3 She **got into** the car and drove to the station. When she arrived she **got out of** the car and locked it.

4 This bus is really old. I think it's going to **break down** any minute.

5 Excuse me. Can you tell me what time the London train **gets in**? I'm meeting somebody on it.

6 They **checked in** their bags and went through passport control.

7 That was a long journey. We **set off** at 7 o'clock this morning and only arrived at 10 pm.

8 I'm tired of working. I want to **get away** for a few weeks, maybe go to the beach.

a start a journey

b enter/leave (a train, bus, boat, plane)

c go somewhere different to have a rest or holiday

d arrive

e show your ticket/give your bags to an official at an airport

f stop working (for a motor or type of transport)

g enter/leave (a car)

h start flying

2a PRONUNCIATION **Look at these sentences. Think about the words in red. When are they verbs and when are they nouns?**

1 We need to **check in** at 7 o'clock.

2 Here's the **check-in** desk.

3 What time does the plane **take off**?

4 What time is **take-off**?

5 The car didn't **break down**.

6 There is a car **breakdown** service.

2b ▶ 09 **Listen to the sentences. Which part of the phrasal verb do we usually stress? Which part of the noun do we stress?**

3 **Complete the text with these words.**

away • down • in • into • off (x 2) • on • out of

Last week my brother and I decided to get
(a) .... for the weekend and go to Brighton.
We set (b) .... early, at 6.30 am. We got
(c) .... my mum's car first because she had
offered to take us to the station. The only problem was that
her car is getting old and it broke (d) .... five
minutes from the station. We got (e) .... the
car, collected our luggage, and ran to the station so that we
didn't miss the train. The train was at the platform when we
arrived. We got (f) .... the train and found our
seats. The train arrived at Brighton station on time – we got
(g) .... at 11 am. We took our luggage and got
(h) .... the train. The only problem we had with
transport all weekend was mum's old car!

4a **Prepare notes about a journey that was special to you. Use some of these questions to help you. Include as many phrasal verbs from 1 as possible.**

1 Where was the journey to?

2 How did you travel?

3 When was it?

4 Who went?

5 Who had chosen the destination?

6 How had you prepared for the journey?

7 What special thing(s) happened on the journey?

8 What were you doing when these things happened?

9 How did the journey end?

10 How did you feel about what had happened?

4b SPEAKING **Work in small groups. Tell each other about your journey.**

Being a responsible T🌀URIST

LIFE SKILLS OBJECTIVES ✗

- To understand the basics of responsible tourism.
- To learn to be a responsible tourist in a specific country.
- To give advice to tourists coming to your country.

KEY CONCEPTS

energy efficient [adj]: *This car is energy efficient because it doesn't need much petrol to travel long distances.* **conserve [v]:** *It's important to conserve water because there isn't a lot and we need as much as possible.* **environmentally friendly [adj]:** *This product is environmentally friendly because it doesn't have any negative effects on the environment.* **damage/harm [v, n]:** *Be careful – that old clock is fragile and you could damage it.* **endangered [adj]:** *That animal is endangered – there aren't many left in the world.* **artefacts [n]:** *You can see many ancient artefacts in a museum.*

1 Work with a partner. Look at the photos. Which ones show responsible tourism? Give reasons.

2 Read the titles from the text below. Match the photos in 1 to four of them.

- **A** Read about your destination before you leave
- **B** Choose the right place to stay
- **C** Choose environmentally-friendly transport locally
- **D** Choose the best way to get to your final destination
- **E** Don't leave rubbish behind
- **F** Think about what you buy
- **G** Learn some of the local language
- **H** Conserve water
- **I** Don't damage things!
- **J** Think about your social impact
- **K** Limit energy use

3 **READING** Read the text and match the titles in 2 with the correct sections.

HOW TO BE A RESPONSIBLE

Before you travel

1. When you're travelling a long distance, flying is usually the fastest way to get to your destination. But it's the worst for the environment in terms of pollution. Some places are difficult to get to by any other means of transport, but if your destination is less than 500 km away, consider catching a train, or even going by car to reduce your carbon footprint. If you need to fly, choose airlines that have energy efficient planes.

2. Knowing about the local culture can help you to be a sensitive, responsible traveller. Researching your travel destination can help you understand what to expect and what is acceptable in that country.

3. Just a few words can help you to communicate. And, apart from that, it can help you and local people feel more comfortable and positive together.

When you are there

1. Try to choose environmentally-friendly accommodation. Look for hotels, hostels or campsites that are energy efficient and that recycle.

2. Help the local environment. One of the easiest but most important things to do is to think about the water you consume. Refill a water bottle instead of continually buying plastic bottles. Limit your use of soaps and reuse your hotel towels.

3. Don't make your hotel room too hot or too cold. Remember to switch off air-conditioning and lights when you're not in your room.

4. People usually go to holiday destinations because they're beautiful. Don't make them ugly and dirty with your rubbish. The message is simple – leave the place the way that you would like to find it.

5. Try to use local public transport or rent a bike – it's a great way to see things. And don't forget you can also walk!

6. Buy locally-made or locally-produced goods. But never buy endangered plants, or products that involve animals or marine life. Check laws about buying historic artefacts, too.

7. Apart from the physical environment, make sure your visit doesn't have a negative effect on local people. Respect local cultures and traditions. Ask permission before you take photographs of people, official buildings, or other special places. Think about the clothes you wear, too.

4 According to the text in 2, are these things good, bad or does it depend? If it depends, what on?

1 Buying old, historic objects
2 Feeding wild animals
3 Using air-conditioning
4 Taking photos of local people
5 Reading about your destination before you go
6 Flying to your destination
7 Picking flowers

5 **SPEAKING** Work with a partner. Which do you think are the three most important or most interesting pieces of advice in the text? Why?

6 Work with a partner. Discuss these questions.

1 What do you know about New Zealand?
2 Would you like to go there for a holiday? Why/Why not?

Greetings from **New Zealand**

TOURIST

8. When you're in a natural area, don't pick flowers. Keep on the paths so you don't damage plants and vegetation, and don't touch, move or take old rocks and other objects in a historic place. Finally, be careful with marine life, and don't feed wild animals because you could harm them.

7 You are going to watch/hear a teenager talking about her recent trip to New Zealand. Read this text. Can you guess any of the missing words?

When you arrive in New Zealand, they check that you don't bring **(a)** ...., **(b)** .... or anything organic into the country. These things can be dangerous for the New Zealand environment.

They even take away outdoor shoes or trainers with **(c)** .... on them which might **(d)** .... the environment.

At Tongariro National Park there is a problem because there is a lot of **(e)** .... there.

If you want to buy something made by Maoris, the original people of New Zealand, look for labels and signs that say '**(f)** ....'. Products that say 'Environmental Choice' on them are more **(g)** .... than other products.

It's fine to bring back souvenirs and local products such as the famous New Zealand **(h)** ....

8 **LISTENING** 10 **Watch the video or listen as many times as necessary and complete the text in 7.**

LIFE TASK

Work in a small group and follow these steps:

1 Think of the area where you live, or an area in your country where tourists go. Make a list of tips to promote responsible tourism in the area. Think about these different topics:

- Transport
- Accommodation
- Energy and water
- Souvenirs
- People and social interaction
- Plants and wildlife
- Food
- Recycling

Use the ideas in the texts on these pages to help you, and search for more ideas on the Internet.

2 Plan and make a presentation about responsible tourism in the area that you chose.

3 Give your presentation to the rest of the class.

Listening

AROUND THE WORLD IN EIGHTY DAYS

1 **Work with a partner. Guess the answers to these questions.**

1 What nationality was the first person to travel around the world?
   a Portuguese
   b Spanish
   c British

2 How long did it take them to travel around the world?
   a about three years
   b about one year
   c about three months

3 Before trains, planes and cars, how long did it take to cross the US?
   a a year and a half
   b a year
   c half a year

4 What made it easier and faster to travel around the world in 1869?
   a the opening of the Suez Canal
   b the invention of the aeroplane
   c the invention of the passport

2 **LISTENING** ▶ **11 Listen to an expert talking about travelling around the world. What answers does she give for the questions in 1?**

3 ▶ **11 There are six mistakes in this text about 'around the world' travel. Listen again and correct the mistakes.**

■ The first person to travel around the world was Elcano and the 20 other people who survived the expedition. They began their journey in 1522.

■ Jules Verne wrote *Around the World in 80 Days* in 1870. He got the idea for writing the novel from a real journey made by George Francis Train. Train was an engineer who worked on the Union Pacific Railroad. After they had built the railroad, you could cross the US in about 14 days.

■ Before 1869, ships had to pass round the bottom of Africa. This was fast. But the problem was that it was dangerous.

■ In 1995 a plane flew around the world in just over two days.

Grammar in context

used to

1a Read the sentences and then match the correct halves of the rules.

Sentences

1 It **used to** take years to travel around the world.

2 Sailors **didn't use to** have an alternative

3 **Did** it **use to** take much longer?

4 People **usually** say that.

5 They **arrived** back home in 1522.

Rules

1 We use **used to** to talk about ....

2 We use the past simple to talk about ....

3 We use the present simple and **usually** to talk about ....

a present habits.

b past habits that do not happen now.

c single actions in the past.

1b What is the negative and question form of this sentence?

They used to travel by horse across the US.

GRAMMAR REFERENCE ➤ PAGE 28

2 **Complete the sentences with the correct form of *used to*.**

1 Transport .... be much slower three hundred years ago.

2 .... people .... think unicorns existed?

3 They .... wear jeans in the thirteenth century.

4 A long time ago people .... believe that the Sun went around the Earth.

5 In England in 1600 most children from poor families .... go to school.

6 .... people .... drive cars in 1750?

7 Before TV, people .... listen to the radio.

8 .... people .... travel by train and ship before the invention of the aeroplane?

9 Fifty years ago, people .... have mobile phones.

10 It .... be important to know how to ride a horse.

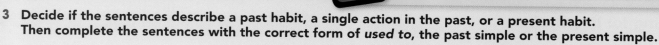
3 Decide if the sentences describe a past habit, a single action in the past, or a present habit. Then complete the sentences with the correct form of *used to*, the past simple or the present simple.

1 My friend .... (go) to Brazil to see the World Cup in 2014.

2 We .... (go) to school by car when we were younger, but now we walk.

3 She usually .... (cycle) to school, but yesterday she caught the bus.

4 I .... (not/like) classical music when I was small but now I love it.

5 They .... (play) football on Wednesdays, but now they play basketball.

6 I .... (not/go) to the cinema at the weekend because it was too expensive, but now I go every Saturday.

4 Look at the scene showing life in the Wild West in 1870. Find eight historical mistakes in the picture and write as many sentences as possible, affirmative and/or negative.

They used to travel long distances by horse.
They didn't use to fly.

would

5 Read the sentences and then choose the correct alternative.

1 In the past, they **would** sail round the Cape of Good Hope.

2 In the past, they **used to** sail round the Cape of Good Hope.

3 It **used to** be dangerous.

4 It **would** be dangerous. ✗

5 In the past, they **wouldn't** fly. ✗

a We *can/can't* use *would* to talk about past habits.

b We *can/can't* use *wouldn't* to talk about past habits.

c We *can/can't* use *would* to talk about past actions.

d We *can/can't* use *would* to talk about past situations and states.

GRAMMAR REFERENCE ➤ PAGE 28

6 Replace *used to* with *would* in these sentences **when possible**.

1 I used to go on holiday with my grandparents.

2 They used to swim at the weekend.

3 We didn't use to travel far.

4 I used to have a white bicycle.

5 My dad used to work on Saturdays.

6 She used to have really long hair.

7a SPEAKING Work with a partner. Make notes with *would* and *used to* about how life was different in your country fifty years ago. Think about these topics.

1 Transport   4 Work

2 Food and drink   5 Health

3 Entertainment   6 Education

7b Report back to the class with your ideas.

Travel would take much longer than now. Fifty years ago people didn't use to fly much.

Asking for information

1 **Look at this train ticket from the UK and complete the information.**

1 Place of departure ....
2 Destination ....
3 When travelling ....
4 Number of people travelling ....
5 Single/Return? ....
6 First class/Standard? ....
7 Price ....

Class	Ticket type		Adult	Child
Standard	Single		1	0

Date 22/9

From	London	Valid Date shown	Price £24.00
To	Oxford	Route Any	

≥ British Rail **SINGLE**

2 **LISTENING** ▶ **12 Listen to a conversation between a girl and a ticket agent. Choose the correct alternative and complete the missing details.**

1 Destination: *Cambridge/Canterbury*
2 When travelling: *Today/Tomorrow*
3 Time of departure: *3.55 pm/6.05 pm*
4 Travel details: *Direct train/Change trains*
  Details: ....
5 Type of ticket: *Single/Return*
  Details: ....
6 Price: *£31/£41*
7 Payment: *Cash/Debit card*
8 Platform: *8/9*

3 ▶ **12 Listen again. Tick (✓) the expressions in the Speaking bank that you hear.**

4 **Make these requests for information more polite using the expressions in the Speaking bank.**

How much is a return?
Could you tell me how much a return is?

1 Is it possible to pay by debit card?
2 What is the cheapest fare?
3 Is it a direct train?
4 What time is it?
5 What time does the train arrive?

5 **Work with a partner. Prepare a dialogue using the guide below.**

Ticket officer:	Offer to help the customer.
Customer:	Ask for the times of trains to Newcastle.
Ticket officer:	Give the time of the next train.
Customer:	Ask if the train is direct.
Ticket Officer:	Say yes.
Customer:	Ask for a ticket.
Ticket Officer:	Ask if the customer wants a single or return.
Customer:	Say you want a return and say when you want to come back.
Ticket Officer:	Give the price.
Customer:	Ask how to pay.
Ticket Officer:	Reply.
Customer:	Find out the platform number.
Ticket Officer:	Reply and say goodbye.

PRACTICE MAKES PERFECT

6 **SPEAKING** **Work with a partner. Prepare another dialogue. Remember to be polite and to ask for clarification by using expressions from the Speaking bank.**

Student A: You are in the UK and you want to buy a train ticket. Look at page 147 for information about the ticket you want to buy.

Student B: You work in the ticket office. Look at page 147 for information about different trains. Begin the conversation: *Good morning. Can I help you?*

✓ EXAM SUCCESS

In this type of exam activity, how important is it to know what specific information you need to ask for and give? Why/Why not?

➤ EXAM SUCCESS page 144

Developing writing

A blog post

1 **SPEAKING** Work with a partner. Imagine your dream holiday. Where would you like to go? What would you like to do there? How would you like to travel? Talk about your different ideas.

2 **READING** Read Ryan's blog post about his dream holiday. What do you think of his holiday?

3 Read the blog again. What did Ryan say about …
  1 the journey?   3 the Dubai Mall?
  2 the Wild Wadi Water Park?   4 skiing?

4 Complete the examples in the Writing bank with words from the blog.

> ### ✎ WRITING BANK
>
> **Useful words and expressions to give emphasis**
> Here are some ways of giving emphasis to what we write, to make our writing more interesting.
> - We can use *What* + (adjective) + noun!, e.g. *What a (a)* _____ !, *What a beautiful day!*
> - We can use *so* + (adjective) or *such* + (adjective) + noun, e.g. *The flight there was so (b)* _____, *We had such (c)* _____ *there.*
> - We can use *do* and *did* in affirmative sentences, e.g. *I (d)* _____ *the Dubai Mall.*

5 Make these sentences more emphatic by using the word given.
  1 It's a busy city. (What)
  2 The flight was great. (such)
  3 We were tired when we arrived. (so)
  4 I love New York. (do)
  5 We had a good time. (did)
  6 We were happy to get back. (so)
  7 It's a great holiday. (What)
  8 It's a fantastic place for shopping. (such)

6 Think of an amazing holiday destination and make notes for a blog post about your holiday there. Use these questions to give you ideas.
  1 Where did you go?
  2 What type of accommodation did you stay in?
  3 How did you get there?
  4 Did anything good or bad happen during your journey there?
  5 What was the place like? Why did you like it?
  6 What did you do there?
  7 What was your favourite moment and why?

Ryan's blog

HOME   BLOG   ABOUT ME   CONTACT

MY DREAM HOLIDAY!

Yesterday we left Dubai. Wow! What a brilliant place! We had such a great time there. I hope I can go back one day.

The flight there was so long! It took about seven hours. But my brother Ben and I watched a couple of films and played video games the whole time.

There were lots of things to do in Dubai. I think my favourite moment was when we went to the Wild Wadi Water Park. We spent hours there trying all the different rides and attractions. When we'd finished, we went shopping. The Dubai Mall is one of the biggest shopping centres in the world. I don't usually like shopping centres, but I did like the Dubai Mall. It had an amazing aquarium, and there was a spectacular show in the evening with fountains and music.

Apart from that, we went to the beach, we had a hot-air balloon trip in the desert and we even skied in Dubai's enormous indoor snow park! We didn't go up the world's tallest tower because we didn't have time.

And now we're here in Doha, another amazing place! We're setting off for the Singing Sand Dunes tomorrow. I'll tell you all about it in my next post.

PRACTICE MAKES PERFECT

7 Look at the task below. Use your notes from 6 to write your blog post. Use the expressions in the Writing bank to add emphasis and interest.

Yesterday you came back from your dream holiday. Write a blog post about it. Write about:
- where you went and where you stayed
- what happened on the journey
- what the place was like
- what you did
- what the best moment was

WRITING BANK ➤ PAGE 150

✔ EXAM SUCCESS

When you finish a piece of writing in an exam, what different things do you need to check before you hand it in?

➤ EXAM SUCCESS page 144

Grammar reference

Past simple

FORM	
Affirmative	I walked to school yesterday.
Negative	You didn't (did not) run yesterday.
Question	Did he run yesterday?
Short answers	Yes, he did./No, he didn't.

Many common verbs are irregular. See the list of irregular verbs on page 149.

USE

We use the **past simple** to:

1 describe finished actions or situations in the past.
   I flew to Russia two years ago.

2 to say that one thing happened after another.
   When the bus arrived, we got on it.

Past continuous

FORM	
Affirmative	He was going.
Negative	They weren't (were not) going.
Question	Were you going?
Short answers	Yes, I was. No, I wasn't.

USE

We use the **past continuous** to:

1 talk about activities in progress at a moment in the past.
   At seven o'clock yesterday I was sleeping.

2 describe scenes in a story or description.
   The boy was wearing a new black coat.

3 talk about an activity in progress when another, shorter activity happened or interrupted it. We know the activity was in progress, but not if it was finished.
   I was talking to my friend when the accident happened.

4 We often use *while* and *as* with the past continuous.
   While/As I was riding my bike, I saw Leo.

5 Some verbs are not usually used in the continuous (see page 16).
   I had a toy car. Not ~~I was having a toy car.~~

Past perfect

FORM	
Affirmative	She had left the station.
Negative	They hadn't travelled far.
Question	Had you bought a ticket?
Short answers	Yes, I had. No, they hadn't.

USE

1 We use the **past perfect** to talk about actions that happened before another action in the past.
   *When I **had done** my homework, I watched TV.*
   (= First I did my homework, then I watched TV.)

2 We often use time expressions such as **when, after, by the time, as soon as** with the past perfect.

used to and would

FORM	
Affirmative	I used to/would play a lot when I was small.
Negative	She didn't use to have so many exams.
Question	What did you use to do?

USE

1 We use *used to* and *would* to talk about past habits, things we did regularly in the past, but not now.
   *I **used to/would** ride my bike to school when I was small.*

2 We cannot use *would* for past states or situations, only for past actions.
   *I **would** play with my toys.* Not ~~I would have a lot of toys.~~

Vocabulary

Transport and travel arrivals • bike • cancel • catch • coach • delay • departures • fare • ferry • hot-air balloon • lorry • luggage • miss • motorbike • platform • return • rocket • single • subway • ticket office • tram • underground • van • yacht

Accommodation bed and breakfast • campsite • caravan • hostel • hotel • motel • tent

Phrasal verbs connected with travel break down • check in • get away • get in • get into/out of • get on/off • set off • take off

Other words and phrases ➤ page 137

Grammar revision

Past simple and past continuous   / 7 points

1 Complete the sentences with the past simple or continuous of the verbs given.

1 We were travelling fast when the train suddenly .... (stop).

2 I met a friend when I .... (wait) for the bus.

3 We .... (put) our coats on and left the house.

4 When the bus stopped we .... (got) off.

5 You looked sad yesterday because you .... (cry).

6 Nobody noticed me because they .... (watch) TV.

7 He .... (drop) it and it broke.

Past simple and past perfect   / 6 points

2 Join the two sentences with a time expression. Put one of the verbs in the past perfect.

1 They left. She arrived at their house.
   By the time ....

2 He finished using the computer. He switched it off.
   When ....

3 They went into the cinema. They bought their tickets.
   After ....

4 She did her homework. She went to bed immediately after.
   As soon as ....

5 We ate our meal. We paid the bill.
   When ....

6 They went into the house. They unlocked the door.
   They ....

used to and would   / 7 points

3 Choose the correct alternative. In one sentence both alternatives are correct.

1 Did people _use/used_ to go on holiday 100 years ago?

2 We _didn't use to/wouldn't_ have short hair.

3 My friend and I _use to/usually_ go to the cinema on Friday.

4 I _used to win/won_ a competition once.

5 It _used to/would_ be very expensive to fly in the past.

6 My best friend and I _used to/would_ talk for hours.

7 Years ago it _would take/usually takes_ days to cross the Atlantic.

Vocabulary revision

TRANSPORT AND TRAVEL   / 8 points

1 Write a simple explanation for each word.

1 coach ....

2 platform ....

3 delay ....

4 fare ....

5 ferry ....

6 a return ticket ....

7 to miss (the bus) ....

8 to cancel (a flight) ....

ACCOMMODATION   / 6 points

2 What are these types of accommodation?

1 A hotel near a big road, for travellers: ....

2 A small hotel that offers a room and a morning meal:
   ....

3 A place where lots of people camp: ....

4 A thing you use to sleep in the countryside: ....

5 A vehicle that you can live in: ....

6 A cheap place where young people can stay: ....

PHRASAL VERBS CONNECTED WITH TRAVEL   / 6 points

3 Choose the correct alternative.

1 We arrived at the airport and checked _in/off_ our bags.

2 It was a long journey so he set _on/off_ early.

3 What time does your train get _in/off_ ?

4 She got _into/on_ the car and started driving.

5 The bus broke _up/down_ so he walked.

6 Let's get _away/around_ from the city this weekend.

Total: .... / 40 points   Unit 2   29

Reading

1 READING **Read the text quickly. Who is Chris Hadfield? Why does he mention each of these places?**

1 Moscow ....

2 Barbados ....

3 Tintagel ....

4 Portugal ....

5 The Caribbean ....

> ▶ **TIP FOR READING EXAMS**
>
> In *True/False* activities, remember …
> First read the text quickly to get a general understanding.
> Then read the sentences that you need to prove true or false.
> Find the parts of the text where you think the information comes and read them again in more detail.
>
> ➤ EXAM SUCCESS page 144

MY LIFE IN TRAVEL: CHRIS HADFIELD

Astronaut Chris Hadfield has walked in space and travelled in a Russian rocket. But what about his travel experiences back down here on Earth?

First holiday memory?
Scuba diving in Barbados. My father was an airline pilot so there was the opportunity for free tickets. We did one
5 very rapid family holiday from Toronto to Barbados. In Bridgetown, there was an introductory scuba diving class. I was only 11, but it was before the rules were so strict. I still scuba dive now because of that first experience.

Favourite place in the British Isles?
10 Tintagel in Cornwall. I set off for a trip along the whole south-west coast of England. It was beautiful and wild. It has ancient Viking and prehistoric sites, all in one beautiful place.

Best holiday?
15 Portugal. My wife and I were going down the coast and east into the country, driving through the hills. We saw everything from the coast of the Algarve to the capital, Lisbon. It was a really
20 unplanned adventure. That's the type of holiday that we like. There was a real sense of discovery.

What do you think travel teaches us?
That the most interesting thing is people. The way we all have the same
25 basic problems in our years on Earth, but the many different ways we resolve those problems. It's fascinating. When you're in space, you travel around the whole world every 90 minutes, so you
30 see the similarities between people and places. It's a very unifying thing.

Ideal travelling companion?
Someone who has a sense of adventure, who has the same daily routine as I do, who knows things I
35 don't, who has their own ideas but who is happy to listen to mine, and who is patient and tolerant of things being different.

Greatest travel luxury?
A really big bed. I stayed at a hotel
40 once which had the most amazing bed and I thought, 'Why don't I have one of these?' So I found the materials and made my own!

Worst travel experience?
When I was a teenager I was travelling
45 across Europe without much luggage, or money. It took six months, so it included some of my best and worst experiences. But I think the worst was a moment when I was at a hostel in
50 Spain. I hadn't had enough money to drink bottled water and the water I drank made me really ill. It was awful!

Favourite city?
Moscow. It's a very friendly city when you speak Russian, which I
55 do. I had spent 20 years studying the language so I could fly a Russian rocket, command the Space Station, and become NASA's director in Russia. Moscow is home to 11 million people
60 and is a thousand years old. It has tremendous history to it. I love the nature and their culture. It's not the easiest or quietest city, but it's my favourite.

Where next?
65 The Caribbean, Las Vegas, California, but a true holiday for me is my home in Canada. I travel a lot so having a peaceful place to relax is
70 really important for me.

2 **Are these statements True (T) or False (F)? Write down the number(s) of the line(s) where you found the answer.**

1 Chris Hadfield's family didn't pay to fly to Barbados.   T / F ....

2 Chris's trip to Barbados began a lifelong hobby.   T / F ....

3 Chris prefers holidays that are carefully planned.   T / F ....

4 Chris thinks that humans all solve problems in the same way.   T / F ....

5 Chris's ideal travelling companion has exactly the same ideas as him.   T / F ....

6 Chris's trip to Europe as a teenager was a completely negative experience.   T / F ....

7 Chris learnt Russian for his job.   T / F ....

8 Chris loves Moscow because life is so relaxing there.   T / F ....

3 SPEAKING **What about *you*?**

Do you know any of the places that Chris Hadfield talks about? Do you like them? Would you like to visit them one day?
Why/Why not?

Speaking

➤ TIP FOR SPEAKING EXAMS

Make sure that, before you begin, you understand the situation and the specific information that you need to ask for or give.

➤ EXAM SUCCESS page 144

4 Look at these questions that Chris Hadfield answered. Make notes for your own answers, but do not write full sentences.

1 What is your first holiday memory?
2 What was your best holiday?
3 What do you think travel teaches us?
4 Who is your ideal travelling companion?
5 What was your worst travel experience?
6 What is your favourite city?

5 Work with a partner. Imagine that this is the 'personal information' part of a speaking exam. Take it in turns to ask and answer the questions. You can use your notes, but don't just read them aloud.

Listening

➤ TIP FOR LISTENING EXAMS

In matching activities, remember …
Before you listen, read the statements. But remember that when you listen you may hear the same ideas expressed in different words.

➤ EXAM SUCCESS page 144

6 Work with a partner. What problems do people sometimes have with travel or accommodation when they go away on holiday?

7 LISTENING ▶ 13 Listen to four people talking about travel problems. Match the statements (a–e) with the person who said them. There is one extra statement.

a I didn't make any plans.
b Bad weather ruined my holidays.
c I couldn't get home on the right day.
d I took the wrong train.
e I had a problem with my luggage.

Speaker 1 ....   Speaker 3 ....

Speaker 2 ....   Speaker 4 ....

Writing

➤ TIP FOR WRITING EXAMS

In writing exams, remember …
When you finish, check carefully for mistakes with punctuation and capital letters, word order, spelling, tenses, vocabulary, missing words and agreement between the subject and verb. Check the style and content, too.

➤ EXAM SUCCESS page 144

8 The people in the photo are some new friends that you made on holiday. Write an email to your family about your new friends.

- Describe their appearance and personality.
- Use *look, look like, look as if, extremely, really* and *quite.*

'CAN DO' PROGRESS CHECK UNITS 1–2   CEF

1 How well can you do these things in English now? Give yourself a mark from 1 to 4.

> **1** = I can do it very well.
> **2** = I can do it quite well.
> **3** = I have some problems.
> **4** = I can't do it.

a I can talk about routines and what's happening now using the present simple and present continuous. ☐
b I can ask for and give personal information. ☐
c I can use synonyms. ☐
d I can understand written and spoken texts about people's identity. ☐
e I can describe people's appearance and personality. ☐
f I can talk about past events, situations and habits using the past simple, past continuous, past perfect, *used to* and *would*. ☐
g I can talk about trips and travel. ☐
h I can understand written and spoken texts about journeys. ☐
i I can ask to buy a train ticket at a station. ☐
j I can write a blog post about a dream holiday. ☐

2 Now decide what you need to do to improve.

1 Look again at my book/notes.
2 Do more practice exercises.
   ➤ WORKBOOK Units 1 and 2
3 Ask for help.
4 Other: ....

3 City to city

Vocabulary

Cities and houses

1 Work with a partner. Match the photos below to these words. There is one word you do not need.

> bungalow • cottage • detached house
> flat/block of flats • semi-detached house
> terraced house

2 ▶ 14 **Listen, check and repeat.**

3 Go round the class. Each person must say a typical room in a flat or a house. How many rooms can you name?

Student A: *bedroom* Student B: *kitchen*

4 SPEAKING Work with a partner. Tell them what type of house you live in and describe it.

> *I live in a terraced house. It's got three bedrooms.*

5 SPEAKING Talk about the photos. Use these words.

> city centre • factory • inner city • outskirts • port
> skyscraper • square • suburbs • town hall

6 Which word in 5 describes …

1 an area of water where ships stop, and the buildings around it?
2 an area near the centre of a big city, traditionally poorer?
3 the part of a city where there are many shops, banks, restaurants or cafés?
4 an open area in a city or town with buildings around it?
5 a richer residential area near a city, but away from its centre with houses and green spaces?
6 the area of a city that is furthest from the centre?

Adjectives describing cities

7a Match six of these words with the definitions.

> busy • clean • crowded • dirty • historic • lively
> modern • noisy • quiet

1 important because it is old and interesting
2 not very busy, or without much noise
3 with rubbish in the streets, for example
4 full of people who are very active and/or having a good time
5 with lots of people in the same place doing things
6 with lots of people in the same place, especially too many

7b What are the opposites of 2 and 3?

8 LISTENING ▶ 15 Listen to four people talking about houses or places in a city. Which place from 1 or 5 does each person talk about?

1 .... 3 ....
2 .... 4 ....

9 SPEAKING Work with a partner. Talk about the area where your school is.

> *Our school isn't in the city centre, but it's quite near. It isn't very noisy. There are a lot of blocks of flats here …*

1 Work with a partner. Take it in turns to describe the photos in the article below. Look at the title of the article. What do you think the article is about?

2 READING Read the article quickly and check your predictions.

MOVING TO THE

Right now, one of the biggest changes in the history of the world is taking place. Yes, an important transformation has already begun and it looks like it will continue for years to come. China is a country where the population is in movement. **(a)** _____ And they are all moving in the same direction – from the country to the city. At the moment, less than half the population of China lives in cities, but that situation is changing and it is changing fast.

Traditionally, the majority of the population of China has lived in quiet, rural areas. But industry is <u>growing</u> so fast that there is constant need for new workers in the city, in factories, construction sites, shops and offices. At the same time, life has become difficult for those living in the country. The traditional way of life is not so easy to follow any more. **(b)** _____ But now there is an <u>urgent</u> need to build, to build big, tall and fast.

(c) _____ Shanghai had none in 1980. Since then, they have built over twice as many as New York! Few Chinese people live in detached or semi-detached houses. So, many large blocks of flats have appeared in the suburbs of these new Chinese megacities to <u>accommodate</u> the new arrivals. But this has led to packed conditions in cities such as Tianjin where over 11 million people live, or in Shanghai itself which has a population of over 22 million.

(d) _____ As the cities <u>increase in size</u>, they eat up historic old buildings and invade the quiet villages <u>nearby</u>. Nearly 160 Chinese cities have passed one million inhabitants in the last 20 years and they continue to grow today.

The future consequences of these enormous changes are still difficult to predict, both for China and for the whole planet.

(e) _____ So they have started designing and building new 'eco-cities'. In these eco-cities there is an emphasis on clean, renewable energy. For example, in one eco-city engineers have just started work on the construction of the world's tallest and greenest skyscrapers, the Phoenix Towers. The idea of these stunning towers is to use solar power for electricity and to collect rainwater for the use of the residents. The walls of the towers even have green plants living on them to clean the air. Hopefully, with plans like this China's megacities can be attractive, clean, modern _and_ good for the environment.

✔ EXAM SUCCESS

You are going to do a missing sentences activity. In this type of activity, you need to find the best place to put different sentences taken from a text. What do you think should be the first thing you do in this type of activity?

➤ EXAM SUCCESS page 144

3 **Complete the text with these sentences.**

1 Luckily, China has already realised the impact that megacities could have on the environment.

2 Until recently there was no need to build such enormous cities in China.

3 Day by day, these lively new megacities keep expanding.

4 Some experts calculate that over 260 million people are moving, more than the entire population of a huge country like Brazil!

5 The rapid growth in the number of skyscrapers is an obvious demonstration of this.

4 **Read the text again and answer the questions.**

1 Where does over 50% of the Chinese population live now?

2 Why are Chinese cities growing?

3 In cities, where do most Chinese people live, and what effect does that have on the cities?

4 How is China trying to fight against the possible negative effects of the new cities on the environment?

5 In what ways are the Phoenix Towers good for the environment?

5 **⚙ CRITICAL THINKING**

Think! Then compare ideas with your class.

■ What do you think of the population moving from the country to the city? Is it a good thing or a bad thing? Why?

6 **What do the <u>underlined</u> words in the text mean? Guess and then check in your dictionary.**

7 SPEAKING **What about _you_?**

1 Would you like to live in a megacity? Why/Why not?

2 Which city in your country is the best to live in? Why?

I wouldn't like to live in a megacity. They're so crowded!

Yes, but they're probably really lively, too, with lots of things to see and do.

Grammar in context

Present perfect simple and past simple

1a Read these sentences and choose the correct alternative.

1 Shanghai **had** no skyscrapers in 1980.
2 Large blocks of flats **have appeared** in the suburbs.
3 They **have started** building new 'eco-cities'.
4 In the past they **lived** in a village but then they **went** to a city.

1 We use the *present perfect/past simple* for actions or experiences which happened at a specific moment in the past, or actions which started and finished in the past.
Examples: sentences *1/2/3/4*.

2 We use the *present perfect/past simple* for actions or experiences which happened at an unspecified moment in the past, actions which started in the past and continue to the present, or past actions which have a result in the present.
Examples: sentences *1/2/3/4*

1b Complete this rule for the formation of the present perfect.

has/have + ...

GRAMMAR REFERENCE ➤ PAGE 42

2 Complete each sentence with the correct form of the present perfect or past simple.

1 The population of India .... (grow) by about 40% between 1990 and 2000.
2 The world population .... (go) up since 1950.
3 When you look around, you can see that this city .... (change) a lot.
4 Just before 2012 they .... (build) a lot of new constructions in London.
5 Renzo Piano is a famous architect. He .... (design) a lot of amazing buildings.
6 Mexico City is enormous. It .... (be) one of the largest cities in the world for many years.
7 Le Corbusier .... (be) a great architect. He died in 1965.
8 I love travelling. I .... (visit) lots of amazing cities.
9 The population of nearly 160 Chinese cities .... (reach) 1 million.
10 Chinese builders .... (build) several eco-cities in recent years.

ever, never, for, since, just, already, yet

3a These words are frequently used with the present perfect. Complete each explanation with the correct word.

already • ever • for • just • never • since • yet

1 We can use .... in questions with the present perfect. It means 'at any time in your life'.
2 We use .... with the present perfect to talk about very recent activities.
3 We use .... with the present perfect to say that something has happened, possibly earlier than we thought.
4 We can use .... to make negative sentences in the present perfect. It means 'at no time in your life'.
5 We use .... and .... with the present perfect to talk about things that started in the past and continue in the present. We use .... with periods of time, and .... with specific moments in time.
6 We use .... with the present perfect to say that something has not happened, but we think it is going to happen soon. We use it in negative sentences and questions.

3b What is the usual position of the words in 3a in a sentence?

1 Words that go just before the past participle:
....
....
2 Words that go just before a time expression:
....
3 A word that usually goes at the end of the sentence: ....

GRAMMAR REFERENCE ➤ PAGE 42

4 Complete the sentences with the present perfect form of these verbs. Put the other word in the correct place in the sentence.

already/visit • ever/live • have/for • just/rain
love/since • never/live • ~~not sell/yet~~

1 They *haven't sold* their flat *yet*.
2 I .... in a big city, but I'd like to.
3 My brother .... New York. He went there for a holiday five years ago.
4 We .... this car .... ten years.
5 Why is it wet here? .... it ....?
6 I .... this city .... the day I arrived here.
7 .... you .... in a cottage?

Developing vocabulary

5 Read about the Shard. Choose the best answer (A, B, C or D) to complete the text.

Have you (1) .... thought about what it's like living in a skyscraper? London didn't (2) .... to have any very tall skyscrapers. But in the last twenty years they have (3) .... appearing in different parts of the city. In the Shard, which is London's tallest skyscraper, there are 13 floors of apartments. They haven't sold them all (4) ...., probably because they are so expensive.

One thing that people who live in the Shard have (5) .... learnt is that you need to think before you leave your apartment. One day a man went down from his flat on the 65th floor to the main door. Then he realised that he (6) .... forgotten his mobile phone! Of course, everybody always asks the same question. What happens if the lift (7) .... work? The good news is that there are 44 lifts in total in the Shard, and they repair broken lifts really quickly. So the people who live there have (8) .... needed to walk up to their flats.

Renzo Piano is the architect who designed the Shard. He (9) .... just won a prize for his work. Some people love the building and others hate it. But it is so famous that it has (10) .... become one of the most iconic buildings in London.

	A	B	C	D
1	yet	ever	just	always
2	use	used	usually	always
3	begin	began	start	started
4	ever	just	yesterday	yet
5	already	ever	never	yet
6	has	had	have	was
7	does	doesn't	hasn't	isn't
8	ever	just	never	yet
9	did	has	have	was
10	already	ever	never	not

Extreme adjectives

1 Match the extreme adjectives (1–10) with the normal adjectives (a–j).

1	ancient	a	bad
2	boiling	b	beautiful
3	dreadful	c	big
4	enormous	d	cold
5	filthy	e	crowded
6	freezing	f	dirty
7	tiny	g	hot
8	silent	h	old
9	stunning	i	quiet
10	packed	j	small

2 Look at the example sentences. Then match the correct halves of the rules.

The film was really bad.   The film was quite bad.
The film was really awful.   The film was very bad.
The film was absolutely awful.

1	We use *totally, completely* and *absolutely*	a	with normal adjectives.
2	We use *very* and *extremely*	b	with normal adjectives.
3	We use *really*	c	with extreme adjectives.
4	We use *quite* and *rather*	d	with both normal and extreme adjectives.

3 Complete the sentences with the correct adjectives from 1.

1 The view from our window wasn't just beautiful. It was absolutely ....

2 The city of Athens isn't just old. It's .... It's existed for over 3,000 years!

3 It was very .... in the city today – over 35°C.

4 At the weekend the shops in the city centre are totally .... with people.

5 The streets are usually quite .... because nobody cleans them.

6 There wasn't a sound in the park. It was completely ....

4a PRONUNCIATION ▶ 16 Listen and check your answers. Which adjectives do we stress more – normal or extreme?

4b Practise saying the sentences in 3 with the correct stress.

5a SPEAKING Write down one place or item for each extreme adjective in 1.

5b Work with a partner. Say the words in random order. Can they guess the extreme adjective?

The North Pole.

Freezing?

Yes!

EXPLAINING STATISTICS

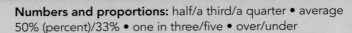

LIFE SKILLS OBJECTIVES	KEY CONCEPTS
■ To look at different ways of presenting statistics. ■ To learn how to talk about and express statistics. ■ To find and present information using statistics.	**Numbers and proportions:** half/a third/a quarter • average 50% (percent)/33% • one in three/five • over/under **Changes:** rise/fall • get higher/get lower • increase/decrease stay the same • change little **Modifying adverbs:** dramatically • gradually • slightly steadily

1 Work with a partner. Guess the answers to these questions about New York.

1 What is the average temperature in January?

2 What is the average temperature in July?

3 Do you think temperatures are getting higher or lower each year?

4 How do you think most New Yorkers travel to work?

5 Do you think there are more tourists in New York now than in the past?

3 Look again at the information in 2. Find ...

1 a pie chart ....

2 a line graph ....

3 a bar graph ....

4 a table ....

2 READING Read the statistics below and check your answers in 1.

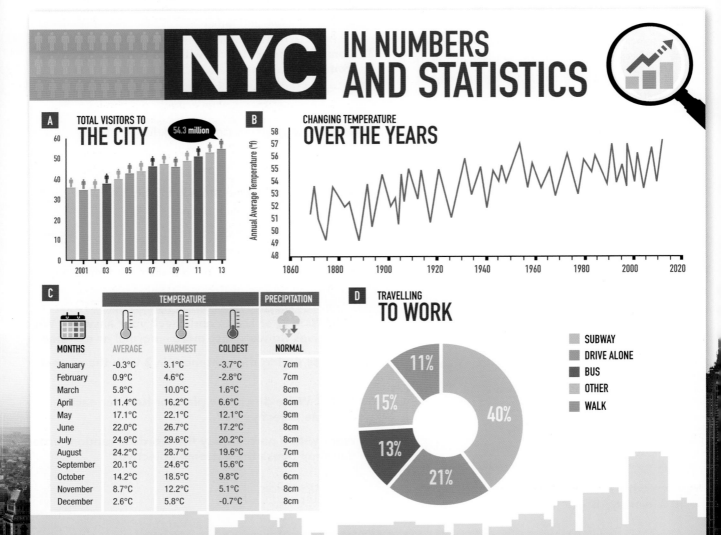

NYC IN NUMBERS AND STATISTICS

A TOTAL VISITORS TO **THE CITY** — 54.3 million

B CHANGING TEMPERATURE **OVER THE YEARS**

C

MONTHS	TEMPERATURE			PRECIPITATION
	AVERAGE	WARMEST	COLDEST	NORMAL
January	-0.3°C	3.1°C	-3.7°C	7cm
February	0.9°C	4.6°C	-2.8°C	7cm
March	5.8°C	10.0°C	1.6°C	8cm
April	11.4°C	16.2°C	6.6°C	8cm
May	17.1°C	22.1°C	12.1°C	9cm
June	22.0°C	26.7°C	17.2°C	8cm
July	24.9°C	29.6°C	20.2°C	8cm
August	24.2°C	28.7°C	19.6°C	7cm
September	20.1°C	24.6°C	15.6°C	6cm
October	14.2°C	18.5°C	9.8°C	6cm
November	8.7°C	12.2°C	5.1°C	8cm
December	2.6°C	5.8°C	-0.7°C	8cm

D TRAVELLING **TO WORK**

SUBWAY 40%
DRIVE ALONE 21%
BUS 13%
OTHER 15%
WALK 11%

4 Read these statements about the information in 2. Choose the correct alternative. Use a dictionary if necessary.

1 The number of tourists is gradually *rising/falling*.

2 Almost *a quarter/a third* of people drive to work alone in New York.

3 Just *over/under* 50% of people go to work by subway or bus.

4 *Just under/Approximately* one in ten New Yorkers walk to work.

5 The average temperature increases *dramatically/slightly* between June and July.

6 The amount of rain *decreases/stays the same* between March and April.

7 The temperatures in New York have *changed little/increased steadily* in the last forty years.

5a Match the parts of the sentences with the diagrams.

a ☐ The average temperature stays approximately the same between …
....

b ☐ Just over a third of New Yorkers …
....

c ☐ Under a quarter of New Yorkers …
....

d ☐ One in ten New Yorkers …
....

e ☐ About two thirds of people in New York don't …
....

f ☐ ....
… is rising.

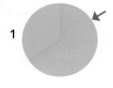 1
 2
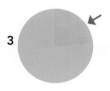 3
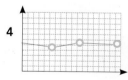 4
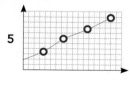 5
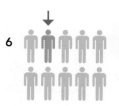 6

5b Complete the sentences in an appropriate way using information from 2.

5c Work with a partner. Compare your sentences.

6 You are going to hear two students presenting information about the use of social media in New York. Before you listen, guess the answers to these questions.

1 In general, which age group do you think is the most frequent user of social media and why?

13 to 17   25 to 34   45 to 54
18 to 24   35 to 44   55 to 64

2 Which age group do you think is the least frequent? Why?

3 Do you think more men or more women use social media?

7 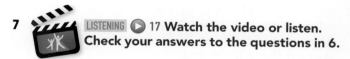 LISTENING ▶ 17 **Watch the video or listen. Check your answers to the questions in 6.**

8 ▶ 17 Watch or listen again. Are these statements True (T) or False (F)? Correct the false statements.

1 About one third of users are between 13 and 34. T/F

2 One in ten users are aged between 13 and 17. T/F

3 Under a quarter of users are people between the ages of 25 and 34. T/F

4 The smallest group of users are between the ages of 45 and 54. T/F

5 The first speaker thinks that the number of older users is going to increase steadily in the future. T/F

6 The number of users rises steadily from the ages of 13 and 17 to the ages of 25 and 34. T/F

7 The number falls very gradually between 34 and 44. T/F

8 There are a lot more women than men using social media. T/F

9 SPEAKING **Work with a partner. Did any of the information surprise you? Why/Why not?**

LIFE TASK

Follow these steps:

1 *Work in a small group. Choose a city. It can be where you live, an important city in your country, or an international city.*

2 *Look for interesting statistics about the city. Try to find a pie chart, a line graph, a bar graph, and a table (for example with temperatures).*

3 *Either individually or as a group, write about the information in the chart, graph or table. Use words from 4.*

4 *Present your information to the class either as a poster or as a computer presentation.*

Listening

1 SPEAKING **Work with a partner. Take turns to describe the photo.**

2 LISTENING ▶ 18 **Listen to part of a podcast where a student called Deniz describes her experience of the Erasmus project. Answer these questions.**

1 Where's Deniz from?
2 Where has she been living?
3 What languages has she been speaking?

3 ▶ 18 **Listen again and complete the notes with one or two words.**

Notepad ✎

Deniz has been living in this new city since
(a) .... and she is leaving at
the end of (b) .... She says the
university there is really (c) ....,
and she likes the city because it's quite small,
but very (d) .... She's seen
two or three good (e) ....
there. She thinks the best part of her
stay has been meeting people from
(f) .... Every night they make
a (g) .... from their country.
It has been difficult for Deniz to understand
explanations of (h) .... in a
different language. Yesterday she finished her
(i) ....

4 SPEAKING **What about you?**

1 Would you like to live and study in another country for a year? Why/Why not?
2 Where would you most like to go and study?

> I'd like to live abroad. And you?

> Yes, I'd like to go to a country where they speak English.

Grammar in context

🎬🔄 *Present perfect continuous*

1a Read these sentences. Which are in the present perfect continuous and which are in the present perfect simple?

1 I**'ve been living** here for four months.
2 I**'ve seen** two or three brilliant concerts.
3 I**'ve made** friends with people from all over Europe.
4 Recently we**'ve been doing** lots of exams.

1b Which of the sentences gives more importance to ...

a the completion and result of an action?
b the process and duration of an action?
c how many times an action has happened?
d the fact that an action is temporary, incomplete or has finished very recently?

1c Complete this rule for the formation of the present perfect continuous.

has/have + ... + ...

GRAMMAR REFERENCE ➤ PAGE 42

2 Look at the photos. What have these people been doing?

1 ....
2 ....
3 ....
4 ....
5 ....

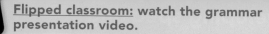
3 Are these sentences grammatically correct or not? Why/Why not? If they aren't correct, change them.

1 Ouch! I've been cutting my finger.

2 We've been studying English for eight years.

3 Have you been crying?

4 She's been reading this book three times.

5 My brother has painted his bedroom, but he hasn't finished.

6 We've been waiting for the bus for half an hour and it still hasn't come.

7 Oh no! I've been breaking the window.

8 This week I've been staying with my grandparents but I'm going home tomorrow.

4 Choose the correct alternative.

1 Stop singing that song. You've *sung/been singing* it all afternoon.

2 That's it. I've *done/been doing* all my homework.

3 It's terrible! Max has *had/been having* an accident.

4 She's *looked/been looking* for her keys all day, but she still hasn't found them.

5 Why are you dirty? What have you *done/been doing*?

6 That actor has *made/been making* twenty films.

7 My eyes hurt. I've *worked/been working* on the computer all day.

8 You've *played/been playing* computer games since ten o'clock this morning. It's time to switch off!

5 Complete the dialogue with the present perfect simple or continuous forms of the verbs given.

6 SPEAKING **Work with a partner. Take it in turns to ask and answer the questions. Use the present perfect continuous or simple in your answers. Decide which answers are the most imaginative.**

1 Why are you hiding behind the sofa?

2 Why are your clothes so dirty?

3 Why are you crying?

4 Why are you so happy?

5 Why are you bored?

6 Why are you so tired?

7 Why aren't you watching your favourite TV programme?

Why are you hiding behind the sofa?

I've been watching a documentary about spiders and I'm really scared of them.

Interviewer:	Silvia, you're Italian, but at the moment you're living here in Bath. How long (a) .... you .... (live) here?
Silvia:	For six months. I (b) .... (study) at the university, but I (c) .... (not finish) my course yet.
Interviewer:	What (d) .... you .... (study)?
Silvia:	Medicine. I (e) .... (work) in a hospital here, too. That finishes next month.
Interviewer:	Where exactly (f) .... you .... (live)?
Silvia:	Well, I (g) .... (make) two really good friends on the course. We (h) .... (live) in a house in the suburbs. I love Bath!

Developing speaking

Describing photos – 1

a

b

1 SPEAKING **Look at the photos. Work with a partner. Write at least four words that you could use to describe each one.**

2 LISTENING ▶ 19 **Listen to someone talking about one of the photos and answer the questions.**

   1 Which photo do they describe?

   2 Which words on your list do you hear?

   3 What does the speaker think of the place in the photo?

3 ▶ 19 **Listen again. Which of the words or expressions in the Speaking bank does the speaker use?**

> 💬 **SPEAKING BANK**
>
> **Useful expressions for describing photos**
> - In the photo I can see …
> - The photo shows …
> - In the foreground …
> - In the background …
> - At the top of the photo …
> - At the bottom of the photo …
> - In the middle of the photo …
> - On the right …
> - On the left …
> - In the top/bottom right/left corner …

4 **Look at photo b and complete the sentences with the words from the Speaking bank.**

   1 .... see a quiet road.

   2 On the ...., there are some people sitting at a table.

   3 In the ...., I can see trees and fields.

   4 In the .... corner, I can see a small blackboard.

   5 In the .... of the photo, there is a blue car.

5 SPEAKING **Tell your partner which place in photos a and b you prefer. Give reasons for your opinions.**

PRACTICE MAKES PERFECT

6 SPEAKING **Work with a partner. Take it in turns to do the task below. Use some of the expressions in the Speaking bank.**

Describe the two photos. Then say which place you would prefer to live in and give reasons for your opinion.

c

d

Developing writing

An informal email describing a place

1 Work with a partner. Do you think these statements about the English city of Birmingham are True (T) or False (F)?

1 Birmingham is the second biggest city in Britain.   T / F
2 Birmingham has more canals than Venice.   T / F
3 Birmingham has a museum and theme park dedicated to chocolate.   T / F
4 Heavy metal music began in Birmingham.   T / F
5 Birmingham isn't on the coast, but it has a beach.   T / F

2 READING **Read this email written by Mia from Birmingham and check your answers in 1.**

✉   ✕

Hi Elena,

Thanks for your last email. It was great to hear from you!

You asked me to tell you something about my home town. Birmingham is actually the second biggest city in Britain. And it has more canals than Venice! In the past, the canals used to be quite dirty because they were next to busy factories. But they've changed a lot.

There's one really famous factory here that everybody likes. It's a chocolate factory. There's even a chocolate museum and theme park. They've just opened a 4D 'chocolate adventure' there!

We also have an enormous shopping centre called the Bullring. It's near the city centre and it's always packed. Oh, and there's a great stadium for concerts, too! People usually say that heavy metal music started in Birmingham.

Some years we've had a beach in the city centre in the summer. Birmingham isn't on the coast, but they fill an area in a main square with sand and you can pretend that you're on a real beach.

Anyway, write back soon. Don't forget to tell me about your home town. Has it changed much in the last few years?

Love,

Mia

---

3 **Would you like to visit Birmingham after reading Mia's email? Why/Why not?**

4 **Look again at the email in 2. Complete the words and expressions in the Writing bank.**

> ✎ **WRITING BANK**
>
> **Useful words and expressions in informal letters and emails**
> - Begin with *Dear* or (a) .... and the person's (b) ....
> - Your first sentences can be *Thanks for* (c) .... and/or *It was great* (d) ....
> - Use contractions (e.g. *they're* or (e) ....).
> - Use short forms of words (e.g. *Thanks* instead of (f) ....).
> - Use interjections like *Well* or (g) ....
> - Use exclamation marks (e.g. *It has more canals than Venice* (h) ....)
> - Use *Any* (i) .... to change the subject.
> - Use *Write* (j) ...., *All the best* and/or (k) .... to end.

5 **Work with a partner. Make notes about your home town. What type of place is it? What is special about it? Has it changed in the last few years? How?**

PRACTICE MAKES PERFECT

6 **Look at the task below and write the email. Include all the information and organise your ideas from 5 into paragraphs. Use words and expressions from the Writing bank.**

An English-speaking friend has asked you to write them an email about your home town. Write the email. Say what type of place your home town is and what is special about it. Describe any recent changes.

WRITING BANK ➤ PAGE 150

Grammar reference

Present perfect simple

FORM

Affirmative	subject + **have/has** + past participle She **has gone** home.
Negative	We **haven't seen** him.
Question	**Have** you **been** there?
Short answers	Yes, I **have**. No, they **haven't**.

USE

We use the **present perfect** to talk about:

1 an experience in someone's lifetime, without saying the exact time when the event occurred.

I've visited Vienna.

2 recent events which have a result in the present.

She's bought a new house.
(= She has a new house now.)

3 actions or situations that began in the past but continue in the present.

Helen's lived here for three years.
(= Helen still lives here now.)

ever, never, for, since, just, already, yet

These words are often used with the present perfect:
We can use **ever** in questions to mean 'at any time in your life'.

*Have you **ever** been to Japan?*

We can use **never** ('at no time in your life') in negative sentences.

*I've **never** lived in a big city.*

We use **for** and **since** with past actions or situations which continue in the present. **For** goes with periods of time and **since** with moments.

*I've lived here **for** three months/**since** January.*

We use **just** to emphasise that something happened very recently.

*We've **just** arrived. (= We arrived only a second ago.)*

We use **already** for something that has happened earlier than we expected.

*I don't need to go there. I've **already** been.*

We use **yet** with questions and negative sentences to ask if something we expect has happened, or to say that it hasn't.

*Have you moved **yet**?*
*I haven't moved **yet**.*

Present perfect continuous

FORM

Affirmative	subject + **have/has** + **been** + -ing She **has been living** in the US.
Negative	We **haven't been studying** French.
Question	**Have** you **been reading**?

USE

We use the **present perfect continuous** when we want to emphasise the process and duration of an action.

I've been living here for a year.

If an action is very short, we cannot use the continuous form.

~~I've been breaking my leg.~~

We also use the continuous to emphasise that an action finished very recently or is incomplete.

*I've been studying. (= I'm tired **because** I finished a second ago or I still haven't finished.)*

If we want to emphasise the completion and result of an action, or how many times an action happens, we must use the **present perfect simple**.

I've washed the dishes. (= They are all finished).

I've written seven books. Not ~~I've been writing seven books~~.

Vocabulary

Cities and houses block of flats • bungalow • city centre • cottage • detached house • factory • flat inner city • outskirts • port • semi-detached house • skyscraper • square • suburbs • terraced house • town hall

Adjectives describing cities busy • clean • crowded • dirty • historic • lively • modern • noisy • quiet

Extreme adjectives ancient • boiling • dreadful • enormous • filthy • freezing • packed • silent stunning • tiny

Other words and phrases ➤ page 138

Grammar revision

Present perfect simple

1 Complete the text with the present perfect simple or past simple form of the verbs given and choose the correct alternative.

I (a) .... (live) in this city (b) *for/since* many years and I love it here. The city (c) .... (change) a lot in the last five years. The biggest change is that the city (d) .... (get) a lot bigger recently. They (e) .... (build) a lot of new offices in the centre, and there are more planned. In 2014 they (f) .... (start) to build a big new sports stadium near the port but they (g) .... (not finish) building it (h) *already/yet*. They have (i) *ever/just* pulled down a lot of buildings in the area. In the past, everybody (j) .... (want) an office there, but not now.

Present perfect continuous

2 Complete the sentences with the present perfect simple or continuous of the verbs given.

1 .... you .... (switch) the light off?

2 You need a rest. You .... (study) for hours!

3 My hands are dirty. I .... (fix) the car.

4 Poor Liam! He .... (break) his leg.

5 Charlie .... (study) in the US all summer, but tomorrow he's coming home.

6 They .... (build) lots of flats here for a while now and I don't think they're going to stop.

7 She .... (make) ten films.

8 I'm sorry. .... you .... (wait) for long?

9 My legs are tired. I .... (walk) all day.

10 That's it! We .... (finish) this exercise.

Vocabulary revision

CITIES AND HOUSES

1 Write the words.

1 A house which is separate, not touching other houses.
....

2 A small house, usually in a village or in the country.
....

3 A building for the offices of the local government.
....

4 The area where ships stop, where there are usually buildings.
....

5 An area where many people live, and there are often social problems there.
....

6 An area away from the centre of the city where people who work in the city live.
....

7 A house which is attached to houses on both sides.
....

8 A tall building where there are many homes.
....

ADJECTIVES DESCRIBING CITIES

2 What adjective can you use in each situation?

1 A concert in a small room with hundreds of people: c.................................

2 A place which nobody ever cleans: d.................................

3 A place which is old and interesting: h.................................

4 A place where there is no noise: q.................................

5 A place where there are a lot of exciting things happening: l.................................

6 A place with lots of people and activity: b.................................

EXTREME ADJECTIVES

3 What is the normal equivalent of these extreme adjectives?

1 stunning ....

2 boiling ....

3 filthy ....

4 dreadful ....

5 enormous ....

6 packed ....

Total: .... / 40 points

4 Feed your mind

Vocabulary

Food and meals

1 Work with a partner. How many of these words can you find in the photos?

> carrot • chicken • cream • lamb • lettuce • oil
> olive • pancake • pea • peach • pie • plum • rice
> semi-skimmed milk • sweetcorn • prawn • tuna • turkey

a 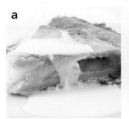   b    c

2 Put the words in 1 in the correct place in the table.

Fruit	
Vegetables	
Meat/Fish/Seafood	
Dairy products	
Sweets/Bakery products	
Other	

3a Read the questions and check that you understand the words in red. Which of the words can you use to talk about the photos in 1?

1 What is a typical **starter** in a restaurant in your country?
2 What is a popular **main course**?
3 What is your favourite national **dish**?
4 What is your favourite **dessert**?
5 When do you usually have a **snack**? What do you have?

3b PRONUNCIATION These words have two syllables. Where is the stress in each word? Which word is the 'odd one out'?

> carrot • chicken • dessert • lettuce • olive
> pancake • starter • sweetcorn • turkey

3c ▶ 20 Listen, check and repeat.

3d SPEAKING Use the questions in 3a to interview your partner.

Describing food

4 Match these words with the definitions.

> baked • boiled • fast • fresh • fried
> frozen • healthy/unhealthy • raw • roast
> spicy • stale • tasty

1 with a hot, strong flavour ....
2 good, with lots of flavour ....
3 not cooked ....
4 good/bad for your body ....
5 preserved by becoming extremely cold
....
6 cooked in hot oil ....
7 cooked in very hot water ....
8 to describe cakes cooked in an oven
....
9 to describe meat cooked in an oven
....
10 recently picked, caught or prepared
....
11 made or served very quickly, e.g. burgers and pizzas ....
12 old and bad, not fresh ....

5 Work with a partner. Think of one or two types of food that go with each word in 4.

boiled – boiled egg, boiled vegetables

6 LISTENING ▶ 21 Listen. For each dialogue, choose a word from 4 to describe the food.

1 ....   4 ....
2 ....   5 ....
3 ....   6 ....

7 SPEAKING Work with a partner. Describe a type of food or drink. Can your partner identify it?

It's a type of meat. It's quite healthy. It comes from a bird that's bigger than a chicken.

Turkey!

1 Work with a partner. Look at the photos and the title of the text. What do you think the text is about?

2 READING Read the article and check your predictions.

THE FUTURE OF FOOD?
ELIMINATE IT!

When you get home this evening, what will you have for dinner? Pizza? A salad? A turkey sandwich? It can sometimes take
5 a long time to decide what to eat. One man who doesn't have that problem is Rob Rhinehart. Rob is the inventor of a product called Soylent, which some people say will
10 be the future of food.

Rob is a software engineer in his twenties. He invented Soylent because he didn't have much money, or much time. Because
15 he didn't have much money, he bought and ate a lot of fast food. And he realised how unhealthy it was
20 making him. Because he didn't have much time, he hated wasting it by cooking, even if it was just frying an egg for
25 breakfast.

Rob's solution to this problem was to create a product that is a mixture of all the nutrients that the body needs to survive. To make the mixture, Rob studied
30 biology and chemistry. He turned his kitchen into a laboratory. Once he had his powder of 35 essential nutrients, he added water and drank it. Since then Rob has had Soylent for 90% of
35 all of his meals for a year.

Some experts say it's impossible to feed on nothing more than powder and water. They say that healthy, fresh food is essential.
40 But Rob believes that you need carbohydrates, not bread, and you need vitamins and minerals, not fruit and vegetables. According to Rob, he feels much healthier with this new
45 diet. He also says he's saved a lot of money because the nutrients are cheaper than either fresh or fast food. And he's saved a lot of time (and energy)
50 because there's no frying, no roasting and no baking.

Some people believe that Soylent will have other, worldwide benefits. When
55 you see the increase in the world population and the effects of global warming, it appears that it's going to be difficult to produce enough fresh
60 fruit and vegetables for everybody. For example, in California there is little water. But 80% of all the water goes to farms. So the agriculture that produces natural food often has
65 a bad effect on the environment. Soylent doesn't. Making it is cheap too, so maybe it could help solve world hunger in developing countries.

> **Most of us don't only eat to survive. Eating tasty food is part of every culture.**

70 But is this a depressing future for food? Most of us don't only eat to survive. Eating tasty food is part of every culture. It's an enjoyable activity and a nice way to spend
75 time. Most people who have tried Soylent say that it doesn't taste bad, that it tastes a bit like pancake mixture. Rob says that he hasn't got tired of the taste yet. But he also
80 admits that other people seem to enjoy food more than he does.

In the next few weeks, scientists are meeting to discuss their detailed research into Soylent. Will it be the
85 future of food or just a passing fad? Only time will tell.

3 Read the text again. Are these sentences True (T) or False (F)? Write the number(s) of the line(s) where you found the answer.

1 An advantage of Soylent is that you don't waste time deciding what to eat. T / F ....

2 Rob Rhinehart wanted to create a healthy alternative to fast food. T / F ....

3 Rob created his product in a professional laboratory. T / F ....

4 Soylent is almost the only thing that Rob consumes. T / F ....

5 Rob believes that our bodies do not need traditional food, they need the nutrients that come from that food. T / F ....

6 According to the text, agriculture is damaging the environment in some places. T / F ....

7 The writer of the text believes that food is just a question of nutrients. T / F ....

8 Rob doesn't like the taste of Soylent. T / F ....

4 ⚙ **CRITICAL THINKING**

Think! Then compare ideas with your class.

- Do you think Soylent is a good idea for society? Why/Why not?

5 What do the underlined words in the text mean? Guess and then check in your dictionary.

6 SPEAKING What about *you*?

1 Would you like to try Soylent? Why/Why not?

2 What other alternatives to the world food problem can you think of?

Grammar in context

will, be going to, present continuous and present simple for future

1a Match the sentences (a–d) with the rules (1–4).

a In the next few weeks, scientists **are meeting** to discuss their research into Soylent.

b When you **get** home this evening, what will you have for dinner?

c Some people say this **will** be the future of food.

d It appears that it's **going to** be difficult to produce enough fresh fruit.

1 We use the **present simple** with time expressions like **when, after, before, as soon as** to talk about the future.

2 We use the **present continuous** to talk about fixed, confirmed future arrangements.

3 We use **will** to make general predictions.

4 We use **be going to** to make predictions based on some sort of evidence.

1b Read the sentences and complete rules (1–4) with *will*, *be going to* or the present simple.

a The conference **begins** at ten o'clock tomorrow.

b I'm **going to** attend the conference.

c It **will** be the second annual conference.

d Hey! I know. I'**ll** invite Scott.

1 We use .... for decisions that we make at the moment of speaking.

2 We use .... to talk about an objective truth, a 'fact'.

3 We use .... to talk about a future event that is part of a timetable or routine.

4 We use .... to talk about plans or intentions.

GRAMMAR REFERENCE ➤ PAGE 54

2 Complete the sentences with the correct form of the present simple or *will*.

1 When the waiter .... (come), we .... (order) our food.

2 My brother .... (call) you back as soon as he .... (finish) his dinner.

3 I .... (do) my homework before my dad .... (make) the dinner.

4 When you .... (go) to the shops tomorrow, ... you .... (buy) some bread?

5 When you .... (come) to my house, we .... (make) a chocolate cake.

6 Before my mum .... (get) home tonight, I .... (clean) the kitchen.

7 When I .... (have) enough money, I .... (eat) out with my friends.

8 I .... (not take) the pie out of the oven until it .... (be) ready.

9 As soon as the adverts .... (come) on, we .... (make) a snack.

10 As soon as the water .... (boil), I .... (add) the peas.

3 What do you think is going to happen in each situation? Use these words to write predictions.

burn • catch • cut • drop

1 ....
....

2 ....
....

3 ....
....

4 ....
....

4 Look at this poster for an event. How many sentences in the present continuous can you make about the event?

Two experts are talking next Monday. They're having the event at the town hall.

FUTURE FOOD
NEXT MONDAY! A TALK BY TWO EXPERTS!

Where? Town Hall

6 pm: Start

First speaker: Film director, Stephanie Brand, talks about her new film: What is in our food?

7 pm: Watch a preview of the film

8 pm: Second speaker: Scientist, Oliver Reeves, explains his solution to the food crisis

8.30 pm: Snack

9 pm: Prize-giving ceremony for school projects

Friday 12th 7 pm: TV programme about the talk on channel 8

5 Read these pairs of sentences and questions. Choose the correct alternative. If you think both are correct, mark both and explain any difference in meaning.

1a What do you do this weekend?
1b What are you doing this weekend?

2a I think it'll rain tomorrow.
2b I think it's raining tomorrow.

3a Someone's calling. I'll see who it is.
3b Someone's calling. I'm seeing who it is.

4a She's going to win the competition.
4b She'll win the competition.

5a When I get home, I'll make a snack.
5b When I will get home, I'll make a snack.

6a What time does your plane leave?
6b What time is your plane leaving?

6a Work with a partner. Make notes on these topics with predictions for this year.

> clothes • entertainment • music • sport technology • your city • your country

6b **SPEAKING** Work in a group. Compare your predictions.

> *Who do you think will win the Champions' League this year?*

> *I think it'll be an English team.*

Developing vocabulary

Prefixes

1a Match these words with the definitions.

> overcooked • precooked • recooked • undercooked

1 not cooked enough ....
2 cooked again ....
3 cooked before ....
4 cooked too much ....

1b What do the prefixes in red do? Do they change the meaning of the word or do they change the type of word (verb, adjective, etc.)?

2 Match these prefixes with their meaning.

Prefix		Meaning	
1	pre	a	again
2	over	b	not enough
3	mis	c	the opposite
4	inter	d	wrong, incorrect
5	dis	e	before
6	co	f	too much
7	re	g	with, together
8	under	h	between

3 Complete the sentences by adding the correct prefix to the word in red.

1 This isn't just a problem for this country. It's an ....**national** problem.

2 You have to ....**do** the exercise because the first time you did it you made a lot of mistakes.

3 Sorry, I ....**understood** what you said. I thought you said 30, not 13.

4 There are lots of advantages and ....**advantages** with genetically-modified food.

5 They've ....**booked** the flight – there aren't enough seats for everyone.

6 Food is still a terrible problem in many countries. Some people ....**estimate** the problem and don't think it's so important.

7 The team need to ....**operate** and work together.

4a Complete these questions with words from 1 and 3.

1 Have you ever .... something that somebody said to you in English? When?

2 Forget the good things. What do you think are the .... of new technology?

3 Do you ever eat .... meals or do you always eat freshly-prepared meals?

4 What do you think is the biggest .... problem at the moment? Which countries does it affect?

4b **SPEAKING** Work with a partner. Ask and answer the questions in 4a.

Preparing FOOD

- To think about why it's important to know how to cook.
- To learn about food safety.
- To learn how to prepare a simple, healthy dish.

KEY CONCEPTS

nutritious [adj]: *This is a nutritious meal because it contains the most important things that we need to be healthy.* **ingredient [n]:** *The main ingredient in paella is rice.* **contaminate [v]:** *When you touch food with dirty hands, you contaminate it and make it go bad.* **food poisoning [n]:** *When you eat food with bad bacteria, you get food poisoning and become ill.*

1 Work with a partner. Discuss these questions.

1 Do you ever prepare your own meals? Which meals can you make?

2 How important do you think it is to learn to cook? Why?

3 Do you think schools should teach teenagers to cook? Why/Why not?

4 Would you like to be able to cook, or cook better? Why/Why not?

2 READING Read this article by a top chef who is interested in getting teenagers to cook and eat healthy food. Match the titles (A–J) with the correct section (1–10).

A Save time
B Improve your social life
C Enjoy yourself!
D Looking after yourself
E Quality control

F Future career?
G Save money
H Taste the difference!
I Travel the world
J Become independent

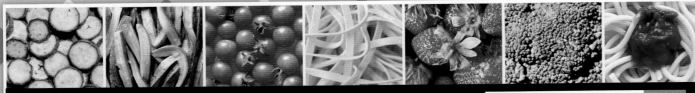

Recipes ▾   How-to ▾   Videos ▾   Chef's blog ▾   [   ] SEARCH

TEENAGERS
Time to cook!

Being able to cook is a useful skill that everyone should learn, and the earlier the better. Here are ten good reasons why!

1 When you learn to cook, you discover that with just a few basic, natural ingredients you can make delicious meals that taste better than typical processed food. You can't compare the flavours of home-cooked meals with meals that come in a packet!

2 Often with pre-packaged, processed foods you don't really know what the ingredients are. But when you cook dishes yourself, you know exactly what they contain, and you can make sure that everything you eat is top quality in terms of taste and nutrition.

3 When you cook at home, you can prepare food in healthy ways, by boiling or baking, for example, instead of frying in lots of oil. You can limit the amount of sugar and fat in each meal. All of this will make it easier to control how healthy you are.

4 Learning to cook can give you a great sense of freedom. Knowing you are able to cook is a great skill to have because you won't need to rely on your parents or others to cook for you. You'll see that you can care for yourself when you live away from home.

5 Everybody knows that eating out is nearly always more expensive than eating at home. The economic factor is important for everyone, but particularly when you're a student.

6 Cooking just one dish can mean you have food for several days. Just increase the quantities and you'll have enough to freeze and eat another day. That means you won't have to depend on unhealthy fast food when you don't have much time.

7 Learning how to cook can be fun! Once you know the basics of cooking, you can create your own dishes and experiment with hundreds of different flavours. You can have a great time just by being imaginative and creative in the kitchen.

8 When you learn to cook, there's nothing better than inviting friends round and letting them try what you've made. It's a great way to make your friends happy and show them your skills, too!

9 Cooking new dishes from around the world can teach you about different countries and cultures. Trying different types of food, flavours and ways of cooking can transport you to places you've always wanted to visit.

10 Who knows where cooking will take you? There are lots of great jobs out there connected with food. Maybe you'll become a professional chef, or perhaps an expert in nutrition, a food blogger, or even a restaurant critic. Many people have taken their love of food and cooking and turned it into their dream job. Just look at me!

3 Read these statements. Which sections (1–10) give us information about these advantages of knowing how to cook? Find the sentences that give you the information.

a   It's cheaper. ....

b   It can be a good way to impress other people. ....

c   You can feel good because you don't depend on other people. ....

d   It can be a great way to spend your free time. ....

e   It could become your job one day! ....

f   You can decide on the quantities to include of ingredients that are not so healthy. ....

g   You can learn to combine ingredients to make really tasty but simple dishes. ....

h   You can learn about the world. ....

i   You know exactly what you are eating because you bought it yourself. ....

j   You can save time by cooking large quantities. ....

4 Work with a partner. Decide what you think are the three best reasons for learning how to cook. Choose the reason you think is the least important. Explain why.

5 LISTENING ▶ 22 **Watch the video or listen. What is each chef making?**

Jasmine: ....

Ben: ....

6 ▶ 22 **Watch or listen again. Both chefs are doing something wrong in the kitchen. Match the person to the problems and make notes about why it's a problem.**

Person	Problem	Why?
....	olive oil	....
Jasmine	apron and hair	....
....	jewellery	....
Ben	knife and chopping board	....

7 Work with a partner. What do you think of the advice in the video? What other 'food safety advice' can you give?

LIFE TASK

Work in a small group and follow these steps:

1 *Find or invent a recipe for a salad that is healthy and tasty.*

2 *Prepare a presentation to your class. In your presentation you need to:*

- *give a list of all the ingredients.*
- *explain why the salad is healthy.*
- *give any special instructions about how to make the salad.*
- *give any necessary 'food safety' advice for preparing and preserving the salad.*

3 *Give your presentation. Vote for the healthiest and tastiest salads.*

Listening

1 SPEAKING Work with a partner. Look at the photos. Take it in turns to describe what you can see.

a

b

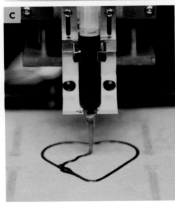

c

d

2 LISTENING ▶ 23 Listen to four experts predicting what we will be eating in 2050. Match each speaker to a photo in 1.

Speaker 1: ....   Speaker 3: ....

Speaker 2: ....   Speaker 4: ....

3 ▶ 23 Listen again. Match the speakers and their opinions.

		1	2	3	4
a	People won't eat out in 2050.				
b	I've eaten the main food of the future and it tastes good.				
c	Not everybody thinks that the food of the future will be healthy.				
d	We won't spend a lot of time cooking in the future.				
e	People already eat this food in some parts of the world.				
f	The only good thing about the food of the future is that it will be good for the environment.				
g	The problem with the food of the future is the opinion that people have of it now.				
h	You'll be able to produce the food of the future very quickly.				

4 SPEAKING What about you?

What do you think of these four predictions? Share your ideas with the rest of the class.

Grammar in context

Future continuous and future perfect

1a Read the sentences. Which are in the future continuous and which are in the future perfect?

1 By 2050 3D printers **will have become** a part of everyday life.

2 That's what we'**ll be eating** in 2050.

3 We'**ll be using** 3D printers at home in the future.

4 By 2050 restaurants **will have disappeared**.

1b Choose the correct alternative.

1 We use the *future continuous/future perfect* to talk about activities in progress at a particular time in the future.

2 We use the *future continuous/future perfect* to talk about activities that will be finished before a particular time in the future.

3 We often use the preposition *by/in* with the future perfect. It means 'some time before'.

1c Complete the rules.

1 To make the future .... we use *will/won't + be + ...*.

2 To make the future .... we use *will/won't + have + ...*.

GRAMMAR REFERENCE ▶ PAGE 54

2a Complete the predictions with these verbs in the future continuous.

> do • eat • have • not drive • not grow
> speak • work

1 We .... our holidays on the moon in 2050.

2 We .... cars that use petrol in 2050.

3 Perhaps we .... genetically-modified food in the future.

4 Most people .... at home via the Internet, not in an office.

5 Everybody in the world .... English in the year 2050.

6 Robots .... jobs like cleaning or building.

7 Farmers .... any fresh fruit or vegetables because there won't be enough water.

2b Which predictions in 2a do you agree with?

3 Complete these predictions about the year 2050 with the future perfect form of the verbs given. Make the sentences affirmative or negative depending on your own opinion.

1   By 2050 we .... (find) a cure for all illnesses.

2   We .... (stop) using mobile phones.

3   Polar bears .... (become) extinct.

4   The North Pole .... (disappear).

5   Astronauts .... (land) on Mars.

6   They .... (invent) clothes that can make you invisible.

7   Temperatures .... (get) much higher.

8   Coasts .... (change) because of the rising water level.

4a Oliver is a busy TV chef. Read his diary for next Monday.

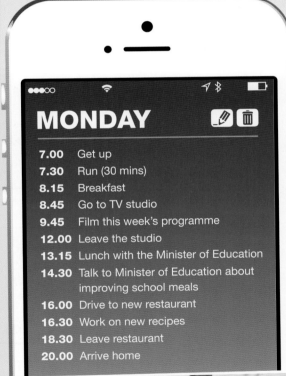

MONDAY

7.00   Get up
7.30   Run (30 mins)
8.15   Breakfast
8.45   Go to TV studio
9.45   Film this week's programme
12.00   Leave the studio
13.15   Lunch with the Minister of Education
14.30   Talk to Minister of Education about improving school meals
16.00   Drive to new restaurant
16.30   Work on new recipes
18.30   Leave restaurant
20.00   Arrive home

4b Complete the sentences with the future continuous or future perfect of the verb given.

1   At half past seven next Monday Oliver .... (get up).

2   At quarter to eight he .... (run).

3   At twenty past eight he .... (have) breakfast.

4   At quarter to nine he .... (have) breakfast.

5   At ten to nine he .... (go) to the TV studio.

6   By twelve o'clock he .... (film) his programme.

7   By quarter to three he .... (eat) with the Minister of Education.

8   At three o'clock he .... (talk) to the Minister of Education.

4c Write one more sentence in the future continuous and one in the future perfect about Oliver's day.

5 SPEAKING Work with a partner. Ask and answer questions about what you *will be doing* or *will have done* at different times tomorrow.

> *What will you be doing at seven o'clock tomorrow morning?*

> *I'll be sleeping.*

6a SPEAKING Think about your life when you're 30 years old. What *will/won't you be doing*? What *will/won't you have done*? Consider these ideas and events.

> become famous • buy a house • get married
> live at home • live in a different country
> make a lot of money • study • work

6b Work with a partner. Ask and answer about 6a.

> *Do you think you'll be studying when you're 30?*

> *No, I think I'll have finished.*

> *Do you think you'll have bought a house when you're 30?*

> *No, but I think I'll have bought a flat.*

Developing speaking

Negotiating

1 SPEAKING **Work with a partner. Look at the photos of places where you can eat. How often do you eat in these places? What do you think of each of them?**

1

2

3

4

5

2 LISTENING ▶ 24 **Listen to two students doing a speaking exam. What question does the teacher ask them? What is their final answer to the question?**

3a ▶ 24 **Listen again. Make notes about what the students say about each place in 1.**

Notepad

1 Fast-food restaurant: *Many people go there. Not very good for a special event.*
2 School canteen: ....
3 Outdoor picnic area: ....
4 Exclusive restaurant: ....
5 Classmate's house: ....

3b SPEAKING **Work with a partner. Compare your notes.**
Do you agree with the opinions and final decision?
Why/Why not?

4 **Write the headings (A–C) below in the correct place in the Speaking bank.**

- **A** Asking other people's opinions
- **B** Responding to other people's opinions
- **C** Giving your opinion

💬 SPEAKING BANK

Useful expressions for negotiating

1 ....
- Personally, …
- I think that …
- In my opinion, …
- I don't think (that) …
- The way I see it, …

2 ....
- Yes, I agree.
- Good idea.
- Yes, you're right.
- Yes, but …
- OK.

3 ....
- What do you think about …?
- What about …?
- Why don't we …?

✔ EXAM SUCCESS

You are going to do an oral activity similar to the one in 2. In this type of activity (called 'negotiating') you usually work with another student. Who should speak more – you or your partner?

➤ EXAM SUCCESS page 144

PRACTICE MAKES PERFECT

5 SPEAKING **Work with a partner. Look at the instructions and diagram on page 148. Give and justify your opinions and come to a decision using expressions from the Speaking bank.**

What do you think about having a school concert?

I think it depends on the type of music.

Developing writing

Replying to informal invitations

1a READING **Read this email invitation. <u>Underline</u> the most important information that Matt wants.**

Hi Sam,

How are you? I haven't seen you since the concert. I hope everything's going well.

Next week my cousin Alfie is staying with me. On Saturday I'm inviting all my friends round to my house so that he can meet them all. I hope you can make it. It'd be great to see you.

There'll be lots to eat. Please bring your MP3 player so we have plenty of good music. We'll be starting to serve food in the garden at about 12.30, so don't be late! In fact, I need one or two people to help me to get everything ready before that. Could you come a bit earlier?

One thing – if it rains on Saturday, we'll change it to Sunday. Are you doing anything then?

Please write back to tell me if you can come or not.

All the best,

Matt

1b Work with a partner. Have you <u>underlined</u> the same information?

2 Imagine you are Sam. What information do you think you should include in your reply? Make notes with your partner.

Tell him how you are

3 Read this reply. Does it include all your information in 2?

Hi Matt,

It's good to hear from you! Everything's fine here.

Thanks for the invitation. I'll definitely be there on Saturday. It'll be good to meet Alfie at last!

I'm sorry but I won't be able to be there before 12.30 because I've got a basketball match in the morning. But, don't worry. I won't be too late! Would you like me to bring anything apart from music? Something for dessert maybe?

I don't think it'll rain on Saturday. I hope not because on Sunday it's my parents wedding anniversary and they're taking us out for the day. Sorry, but I won't be able to come if it isn't on Saturday.

Thanks again for the invitation. I'm really looking forward to it!

All the best,

Sam

4 Are the invitation and reply formal or informal? How do you know?

5 Look again at the invitation and reply and complete the examples in the Writing bank.

✏ **WRITING BANK**

Useful expressions in informal invitations and replies

Invitations:

- Please come!
- I hope you (a) ....
- It'd be great (b) ....
- I'd love to see you there.
- Please write (c) .... to tell me if you can come or not.

Replies:

- (d) .... for the invitation.
- I'm (really) (e) ...., but I won't be able to (be there/come) because …
- (f) .... you like me to bring anything?
- I'm really (g) .... to it!

✔ **EXAM SUCCESS**

You are going to do a piece of writing where you need to reply to an email and give specific information that the writer of the email needs. How do you know what information to include and what style (formal or informal) to use?

➤ EXAM SUCCESS page 145

PRACTICE MAKES PERFECT

6a Read the email invitation below. <u>Underline</u> the important information that the writer wants from you.

Hi!

How are you? Are you doing exams at the moment or have you already finished? I finished yesterday.

In a couple of weeks my brother is going to the US to study. We're having a party next Saturday so that people can say goodbye to him. We'd love to see you there. Please come!

We'll have lots of soft drinks. But if you remember, can you bring some snacks – some sandwiches or cakes or something? The party will be starting at 6 pm. What time do you think you'll be coming? I'll probably need one or two people to help me to tidy up after. Do you think you'll be able to stay and help?

Anyway, I hope you can make it! Please write back to tell me if you can come or not.

All the best,

Ella

6b Write a reply to the email invitation. Invent and include all the information that the writer wants from you. Write in the correct style and use expressions from the Writing bank.

WRITING BANK ➤ PAGE 150

Grammar reference

be going to and will

We use **be going to** for plans and intentions which we have already decided to do in the future.

We've decided that we're going to eat out.

We can also use **be going to** to make predictions about the future, particularly when we have evidence for the prediction.

I've studied hard for this exam. I think I'm going to pass.

We use **will** and **won't** to make general predictions about the future. We often use **think, hope, expect** etc. with **will** and **won't** to express our opinion.

I think our next exam will be easy.

We also use **will** and **won't** when we decide to do something at the moment of speaking.

You look tired. I'll make the dinner tonight.

We use **will** and **won't** to talk about the future when it is an objective truth.

It's my birthday next week. I'll be seventeen.

Present continuous and present simple for future

We use the **present continuous** to talk about future arrangements or plans that have been confirmed.

Tomorrow we're eating at an expensive restaurant. My parents booked last week.

We use the **present simple** directly after time expressions like **when, as soon as, until, after** and **before**. We cannot use **will** with these time expressions.

When I go to the shops, I'll buy something to eat.

We can also use the **present simple** to talk about the future when the action is part of a timetable or routine.

My class starts at 8 am tomorrow.

Future continuous

FORM

Affirmative	subject + **will** + be + -ing She **will be** having lunch at one o'clock tomorrow.
Negative	We **won't be** having dinner at 6 pm tomorrow.
Question	**Will** you **be** having breakfast at this time tomorrow?
Short answers	Yes, I **will**. No, they **won't**.

USE

We use the **future continuous** to talk about activities in progress at a particular time in the future. The activities are in progress and so they are unfinished.

Future perfect

FORM

Affirmative	subject + **will** + **have** + past participle She **will have had** lunch by 3 pm.
Negative	We **won't have finished** the exam by half past nine.
Question	**Will** you **have done** your homework by 9 pm tonight?
Short answers	Yes, I **will**. No, we **won't**.

USE

We use the **future perfect** to talk about activities that will be finished by a certain time in the future.

We often use the preposition *by* with the future perfect. It means 'some time before'.

Vocabulary

Food **Dairy products:** cream • semi-skimmed milk • **Fruit:** peach • plum • **Meat/fish/seafood:** chicken • lamb prawn • tuna • turkey • **Sweets/bakery products:** pancake • pie • **Vegetables:** carrot • lettuce • olive • pea sweetcorn • **Others:** dessert • dish • main course • oil • rice • snack • starter

Describing food baked • boiled • fast • fresh • fried • frozen • healthy/unhealthy • raw • roast • spicy stale • tasty

Prefixes cooperate • disadvantage • international • misunderstand • overbook • overcooked • precooked recooked • redo • undercooked • underestimate

Other words and phrases ➤ page 138

Grammar revision

Present simple for future   / 6 points

1 **Complete the dialogue with the present simple or *will*.**

Alex: What time **(a)** .... your train .... (leave) tomorrow?

Liam: I don't know. When I **(b)** .... (arrive) at the station tomorrow, I **(c)** .... (look) at the information screen.

Alex: **(d)** .... you .... (remember) to call me as soon as you **(e)** .... (get) there?

Liam: Don't worry. I **(f)** .... (call) you.

will, be going to, present continuous for future   / 7 points

2 **Choose the correct alternative.**

1 **A:** What are you going to do this weekend?

B: I*'ll have/'m having* a party. I've invited fifty people! And you?

A: I haven't made any plans. I know! I*'ll call/'m calling* Brad.

2 **A:** Look at the clouds.

B: Yes. It's *raining/going to rain* this afternoon.

3 I think temperatures *will get/are getting* higher in the future.

4 Tomorrow Jo *will be/is being* twenty-one.

5 I'm sure that Mo *will win/is winning* the race tomorrow.

6 I can't see you tomorrow. I*'ll go/'m going* to visit my cousin.

Future continuous and future perfect   / 7 points

3 **Complete the sentences using the future continuous or future perfect form of the verb given.**

1 I'll do my homework between 6 pm and 8 pm.
By 9 pm .... (do my homework)

2 She's going to study English for one month next August.
On 15ᵗʰ August .... (study English)

3 Tomorrow I'll get up at 11 am.
At 10 am .... (sleep)

4 Tomorrow I have an appointment at the dentist from 4 to 4.30 pm.
By 5 pm .... (leave the dentist)

5 We need to give him the money before Thursday.
By Friday .... (give him the money)

6 I'm going for a run tomorrow between 5 and 6 pm.
Tomorrow at 5.15 pm .... (run)

7 He's reading the last pages of the book now.
By tomorrow .... (read the book)

Vocabulary revision

FOOD   / 7 points

1 **Put the letters in order to make food. What type of food is each one (e.g. meat, fish, etc)?**

1 cutlete ....

2 yerkut ....

3 torcar ....

4 mulp ....

5 marce ....

6 warpn ....

7 pecanak ....

DESCRIBING FOOD   / 6 points

2 **Complete the sentences with these words. There are two words you don't need.**

boiled • fresh • fried • raw • roast • spicy • stale • tasty

1 Waiter! This fish isn't .... It smells terrible.

2 This bread is .... It's at least a week old!

3 Don't eat too much .... food. A lot of oil can be bad for you.

4 Take the egg out of the hot water. I think it's .... now.

5 **A:** Why are you crying?
B: I'm not. It's this dish. It's really hot and ....

6 They make sashimi with .... fish. They don't cook it.

PREFIXES   / 7 points

3 **Underline the prefix. Then write the meaning of the prefix next to each word.**

1 disadvantage ....

2 recook ....

3 cooperate ....

4 underestimate ....

5 international ....

6 misunderstand ....

7 overbook ....

Reading

1 You are going to read about the coldest city on Earth. Work with a partner. Make predictions about life there.

2 READING **Read the text and check your predictions.**

YAKUTSK:
life in the coldest city on Earth

At -45ºC wearing glasses is not a good idea. **1** .... I know this because I've just arrived in Yakutsk, a place where friendly local people suggest not wearing glasses when you go outside.

2 .... It's famous because it is probably the coldest city on Earth. In January, the most freezing month, the *highest* temperature is -40ºC. Today it is -43ºC and the city is covered in freezing fog which only allows you to see ten metres in front of you. I decided to come to Yakutsk myself to find out how people can survive in the coldest city on Earth.

In January, the highest temperature in Yakutsk is -40°C

I soon discover that local people describe -40ºC as 'cold, but not very cold'. **3** .... Before I go outdoors in Yakutsk for the first time I put on two pairs of socks, long underwear, two big jumpers, a heavy winter coat with hood, two pairs of gloves, and a hat. And when I walk out, I feel … fine. In fact, I feel good.

4 .... Then I just can't feel it, and that is dangerous. Then the cold penetrates my two pairs of gloves and starts to attack my fingers. Next it's my ears. And then my legs. Finally my whole body hurts and I decide to go back indoors. I look at my watch. I've been outside for just 13 minutes.

5 .... Now it takes six hours by plane. There are no trains to Yakutsk. The other alternatives are a 1,000 mile boat ride up the Lena River (only during summer, when the river isn't frozen) or a 1,200 mile drive on the 'road of bones' (only during winter), which runs over frozen rivers.

6 .... Workers continue working on building sites up to -50ºC. When it gets colder than this the metal becomes too fragile to work with. Children go to school unless it's below -55ºC. 'Anyway, it's a nice cold here, because we don't have wind,' says university professor Vasily Illarionov. 'When it's -40ºC I like to walk to work. I like our weather, but I don't think I could live somewhere windy.'

7 .... There are two or three weeks when the temperatures rise to 30 or 35ºC. None of the buildings have air-conditioning and the air is full of mosquitoes and other insects. And there's just time to make repairs and prepare for the next winter. 'Of course it's difficult to live here' says Vladimir Fyodorov, editor of the regional newspaper. 'But the people here were born here. It's our home. What can you do about it?'

3 **Read the text again. Complete it with sentences a–g.**

a The inhuman temperatures are just part of daily life for the residents of the city.

b In the past it took more than three months to get to Yakutsk from Moscow.

c In fact one person told me that last November was exceptionally warm – -25ºC!

d Yakutsk is a remote city in eastern Siberia with a population of 200,000.

e But after a few minutes, the cold weather starts to make my face feel uncomfortable.

f The metal sticks to your face and it's extremely painful when you try to take your glasses off.

g Unfortunately, the summers in Yakutsk sound worse than the winters.

Speaking

4 **Work with a partner. Make a list of six different places or things to visit in or near where you live.**

5 SPEAKING **Imagine that a friend from the US called Tom is going to come and visit you for a day. You and your partner must decide which are the two best places in your list in 4 to take your friend and why. Ask for your partner's opinions and respond to them.**

What do you think about going to the river with Tom?

Good idea. But to go to the river we need good weather.

Use of English

➤ **TIP FOR USE OF ENGLISH**

In multiple-choice cloze activities, remember ...
Read the complete text first without thinking about the gaps. Then read again and think of words that could go in each gap. Look at the alternatives. Are any words the same as yours?

➤ EXAM SUCCESS pages 144

6 **Read this text about genetically-modified foods. What are they? What good and bad aspects of these foods appear in the text?**

Genetically-modified (GM) foods are foods which come from plants and animals that scientists (1) .... changed through genetic engineering. For example, you can make a strawberry plant more resistant to the cold by adding a gene from an alpine plant that is able to live even when the weather is (2) .... freezing. These organisms are stronger than natural organisms so they can grow in difficult conditions. The biotech companies that make GM organisms say that they will help to end world hunger. But organisations like Greenpeace are (3) .... that the real reason for their development is so that multinational biotech companies can control food production in the world and make money.

The truth is that nobody knows what the effects of GM foods may be. Scientists have (4) .... investigating the possible consequences (5) .... more than ten years, but they still can't predict all the possible impacts on plants, animals and human health. They say that by the time we understand the effects, it will probably be too late and the biotech companies will (6) .... contaminated the environment so badly that it will be impossible to fix the problem. Because GM organisms grow faster and stronger (7) .... natural organisms, once they mix with other natural varieties they will probably change these natural species forever. But some scientists have already predicted that we will all (8) .... eating GM foods in the future because they will be so good for our health.

7 **Read the text again. Choose the best answer (A, B, C or D) to complete the text.**

	A	B	C	D
1	are	has	have	will
2	really	extremely	quite	very
3	true	convinced	thinking	seeing
4	wanted	had	been	already
5	for	since	already	yet
6	finish	have	be	already
7	that	then	than	with
8	be	are	have	can

Writing

➤ **TIP FOR WRITING EXAMS**

In transactional activities, remember ...
It is essential to write in the correct style – informal, semi-formal or formal. Only use contractions and informal expressions in informal texts.

➤ EXAM SUCCESS page 145

> ✉   ✕
>
> Hi!
> I'm having a party at 8 pm on 18th June to celebrate the end of term and I'd love you to come. You don't need to bring drinks, but I'm asking everyone to bring food. And can you come early to help me get everything ready?
> Hope you can make it!
> Matt

8 **Write a reply to Matt's invitation.**

- Tell Matt what food you are going to bring.
- Explain why you can't come early to help.
- Ask if you can bring a friend to the party.
- Offer to help tidy up after the party.

'CAN DO' PROGRESS CHECK UNITS 3–4   CEF

1 **How well can you do these things in English now? Give yourself a mark from 1 to 4.**

> **1** = I can do it very well.
> **2** = I can do it quite well.
> **3** = I have some problems.
> **4** = I can't do it.

a I can talk about past activities using the present perfect simple and continuous. ☐

b I can describe cities and use extreme adjectives. ☐

c I can understand written and spoken texts about city life. ☐

d I can describe different parts of a photo. ☐

e I can write emails describing places. ☐

f I can talk about the future using different verbs and tenses. ☐

g I can talk about meals and describe food. ☐

h I can form new words by adding prefixes. ☐

i I can negotiate with somebody by asking for, giving and responding to opinions. ☐

j I can write simple replies to invitations. ☐

2 **Now decide what you need to do to improve.**

1 Look again at my book/notes.
2 Do more practice exercises.
   ➤ WORKBOOK Units 3 and 4
3 Ask for help.
4 Other: ....

5 Lifelong learning

Vocabulary

School and university subjects

1 **Work with a partner. Look at these subjects. Where do you usually study them for the first time – at nursery school (3–4 years old), primary school (5–10), secondary school (11–18) or at university? Complete the table.**

architecture • art • biology • business studies
chemistry • computer science • drama
engineering • English • geography • history • law
literature • maths • media studies • medicine
music • PE (physical education)
physics • psychology

Nursery	Primary	Secondary	University
art	English	biology	architecture

2a **PRONUNCIATION Mark the stress on each word in 1 that has more than one syllable.**

árchitecture

2b ▶ 25 **Listen, check and repeat.**

3 **LISTENING ▶ 26 Listen to four teachers giving instructions and asking questions. What subject is each one teaching?**

1 .... 3 ....

2 .... 4 ....

4 **SPEAKING Work with a partner. Ask these questions.**

1 Which of these subjects do/don't you like?
2 Would you like to study any of these subjects in the future?
3 Which of the subjects do you think will be useful in life after school/university?

Words connected with studying

5 **Complete the sentences with these words.**

assessment • assignment • coursework • essay
fail • mark/grade • scholarship
terms • timetable • resit

1 In my last history class I wrote a(n) .... about the Roman Empire.
2 9 out of 10 is a really good ....
3 I didn't do the exam very well so next week I'll probably need to .... it.
4 What lesson do we have now? I didn't bring my

   ....
5 My sister doesn't pay the full amount for her studies because they gave her a(n) ....
6 When you get less than 50% in an exam you usually

   ....
7 Our school year is divided into three ....
8 The teachers evaluate us by looking at our exams and the work we do all year, which is called our

   ....
9 We're going to do a(n) .... on Shakespeare. We have a month to prepare it and then we present it.
10 Exams are not usually the only form of

   .... at school.

6a **SPEAKING Work with a partner. Ask and answer the questions.**

1 What is your school timetable for Tuesday? What do you think of it?
2 Which is your favourite term and why?
3 What's your best mark in an exam this year?
4 Did you have to resit any exams last year? Which one(s)?
5 Do you prefer assessment with exams or with coursework? Why?
6 What was the last essay that you wrote?
7 How often do you get assignments? In what subjects?

6b **Compare your answers with the rest of the class.**

1 Work with a partner. Look at the photo and the title of the text. What do you think the text is about?

2 READING Read the text and check your predictions.

Green school in the city

How one inspirational teacher is changing lives

When you think of the Bronx in New York, green is probably not the first colour you think of. But one inspirational teacher and instructor, Stephen Ritz, is doing something to change that.

It all began by accident. Stephen was teaching at a school in the South Bronx. Somebody had sent him a box of flower bulbs. Stephen didn't really know what they were so he hid them behind a radiator in his classroom. Then one morning there was a moment of real surprise and excitement when he and his class suddenly noticed all the flowers that had grown next to the radiator.

That gave Stephen an idea. He decided to do something to improve the area where his students live, so he and his class worked on a project in their own neighbourhood. They planted flowers and vegetables and managed to transform some

depressing spots into green areas where local people could meet.

Next, Stephen brought plants back into the classroom. The students planted vegetables in special towers and created an 'edible indoor wall' in the science room. It was a great success.

Although all students under 16 must attend school, in a difficult area like the Bronx students often miss classes. But thanks to his classroom project, attendance in Stephen's classes went up from around 40% to 93%. The students feel responsible for their plants. They realise they have to water them and look after them every day, so they also see that they mustn't miss school. And with better attendance their marks go up.

Importantly, the students also begin to learn about natural, healthy food. As they started to grow their own vegetables, they became more interested in following a healthy diet instead of eating the typical fast food they had eaten before. In fact, the edible indoor wall in Stephen's classroom produces enough food to feed healthy meals to 450 students! The students can even sell some of their vegetables to local shops. Some of his older students have worked as employees of a new company as technicians creating green walls for other schools around the country.

Stephen began his project with older students, but he now teaches younger students, too. He believes young people ought to start learning about healthy diets as early as possible so that they don't pick up bad habits which are then difficult to change.

Many of Stephen's students have special educational needs or are homeless. Stephen's project has really affected them. They have learnt lessons that will help them throughout their lives. They have learnt about responsibility. They have also realised that they'd better eat well if they want to stay healthy. And, finally, they've learnt that you don't have to be a farmer out in the country to grow plants. Anybody can do it. But you must believe that you can make a difference. By teaching all of this, Stephen Ritz is making a massive difference to the lives of his students.

Material courtesy of Green Bronx Machine

Stephen Ritz (second from left) with his students

3 Read the text again and answer the questions.

1 How did the students react to the first plants in their classroom?

2 Why did Stephen and his students plant flowers and vegetables in areas of the Bronx?

3 What did Stephen's students do in the science room?

4 What effect did Stephen's project have on attendance of his classes and why?

5 What effect did the project have on his students' eating habits?

6 Why does Stephen think it's important to teach very young students?

7 What are two of the things that Stephen's students have learnt from this project?

4 ⚙ CRITICAL THINKING

Think! Then compare ideas with your class.

■ What message(s) do you think the text gives about bringing the outside world into the classroom? Give reasons for your answer.

5 What do the underlined words in the text mean? Guess and then check in your dictionary.

6 SPEAKING What about *you*?

1 Would you like to work on a school project like Stephen Ritz's? Why/Why not?

2 Does your school ever organise lessons or activities that take place outside the classroom? If so, explain what they are.

Grammar in context

Modal verbs of obligation, prohibition, advice and permission

1a **Read the sentences and complete the rules with the words in blue.**

  a Students **shouldn't be** forced to leave their own community.

  b All students under 16 **must** attend school.

  c They **have to** look after the plants.

  d They **mustn't** miss classes.

  e They **can't** miss school.

  f The students **can** sell their vegetables.

  g Young people **ought to** start learning about healthy diets.

  h They **had better** eat fresh food.

  i You **don't have to** be a farmer to grow plants.

  1 We use .... and .... for obligation.

  2 We use .... when there is no obligation.

  3 We use .... and .... for prohibitions or when there is no permission to do something.

  4 We use ...., ... and .... for advice and recommendations.

  5 We use .... to give permission.

1b Are these sentences True (T) or False (F)?

  1 The contraction for **had better** is **'d better**.   T / F

  2 We use **to** with **ought**, but not with **should** or **'d better**.   T / F

  3 We usually use **must** in questions.   T / F

  4 The correct question is **Do you have to (go)?** not **Have you to go?**   T / F

GRAMMAR REFERENCE ➤ PAGE 68

2a Complete the sentences using the correct form of the word(s) given and any other words.

  1 It is obligatory to be at least 17 to drive a car.

     You .... at least 17 to drive a car. (*have to*)

  2 It is obligatory to go to school until you are at least 16.

     You .... to school until you are at least 16. (*have to*)

  3 Voting in a general election is prohibited until the age of 18.

     You .... in a general election until you are 18. (*can*)

  4 It is possible to ride a moped when you're 16.

     You .... 18 to ride a moped. (*have to*)

  5 It is obligatory to be 18 before you can get married without your parents' permission.

     You .... 18 before you can get married without your parents' permission. (*must*)

  6 It is impossible to change your name until you are 16.

     You .... your name until you're 16. (*can*)

  7 It is possible to buy a ticket in the National Lottery when you are 16.

     You .... 16 to buy a ticket in the National Lottery. (*have to*)

2b Do you know if the legal ages for these things are similar in your country?

3 Complete the sentences for these situations. Use *should, shouldn't, ought to, had better* and expressions from the box.

> get ready to go
> go out without an umbrella
> look for a job there • rest and have a coffee
> study all night • use a dictionary
> walk to school

  1 A friend has an exam tomorrow, but says he isn't going to sleep tonight because he needs to study.

     He .... because he'll be tired for the exam.

  2 Your sister wants to study English in the US in the summer, but she hasn't got any money.

     She ....

  3 You have received an email in English, but there are words you don't understand.

     You ....

  4 Your friend is very unfit because his parents always take him to school by car.

     He ....

  5 We're at a party. We promised to be back home at 9.30 and it's 9.10 now.

     We ....

  6 You're going to walk to school, but the sky is very black.

     You ....

  7 Your dad is driving, but he's feeling a bit tired.

     He ....

4 Write rules for your school using *must*, *mustn't*, *can*, *can't*, *have to*, *don't have to* and these verbs.

> arrive early • carry ID • cheat in tests
> eat or drink in class • participate in class
> put make-up on • use mobile phones in class
> wear school uniform • wear special clothes for PE

5 Read the text and choose the correct alternative.

Secondary students usually (a) *have to/mustn't* do lots of homework and lots of exams. This can be stressful. That's one of the reasons why some schools in the UK now teach a thing called 'mindfulness'. The idea is that the students (b) *should/ought* pay attention to what is happening right now. They (c) *had better/shouldn't* think about the past or the future, just the present. One activity that is part of mindfulness is 'beditation'. This is like meditation but you (d) *better/have to* do it lying down to get the full benefits. The idea of mindfulness originally came from Buddhist thinking and meditation, but, of course, you (e) *don't have to/mustn't* be a Buddhist to practise mindfulness. Many experts think that they (f) *ought/must* to teach mindfulness in all schools. There are certainly lots of good reasons to try it. But you (g) *had/would* better find a clean floor to practise!

6a SPEAKING Work with a partner. You have a friend who wants to become a maths teacher one day. Think of advice to give them. Use *must, mustn't, have to, should, shouldn't, had better, ought to.* Make a list of your ideas.

6b SPEAKING Compare your list with another pair. Are your ideas similar?

You have to get very good marks in maths. You should be patient with people when they don't understand.

Noun suffixes

1 Read these words. They all have suffixes which make nouns. Are they nouns for people or things?

> direct**or** • employ**ee** • farm**er**
> instruct**or** • scient**ist** • technic**ian**

2 Match these words and the words from 1 with the definitions. Check that you understand the other words.

> electric**ian** • employ**er** • journal**ist** • librar**ian**
> photograph**er** • physic**ist** • profess**or** • train**ee**

1 somebody who teaches at a university
2 somebody who teaches you to do a particular skill, e.g. ski or play a sport
3 somebody who pays someone to work for them
4 somebody with technical training who works with special equipment or machines
5 somebody whose job is to report the news
6 somebody who is training for a job

3a PRONUNCIATION ▶ 27 Listen to the words in 1 and 2. Mark the stress in each word. Which is the only noun suffix we stress?

3b Practise saying the words with the correct stress.

4 Match one word from each list.

List A:
TV
wildlife
company
university
driving
computer
TV journalist

List B:
photographer
journalist
technician
director
professor
instructor

5 SPEAKING Work with a partner. Which of the jobs in 4 would you like or dislike? Why?

> *I think I'd like to be a TV journalist. You probably meet interesting people all the time.*

Get the best from the Web

LIFE SKILLS OBJECTIVES

- To learn how to evaluate web sources of information.
- To think about good use of the web for schoolwork.
- To practise evaluating and using web sources of information.

KEY CONCEPTS

source [n]: *An encyclopaedia is a great source of information – you can find almost everything in there.* **link [n, v]:** *When you click on this link, it takes you to a history website.* **cut and paste [v]:** *He cut and pasted the text, moving it from one document to another.* **update [v]:** *This website has to update its information all the time so that people know the latest news.* **plagiarism [n]:** *They accused the student of plagiarism – his work used lots of texts written by other people.*

1 Work with a partner. Discuss these questions.

1 When was the last time you used the Internet for schoolwork or an assignment?

2 Which website(s) did you find the most useful? Why?

2 READING Read the first part of the website article on this page and answer the questions.

1 What does 'critical' mean in this text?

2 Why does the writer say it is important to be critical using the Internet?

3 What different things can the URL of a website tell you about the website?

3 Find three URLs connected with global warming. What do you know about each one? Do you think they will be good sources of information for an assignment about global warming? Why/Why not?

EVALUATING WEB SOURCES

Nowadays the Internet is one of our main sources of information, but because of the freedom of the Internet, anybody can put up information on a website. Just because the information is on the Internet does not mean that it's true. So we need to be 'critical' about what we read and find on the Internet.

'Critical' in this context means being thoughtful, asking questions, and not just believing everything we read or hear immediately.

Here are some things that can help us to evaluate web sources.

Every web page has its own URL, an address used on the Internet. The URL gives us some initial information about the website or page. The information is not completely reliable because people can invent some parts of the URL. But the URL is useful as a starting point.

Take this example:

the main part of the address

http://www.wwf.org.mx/

shows the country where the organisation is, in this case Mexico

shows that it is a charity, or non-profit organisation

Here are the most common elements of a URL.

.COM (US or anywhere) **.CO.UK** (UK)

.FR, .AU

.GOV

.ORG

.EDU (US), **.AC.UK** (UK)

The country where the organisation is: France, Australia

A government agency

Academic institutions

A non-profit organisation

Commercial organisation or company, big or small

4 READING **Read the second part of the website article below. Are these statements True (T) or False (F)?**

The writer says …

1 it's important to know if you are reading facts or opinions.　　　　　　　　　　　　　　T / F

2 it isn't necessary to compare the information in one website with information from a different place.　T / F

3 you should read the 'About us' section of a website, for example to find out why they have created the website.　　　　　　　　　　　　　　T / F

4 it's possible that the creator of the website wants to make you buy something.　　　　　　T / F

5 it's important to know how old the information on a website is.　　　　　　　　　　　T / F

6 you should always contact the creators of the website.　　　　　　　　　　　　　T / F

> Now you're ready to look at the website
> Ask yourself these questions, and after each one, ask yourself the important question: What are the implications?

1 What is being said?

- Are you reading facts? How do you know they are correct?
- Are you reading opinions? Whose opinions? What is their argument?
- Does it show where the statements or data are from? Are there any references or useful links?
- Does the information here seem similar to what you already know?
- Check the information using a different source. Does that source give the same information?

2 Why is it there?

- What is the aim of the site? See if there is a section that says 'About us' and read it.
- Why did they put this material up? To give access to information, or to explain, persuade, or maybe sell you something?

3 Who produced the site?

- An individual? An organisation? Who are they? Can you contact them?
- How are they qualified to produce this material?
- Do they produce material in other formats – books, reports …?
- What sites does it link to?

4 How good is it to use?

- Is it easy to use?
- Is it logical and easy to navigate?

6 When does the information date from?

- Does the material/data and its sources have dates?
- When was the information last updated?
- Do the links still work?

5 Where is the organisation or person?

- Do they have a real address and telephone number? Look for an 'About us/Contact us' section.

---

5 Work with a partner. Look at one of the websites you found in 3. Use the questions in the text to evaluate the website. Is it a good site to use? Why/Why not?

6 SPEAKING **You are going to watch or listen to two students answering questions about how to use web sources. Work with a partner. What do you think they are going to say about …**

a) university or museum websites?

b) online encyclopaedias?

c) expressing things in your own words?

d) cutting and pasting?

7a LISTENING 28 **Watch the video or listen. What order do they mention the things in 6? Do they include any of your ideas?**

1 _____　2 _____　3 _____　4 _____

7b 28 **Watch or listen again. Answer the questions.**

1 What type of online encyclopaedia do they recommend?

2 Why do they mention Einstein's Theory of Relativity?

3 What do they say about including other people's words or ideas in your assignment?

4 According to the students, why is it easy for teachers to detect plagiarism?

LIFE TASK

Do you have any assignments that you need to research for school at the moment? Ask your teachers. If you don't, choose one of these assignments.

- A famous play by Shakespeare
- Radioactivity
- The future of the Amazon region
- The life of a famous king or queen

Now follow this plan.

1 *Work in a group with people who have the same assignment.*

2 *Each person in the group should find one website that gives you information about the topic of your assignment. Use the questions in the text on this page to evaluate how good, useful and reliable it is. Make notes.*

3 *Work together and compare what you have found.*

4 *Use your good web sources to prepare a text with five interesting pieces of information about your topic. Write the information in your own words, but include a note of the sources you used at the end of your text.*

5 *Present some of your information to the class.*

Listening

1a
Work with a partner. What extracurricular activities can you do at school?

1b
Look at these extracurricular activities. What do you think they are?

a

b

c

d

2
LISTENING ▶ 29 Listen to four dialogues about extracurricular activities. Match each dialogue to a photo. What is the activity?

1 .... 2 .... 3 .... 4 ....

3
▶ 29 Listen again and complete the sentences with one or two words.

Notepad

1 This activity is a mixture of martial arts, (a) ...., gymnastics and music. The classes are at 7 pm on Mondays and (b) .... The boy may join, but he doesn't know his (c) ....

2 They play this activity on a (d) .... You have to (e) .... a lot when you do the activity. The speaker thinks you have to (f) .... when you're a student or you get too stressed.

3 This society is one of the (g) .... at the college. (h) .... are welcome at the society. They teach ballet, (i) .... dance and (j) .... dance.

4 This person joined the club because he (k) .... do the activity at the moment. He doesn't want to (l) .... everyday when he's away from home. Sometimes everybody in the club eats (m) ....

4
SPEAKING **What about you?**

1 Do you think that it's important to do extracurricular activities? Why/Why not?

2 Which of the extracurricular activities in 2 would you like to try? Why?

Grammar in context

Zero, first and second conditionals

1a
Read these sentences. Which are zero, first or second conditionals?

1 It would be great if it was like in the films.

2 If I'm free then, I'll think about it.

3 If I were you, I'd stop reading those Harry Potter books.

4 If you don't find time to relax, you become stressed.

1b
Read the rules and write Z (zero conditional), F (first conditional), S (second conditional) or A (all).

1 It describes an improbable or imaginary situation in the present or future and its consequence.
....

2 It describes a possible situation in the present or future and its consequence. ....

3 It describes a situation which has a consequence that is generally or always true. ....

4 We use the present simple in the half of the sentence with if, and **will/won't** + *infinitive* in the other half. ....

5 We use the present simple in both halves of the sentence. ....

6 We use the past simple in the half of the sentence with if, and **would/wouldn't** + *infinitive* in the other half. ....

7 The half of the sentence with if can come after the other half, but we don't use a comma. ....

8 We can use it to give advice when we have **If I were/was you** in one half of the sentence. ....

GRAMMAR REFERENCE ➤ PAGE 68

2
Complete the zero or first conditional sentences with the correct form of the verb given.

1 My friend Omar wasn't at school yesterday. If he .... (not come) today, I .... (ring) him to find out how he is.

2 At our school, if you .... (not go) to class, the school .... (call) your parents.

3 Don't worry. If the exam .... (be) tomorrow, I .... (lend) you my notes.

4 If they .... (have) a party for new students tonight, I .... (go).

5 Usually if you .... (not get) over 50% in an exam, you .... (fail).

6 If we .... (arrive) late today, the teacher .... (get) angry.

3 Complete the dialogues with these verbs in the second conditional.

be • do (x2) • get • go • have • spend

1 Ben: What (a) .... you
            .... to improve the
            world if you (b) .... a
            world leader?
   Bethany: I (c) .... more money
            on schools and universities.

2 Emma: You never do any schoolwork
            at the weekend. If you
            (d) .... more, you
            (e) .... higher marks
            in your exams.
   Megan: I know, but I have to train with
            the swimming team at the pool.
            If I (f) .... there, I
            (g) .... time to study.

4 Complete the text with the zero, first or second conditional using the correct form of the verbs given.

My name's Jeff. I've just started university. There are hundreds of extracurricular activities on offer, but right now I can't decide which ones I want to do. One problem is that I'm not very good at sport. If you (a) .... (not like) sport, it (b) .... (limit) the number of clubs you can join. I suppose that if I (c) .... (be) good at sport, I (d) .... (play) tennis or basketball or something like that. Another problem is that I haven't got much money. If you (e) .... (not have) much money, there (f) .... (be) some activities that you can't do. If money (g) .... (not be) a problem, I (h) .... (think) about joining the Diving Club. They organise lots of trips to the coast. The thing is, if we (i) .... (be) closer to the coast, it (j) .... (not cost) so much but we're about 150 kilometres away! It's true that there are usually special prices for students. If you (k) .... (show) your student card, you always (l) .... (pay) less. Also, if I (m) .... (visit) my sister in Australia next year, I (n) .... (be able to) dive at the Great Barrier Reef. Anyway, I'm going to make my final decision next Tuesday. If I (o) .... (have) problems deciding, I (p) .... (talk) to my older sister, but I don't think that'll be necessary in the end.

5a Complete these sentences with your own ideas.

1 If a Martian stole my homework on the way to school, …
   ....

2 If I pass all my exams, … ....

3 If I haven't got any homework this weekend, … ....

4 If I have time this weekend, … ....

5 If I had enough money, … ....

6 If I became famous, … ....

7 If I was a superhero, … ....

8 If I go out this weekend, … ....

5b Work with a partner. Compare your sentences and choose the best three.

6a Write six questions: three beginning with *What will you do if* and three beginning with *What would you do if*.

What will you do if you don't have any homework this weekend?

What would you do if you found a bag full of money in the street?

6b SPEAKING Ask different people your questions. Choose the best answers and report them to the class.

Developing speaking

A presentation

1 SPEAKING **Work with a partner. What do you think are the advantages and disadvantages of homeschooling? Make notes of your ideas. Do you think there are more advantages or disadvantages?**

2 LISTENING ▶ 30 **Listen to a student giving a presentation on homeschooling. Does she think it's a good idea or a bad idea? Does she include any of your ideas?**

3 ▶ 30 **Listen again and tick (✓) the expressions in the Speaking bank that you hear.**

> ### 💬 SPEAKING BANK
>
> **Useful expressions in presentations**
> **Beginning a presentation**
> - I'd like to begin by saying …
> - I'm going to talk about …
>
> **Introducing arguments**
> - Firstly,
> - First of all,
> - Secondly,
> - Another thing is that …
> - It's also true that …
> - Furthermore,
> - What's more,
>
> **Giving examples**
> - For example,
> - For instance,
> - Look at the case of …
> - Take …
>
> **Concluding**
> - In conclusion
> - Finally,
> - To sum up,
> - Last but not least
> - The point (that) I'm trying to make is …
> - In short,

> ### ✔ EXAM SUCCESS
>
> What other advice would you give to somebody who is about to give a presentation to the class in English? Think about your voice, the position of your body, visuals, the language you use, etc.
>
> ➤ EXAM SUCCESS page 145

PRACTICE MAKES PERFECT

5a Choose one of these topics and prepare a presentation. Use the relevant advice in 4 to help you.

1 Should students be paid for going to school?
2 Is it a good idea to separate boys and girls into different classes at school?
3 Should homework exist?
4 Are exams the best way to evaluate students?
5 Should the use of mobile phones be permitted in class?
6 Are school uniforms a good idea?

5b SPEAKING **Give your presentation to the class. Use the advice in 4 and expressions from the Speaking bank.**

4 SPEAKING **Work with a partner. Put these stages of giving a presentation in the correct order.**

a During your talk, use your notes to remember what comes next, but don't just read things aloud. ....

b Organise your notes in a logical way. ....

c Finish your presentation at the right time. ....

d Look at the question which you have to talk about. ....

e Make notes with your ideas and arguments. ....

f Begin your presentation and look up at the audience. ....

g Think of a short introduction and a conclusion. ....

Developing writing

A formal letter of application

1 READING **Read this information about a scholarship. Underline the qualities of an ideal candidate. Would _you_ be a good candidate for the scholarship? Why/Why not?**

English College
Summer scholarships

A number of scholarships are given to students of English who have a special interest in British history and who would like to study in England. Applicants must have good grades, especially in English and history, and should be active in extracurricular activities such as sports and debating and also have an interest in travel. Please send a letter of application to this address.

2 READING **Read the letter of application for this scholarship. Do you think Marcus is a good candidate? List reasons for your answer.**

Dear Sir or Madam,

I am writing to apply for the scholarship which I saw advertised on your website.

I believe I would be perfect for this scholarship for the following reasons. Firstly, my best subjects at school are English and history and my ambition is to study one day in the United Kingdom to discover more about the people, places and traditions. My grades this year have been very good, with an average mark of 80% in my exams.

I also love sports, particularly football. I am the captain of my school football team. As captain of the team, I am responsible for organising social activities such as parties and events to raise money for the team.

I would be very grateful to receive the chance to study at your school with a scholarship and I am sure that I could make a good contribution to the English department.

I look forward to receiving your reply.

Yours faithfully,

Marcus Reeves

M. Reeves

3 **Look again at the letter in 2 and complete the information in the Writing bank.**

WRITING BANK

Useful expressions and conventions in a formal letter

- If we know the name of the person we are writing to, we begin _Dear Mr/Mrs/Ms_ and their surname. We finish _Yours sincerely_.
- If we don't know the name of the person we are writing to, we begin _Dear_ (a) .... or (b) .... We finish _Yours_ (c) ....
- In formal letters we do not use (d) ...., e.g. we write _I would_, not _I'd_.
- We often use more formal words and expressions, e.g. (e) .... instead of _I'd be really happy to get the chance_.
- We often start formal letters with _I am writing to …_ and then explain why we are writing.
- We often end formal letters with expressions like _I_ (f) .... _to receiving your reply_.

PRACTICE MAKES PERFECT

4a **Read the information below about a scholarship. Write a letter of application using expressions and conventions in the Writing bank to help you. Include information to make yourself the ideal candidate. Write between 150 and 180 words.**

Combined English Scholarship

We have two scholarships for students who are interested in combining their chosen subject (any subjects are possible) with an English Studies programme. Applicants must have good academic marks and should have interests in extracurricular activities such as music, theatre, or literature. Active participation in a sport is also an advantage. Send your letter of application to this address.

WRITING BANK ➤ PAGE 150

4b **Exchange your letter with a partner. Prepare five questions to ask them in an interview to get the scholarship.**

In your letter you say that your marks are usually high. Which are your best subjects?

4c SPEAKING **Role-play your interviews. Would you give your partner the scholarship?**

✓ EXAM SUCCESS

Who are you writing to in this task? What style (formal or informal) should you use? Why is it important to know this in an exam?

➤ EXAM SUCCESS page 145

Grammar reference

have to, don't have to, must, mustn't, can, can't

FORM	
Affirmative	You **have to** go to school until you're 18.
Negative	You **don't have to** go to school when you're 21.
Question	**Do** you **have to** go to school?
Short answers	Yes, I **do**. No, I **don't**.

Affirmative	You **must** listen to the teacher.
Negative	You **mustn't (must not)** cheat in exams.

Affirmative	You **can** use the computers here.
Negative	You **can't (cannot)** eat or drink here.

USE

We use **have to** to talk about things which are obligatory or necessary. It often describes obligations imposed on us by other people and authorities.

You have to show your ID to enter the building.

We use **don't have to** to talk about things which are not obligatory or necessary.

Students don't have to carry ID at school.

We use **must** to talk about rules, regulations, and obligations. It often describes obligations that come internally, from ourselves.

I must remember to take my ID.

We use **mustn't** to talk about prohibitions.

You mustn't enter without your ID.

We use **can** to give permission and **can't** to refuse permission.

You can use the library but you can't eat there.

should, shouldn't, ought to, had ('d) better

FORM	
Affirmative	You **should/ought to/had better** do your homework.
Negative	You **shouldn't** hand work in late.
Question	**Should** I write it by hand?
Short answers	Yes, you **should**. No, you **shouldn't**.

USE

We use **should, shouldn't, ought to, had ('d) better** to give and ask for advice and recommendations.

You ought to arrive on time.

Zero, first and second conditionals

FORM	
Zero conditional	If + present simple, present simple
First conditional	If + present simple, *will/won't* + infinitive
Second conditional	If + past simple, *would/wouldn't* + infinitive

If can go at the start of the sentence or in the middle. If it goes at the start, we must use a comma before the second half of the sentence.

USE

We use the **zero conditional** for situations that are generally or always true.

If you go to the US, you need a passport.

We use the **first conditional** for possible and probable situations in the future, and their consequences.

*If you **aren't** careful (possible future situation), you **will have** an accident (the consequence).*

We use the **second conditional** for imaginary or improbable situations and their consequences. The situations are in the present or future, NOT in the past.

*If I **made** films (imaginary present situation), I **would live** in Hollywood (the consequence).*

We use **If I were/was you, I'd ...**, to give advice.

Vocabulary

School and university subjects architecture • art • biology • business studies • chemistry • computer science drama • engineering • English • geography • history • law • literature • maths • media studies • medicine music • PE (physical education) • physics • psychology

Words connected with studying assessment • assignment • coursework • essay • fail • mark/grade scholarship • terms • timetable • resit

Noun suffixes director • electrician • employee • employer • farmer • instructor • journalist   librarian photographer • physicist • professor • scientist • technician • trainee

Other words and phrases ➤ page 139

Grammar revision

have to, don't have to, must, mustn't, can, can't

/ 7 points

1   Rewrite these sentences with have to, don't have to, must, mustn't, can, can't.

1   I haven't got permission to go to the match.
    I ....

2   It isn't necessary for students to wear a uniform.
    Students ....

3   Making a loud noise is prohibited.
    You ....

4   It is obligatory to write your name here.
    You ....

5   Copying is not allowed in exams.
    You ....

6   It's essential for me to leave now.
    I ....

7   My little brother has permission to ride his bike alone.
    My little brother ....

should, shouldn't, ought to, had ('d) better

/ 5 points

2   Are these sentences correct or not? If not, correct them.

1   They shouldn't to go out at the weekend.

2   You would better walk to school.

3   I think you ought go to the dentist.

4   What should I say when I see her?

5   We'd better leave now if we want to arrive on time.

Zero, first and second conditionals

/ 8 points

3   Complete the sentences with the correct form of the verbs given.

1   If I were you, I .... (tell) her the truth.

2   Leo .... (buy) me a souvenir if he goes to Mexico.

3   What .... you .... (say) if I told you I was a superhero?

4   In her school they .... (give) you a prize if you get 100% in all your exams.

5   Connor wouldn't be angry if you .... (ask) him for a favour.

6   If I .... (be) you, I would go to bed early tonight.

7   Where will your parents go on holiday if you .... (not go) with them?

8   If I .... (have) time, I'd learn to play the guitar.

Vocabulary revision

SCHOOL AND UNIVERSITY SUBJECTS

/ 7 points

1   In which subject do you learn about ...

1   the theories of Isaac Newton? ....

2   becoming a doctor? ....

3   TV, newspapers, radio? ....

4   designing and making buildings?
    ....

5   the legal system? ....

6   designing and building structures and machines?
    ....

7   stories, poems, plays? ....

NOUN SUFFIXES

/ 6 points

3   Add the suffixes -er, -or, -ist, -ian, -ee to these words to make nouns for people.

1   scient ....

2   instruct ....

3   technic ....

4   employ ....

5   employ ....

6   librar ....

WORDS CONNECTED WITH STUDYING

/ 7 points

2   Write a simple explanation for each word.

1   assessment ....

2   scholarship ....

3   fail ....

4   resit ....

5   assignment ....

6   timetable ....

7   mark ....

Total: .... / 40 points

6 Pure science

Vocabulary

Everyday inventions

1a SPEAKING **Work with a partner. How many of these words can you use to talk about the things in the photos?**

> digital camera • dishwasher • e-reader
> fridge-freezer • headphones
> home cinema system • laptop
> microwave oven • mobile phone
> MP3 player • music system
> remote control • satnav • speaker
> vacuum cleaner • washing machine

There's a mobile phone.

You can use a mobile phone as an MP3 player.

1b **Check that you understand all the words. Use a dictionary if necessary.**

2 SPEAKING **Work with a partner. Take it in turns to say what you can do with the items in 1a. Can your partner identify the word?**

You use it to clean carpets and the floor.

A vacuum cleaner.

3 SPEAKING **Work with a partner. Ask and answer the questions.**

1 Which of the inventions in 1a do you use the most? Why?
2 Are there any inventions in 1a that you never use? Why not?
3 If you lived alone and only had money for five of the inventions in 1a, which would you buy and why?

Which of the inventions do you use the most?

Maybe my MP3 player because I use it to listen to music every day on my way to school.

Operating technology

4 **Match these words to the pictures.**

> charge/recharge (a battery) • connect X to Y • insert
> plug in • press a button (e.g. play/stop)
> select (a network/a programme/a track/a function)
> switch/turn on/off • tap (the screen)

5 ▶ 31 **Listen and check your answers.**

6 LISTENING ▶ 32 **Listen. Which everyday invention are they talking about?**

1 .... 2 .... 3 ....

7a SPEAKING **Work with a partner. Write basic instructions for how to operate these items. Use as many words from 4 as possible.**

1 a music system 2 a microwave oven 3 a mobile phone

7b **Work with a partner. Read out one set of instructions. Can your partner identify the invention?**

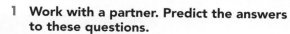

FIRST LAUGH, THEN THINK!

A A group called Improbable Research celebrates unusual research by giving out Ig Nobel prizes. These are given annually to scientists whose work is funny and different. The aim is to make people aware of scientific investigation which 'makes people laugh, but then makes them think'. Only work that has been published in a serious scientific journal can win. Here are some past winners.

B In 2012 an Ig Nobel prize was won by Kazutaka Kurihara and Koji Tsukada. They created a machine called the SpeechJammer. The device stops people talking when you don't want to listen to them. It records the person's voice with a microphone. Just a few milliseconds later, you press a button and it plays back the recording through a speaker. When you hear yourself in this way it becomes very difficult, confusing and stressful to continue talking … so you stop. The machine works at a distance of up to 30 metres.

C Johan Pettersson won the Chemistry Ig Nobel prize in 2012. He helped the people of Anderslov in Sweden with an unusual problem. Some people in the town found that when they washed their hair, it turned green. Originally people thought that there was probably some copper in the drinking water. But the water was analysed before it reached people's houses and it was found to be normal. However, when hot water came out of the taps in the morning, for example in the shower, they found lots of copper. The problem came from hot water reacting with copper in the pipes. So now people in the town have to wash their hair in cold water!

D Lots of interesting research is being done by psychologists at the moment. One Ig Nobel prize was given to a team of psychologists who discovered that if you move your head slightly to the left, the Eiffel Tower seems smaller! When we write numbers in order, we begin with small numbers on the left and they get bigger when they go to the right. The psychologists were interested in seeing if the way that we see numbers in our mind would make a difference to calculating size and height. Their experiment showed they were right. When you move your head slightly to the left, things seem smaller because we begin with small numbers on the left.

E Catherine Douglas and Peter Rowlinson of Newcastle University won an Ig Nobel prize for a research project which involved cows. They discovered that cows that have names produce significantly more milk than cows that don't have names. It seems that cows feel happier and more relaxed when they are given individual attention. And when they are happier and more relaxed, they produce more milk.

F Other Ig Nobel prizes have been won by inventions. Eduardo Segura from Spain won a prize for inventing a washing machine for cats and dogs. Simply insert your pet, select a function, and you're ready for action! An automatic translation device called Bow-Lingual also won a prize. Switch it on and you can understand what your dog is 'saying'. It's true that these inventions probably won't be used much in the future. But, like all the Ig Nobel prize winners, they certainly make you laugh … and then think.

1 Work with a partner. Predict the answers to these questions.

1 What happens when you hear what you are saying just a few milliseconds after you say it?

2 How can your hair turn green?

3 Does the Eiffel Tower look bigger or smaller when you move your head slightly to the left? Why?

4 Who produces more milk – cows with names or cows without names? Why?

2 READING **Read the text and check your answers.**

✔ **EXAM SUCCESS**

You are going to do a matching activity. In this type of activity, you say which text or part of a text contains a specific piece of information. After reading quickly to get a general idea, what should you do next?

➤ EXAM SUCCESS page 145

3 Which paragraph (A–F) tells us about …

1 the philosophy behind the Ig Nobel prizes? ....

2 a discovery that is explained by the way we see numbers in our mind? ....

3 an invention that makes it hard to do something that is usually simple? ....

4 a domestic problem in a particular place in the world? ....

5 something that allows animals to talk to humans? ....

6 how to win an Ig Nobel prize? ....

7 a physical action that can make you think differently? ....

8 a discovery that could be very important for farmers? ....

4 ⚙ **CRITICAL THINKING**

Think! Then compare ideas with your class.

■ The text says that the Ig Nobel prizes have a useful or serious side because they make you think. What useful or serious side can you find for any of the discoveries or inventions in the text?

5 **What do the underlined words in the text mean? Guess and then check in your dictionary.**

6 SPEAKING **What about you?**

Which scientific research or invention in the text did you like the most? Why?

Grammar in context

The passive

1a Read the sentences. Which sentence is *not* in the passive?

1 The prizes are given to scientists.
2 An Ig Nobel prize was won by two Japanese scientists.
3 Johan Pettersson won the Chemistry Ig Nobel prize.
4 These inventions won't be used much.
5 Lots of interesting research is being done at the moment.
6 Their machine has been taken.

1b Choose the correct alternative for each rule.

1 We use the passive when we are interested mainly in the *action/person who does the action*.
2 We use the passive when it *is/isn't* obvious who does or did the action.
3 When we use the passive we *always know/don't always know* the person who does the action.

1c Read the sentences in 1a again and answer the questions.

1 Which tense is each passive sentence written in?
2 What changes in different tenses of the passive – the verb **to be** or the past participle?
3 What preposition do we use to introduce the agent (the person or thing which does the action)?

GRAMMAR REFERENCE ➤ PAGE 80

2a PRONUNCIATION Read the sentences. Which words do you think are stressed in each one? Why?

1 The gadget was invented last year.
2 The new phones are sold here.
3 Ten prizes were given.
4 The disc was inserted.
5 Emails are sent every day.

2b ▶ 33 Listen and check your answers. What happens to the pronunciation of the verb *to be*?

2c ▶ 33 Listen again and repeat the sentences. Make sure to stress the correct words.

3 Add one word in each sentence to make a correct passive sentence. Then write which tense each sentence is in.

1 The radio was invented ..*by*.. Marconi. *past simple*
2 Many new gadgets .... been invented in the 21ˢᵗ century.
   ....
3 Many jobs .... be done by robots in 2025. ....
4 Velcro, penicillin and the microwave oven .... invented by accident. ....
5 Millions of dollars .... spent on video games every year.
   ....
6 Football is .... by millions of people on TV each weekend.
   ....
7 The novel *The Fault in Our Stars* .... written by John Green in 2011. ....

4 Change these sentences from active to passive.

1 Alfred Nobel invented dynamite in 1867.
2 They gave the first Nobel prizes in 1901.
3 The Hurley Machine Company of Chicago produced the first electric-powered washing machine in 1908.
4 People have used this invention since 1908.
5 People are using this invention right now.
6 Perhaps people won't use electricity in the future.
7 Joseph Niépce took the first photo in 1826.
8 People take lots of photos on holidays.

5 Decide if the sentences are active or passive. Complete them with the correct form and tense of the verb given.

1 Usually cars .... (build) by robots.
2 Yesterday the president of the society .... (give) the prize to the scientist.
3 Since they began, many Ig Nobel prizes .... (win) by Japanese scientists.
4 The first science fiction film .... (make) in 1902.
5 Sir Isaac Newton .... (discover) the three laws of motion.
6 At this very moment, this programme .... (watch) by hundreds of thousands of people.
7 In the future, a lot of money .... (spend) on sending humans to Mars.
8 Stan Lee .... (create) many superheroes like Spiderman, Iron Man and Thor.

6 Complete the text with the passive or active form of the verb given.

Today, Post-it Notes **(a)** .... (find) everywhere. Thousands of different Post-it products **(b)** .... (use) around the world right now. For example, many students often **(c)** .... (put) them in their text books, to mark important pages or information. Did you know that they **(d)** .... (invent) by accident? Dr. Spencer Silver, a scientist at 3M, **(e)** .... (make) a type of glue that wasn't permanent. His discovery didn't seem very useful at the time. Six years later, Art Fry had the idea to use the adhesive on paper as a bookmark. The Post-it Note **(f)** .... (introduce) in the US in 1980. Since 1980, millions of notes **(g)** .... (sell) all around the world. A famous fashion designer called Ashley Isham even **(h)** .... (design) a dress which **(i)** .... (inspire) by Post-it Notes! Who knows? Maybe one day Post-it Note dresses **(j)** .... (be) available to buy in the shops!

7a SPEAKING **Work with a partner and discuss the questions.**

1 Who was the 2014 World Cup won by?
2 Who was *The Hunger Games* written by?
3 Who were *We will rock you* and *We are the champions* sung by?

7b Work with a partner. Prepare a quiz using this table.

Who	was were	X X and Y	invented discovered written sung composed directed drawn painted created won	by?

7c SPEAKING **Ask another pair of students your questions.**

Prepositional phrases with adjectives

1 What preposition do we usually use after these adjectives? If you don't know, check in the text on page 71.

aware • interested • ready

2 Match the adjectives with the prepositions. Check that you understand the meaning.

Adjective		Preposition
1 good	a	of
2 bored	b	for
3 worried	c	to
4 tired	d	at
5 afraid	e	with
6 responsible	f	about
7 similar	g	from
8 different		
9 pleased		

3 Complete the questions with the correct prepositions.

1 Are you good .... maths?
2 Are you interested .... music?
3 Are you aware .... the latest fashions?
4 Are you tired .... people talking about football?
5 Are you pleased .... your progress in English this year?
6 Are you ready .... a holiday?
7 Are you afraid .... spiders?
8 Are you similar .... anyone in your family or are you very different .... them all?
9 Are you worried .... your next exam?
10 Are you responsible .... looking after any pets?
11 Are you bored .... celebrities?

4 SPEAKING **Work with a partner. Ask the complete questions in 3. How many of your answers are the same?**

Are you good at maths?

Yes, quite good. And you?

Not really. I'm better at language and literature.

Brainstorming

LIFE SKILLS OBJECTIVES

- To learn about brainstorming as a way of creative thinking.
- To analyse a brainstorming session.
- To practise brainstorming and creative thinking.

KEY CONCEPTS

generate [v]: *The meeting of so many top inventors generated lots of good ideas.* **innovative [adj]:** *It was a totally innovative invention, nothing similar had ever existed before.* **fix/solve [v]:** *My phone doesn't work. I need to solve the problem/fix it fast so that I can make a call.* **inspire [v]:** *A falling apple inspired the thought behind Newton's Law of Gravity.*

1a Work in a small group. Do this activity to help you start thinking creatively. Give your group one point for each idea, even if it's crazy!

1 You have two minutes to think of as many different uses as possible for a brick.

2 Now do the same for a coffee mug.

1b Share your answers with the class. Who has the most points?

2 READING Read the article below about a creative thinking technique. Put these sentences in the correct place.

A Quantity helps to get quality.

B All ideas are welcome, even crazy ones.

C No criticism of ideas is allowed.

D It's OK to 'steal' other people's ideas.

3 Are these statements True (T) or False (F)?

1 You should tell somebody that they have had a good idea when you are brainstorming.   T/F

2 It's important to think carefully and only suggest really good ideas in a brainstorming session.   T/F

3 Using other people's ideas to inspire a new idea from you is a positive part of brainstorming.   T/F

4 You should be serious and logical when you brainstorm.   T/F

Brainstorming: Principles

There are many situations in life where we need to think creatively, to find new solutions to problems. Creative thinking is a key part of scientific research and invention, for example. It is also essential when a company starts designing a new product or decides how to sell it. The good news is that young people are usually very creative. The only problem is that sometimes our creative side is controlled by our 'sensible' side, the side that wants to keep our new ideas in order and under control. But here's one technique which helps you to let those original ideas out. It's called 'brainstorming'.

'Brainstorming' was introduced by Alex Osborn in his book *Applied Imagination*. He was looking for a process to give people the freedom to generate new ideas and find solutions to problems in groups, and came up with a simple but successful method. There are some basic principles:

1 People in the group can call out any ideas, but during the brainstorming session people should not make either positive or negative comments. This is because these comments can stop other people from suggesting new ideas.

2 In a brainstorming session, you want lots of ideas. Usually people say all the most usual, least imaginative things at the start, but, later, more original, innovative ideas come out. These are the ideas you want. So if you get lots of ideas, it's more likely that there will be interesting ideas.

3 Everybody is allowed to take somebody else's idea and adapt it or change it. This is all part of the group creativity.

4 The ideas can seem to be mad, humorous, stupid or unimportant. Who knows? Maybe when you think more about it there's something brilliant inside that mad idea!

So, how do you organise a brainstorming session? We suggest you follow this procedure.

1 In a small or large group, select a leader and a secretary (they may be the same person). The leader guides the brainstorming session. The secretary makes notes of all the ideas.

2 Define the topic to be brainstormed and make sure everybody understands clearly what the topic is.

3 Make the rules for brainstorming clear. Everybody is allowed to contribute. No answer is wrong, and nobody should laugh at or criticise anybody for their ideas. Set a time limit and respect it.

4 Start the brainstorming. The secretary should write down all the ideas, unless they are repeated. It's good if everybody can see the secretary's notes.

5 During brainstorming, the idea is to get as many ideas as possible. After brainstorming, the evaluation stage begins. Analyse the ideas and decide if each idea is excellent, interesting, or not useful. The excellent ideas may work immediately. The interesting ideas will need further development. Hopefully, one of those excellent or interesting ideas will be a solution to your initial problem.

4 READING **Read the rest of the article on this page and answer the questions.**

1 What does the secretary do in a brainstorming session?

2 How should people in the group treat each other?

3 What ideas are written down in a brainstorming session?

4 What happens immediately after the brainstorming session?

5 How is the last part of the procedure different from the brainstorming session?

5a LISTENING ▶ 34 **Watch or listen to a group of students brainstorming a topic. Answer the questions.**

1 What topic are they brainstorming?

2 Do they follow the principles and procedure suggested in the texts?

5b Work with a partner. Discuss your answers and justify your answer to question 2 in 5a.

They had a leader and a secretary.

6a ▶ 34 **Work in groups of three. Watch or listen again.**

Student A: Write down any ideas you hear for who should get the prizes.
Student B: Write down any ideas you hear for what the prizes could be.
Student C: Write down any ideas you hear for the ceremony.

6b Compare your notes.

LIFE TASK

Work in small groups. Follow this plan:

1 *Look at the ideas from the video. Brainstorm more ideas for a prize ceremony at your school. Who are the prizes for? What are they? What could happen at the prize ceremony? Accept all ideas at this stage. Make sure you have a leader/secretary.*

2 *Analyse all the ideas. Decide which ones you think could realistically work and which ones could be developed.*

3 *Present your ideas to the rest of the class.*

1 SPEAKING **Work with a partner. Discuss what you think a smart home is, and what technology it could have.**

2 LISTENING ▶ 35 **Listen. Do they mention any of your ideas in 1?**

✓ EXAM SUCCESS

You are going to do a multiple-choice listening activity. In this type of activity you have three or four answers and you choose the best answer. When should you read the answers for the first time? Do you think the questions are usually in the order that you hear them?

➤ EXAM SUCCESS page 145

3 ▶ 35 **Listen again and choose the best answers.**

1 Smart fridges …

  a tell you what you must eat.
  b can prepare your dinner.
  c can help to improve your diet.

2 Smart fridges can also …

  a say who has taken something from the fridge.
  b make it unnecessary for you to go to a food shop.
  c tell you which is the best and nearest food shop.

3 To control cameras, lights and heating in a smart home …

  a you have to use a special mobile phone.
  b you need to use a special remote control from inside the house.
  c it doesn't matter where you are.

4 The first smart houses …

  a appeared a few years ago.
  b have just been built now.
  c will exist in a year or two in the future.

5 Soon vacuum cleaners …

  a will not just clean floors.
  b will be frightening in some ways.
  c will not need humans to operate them.

6 The expert, Jane, says that …

  a she doesn't like making breakfast.
  b smart homes will make us lazy.
  c we can do more when we live in smart homes.

4 SPEAKING **What about *you*?**

1 Have you seen or used any of this technology?

2 Would you like to live in a smart home? Why/Why not?

🎬 *have something done*

1a Read the sentences. Who does the action – the subject at the start of the sentence or somebody/something else?

1 You have all your food delivered to your house.

2 Bill Gates had a smart house built.

3 We'll get everything done for us by robots.

1b Read the sentences again and answer the questions.

1 What comes after the verbs **have** or **get** – the subject or the object of the sentence?

2 Which part of the verb are **delivered**, **built** or **done** in these sentences?

3 Can we use **have** or **get** in different tenses in this type of sentence?

4 What does **by** introduce in this type of sentence?

GRAMMAR REFERENCE ➤ PAGE 80

2 What did these people have/get done last week? Make sentences using these verbs.

cut • deliver • fix • make • paint • test

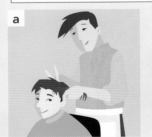

He had his hair cut.

3 Put the words in order to make questions.

1 cut often you do get How hair your?
....

2 yourself fix you Can computer your?
....

3 ever Have delivered your house to pizza had you a?
....

4 When your you eyes time was last the had tested?
....

5 Do your photo you taken like having?
....

6 for Have ever had made clothes you you?
....

4 Rewrite these sentences using *have something done* in the correct tense. If we know who did the action, include them with *by*.

1 They're painting the kitchen on Saturday.
We ....

2 They're going to service my sister's car next week.
My sister ....

3 Her parents pay her mobile phone bills.
She ....

4 Last summer they built a swimming pool in my friend's garden.
My friend ....

5 They fixed our computer last week.
We ....

6 They've reinstalled the operating system on his computer.
He ....

7 A computer specialist rescued my files.
I ....

5a SPEAKING Work with a partner. Ask the questions in 3. Then ask questions to find out extra information. Use *Who?*, *What?*, *Why?*, *When?*, *Where?*, *How often?*.

5b Tell the class three interesting things you found out about your partner.

Gerunds and infinitives

6 Match the sentences (a–f) with the rules (1–6). Choose the correct alternative in each rule.

a That will give us more time to go **running**. ....
b I'd be interested in **finding** a solution. ....
c I don't like **doing** housework. ....
d I think **cleaning** will be a thing of the past.
e You use a fridge **to keep** your food cold. ....
f That's easy **to fix**. ....

1 We use the *infinitive/gerund* after prepositions (except *to*).

2 We use the *infinitive/gerund* immediately after adjectives.

3 We use the *infinitive/gerund* with *go* to talk about physical activities.

4 We use the *infinitive/gerund* after verbs of liking or disliking (except *would like*).

5 We use the *infinitive/gerund* to explain why we do something.

6 We use the *infinitive/gerund* as the subject or object of the sentence.

GRAMMAR REFERENCE ➤ PAGE 80

7 Complete the sentences with the correct form of the verb given.

1 I go .... (cycle) at the weekend.

2 I'm interested in .... (learn) to play the guitar one day.

3 I think .... (read) is a great way to spend your free time.

4 I love .... (play) tennis.

5 I think it's difficult .... (learn) new vocabulary in English.

6 I want to go to university .... (get) a good job.

8 SPEAKING Work with a partner. Talk about the sentences in 7. Are they true for you or not?

Developing speaking

Comparing and contrasting photos

1 [SPEAKING] **Work with a partner. Look at the photos of lessons at school. Which of the two lessons would you prefer and why?**

1

2

2 [LISTENING] ▶ 36 **Listen to a student talking about the two photos. Which lesson does she prefer and why? Do you agree with her? Why/Why not?**

3 ▶ 36 **Listen again and complete the sentences.**

1 .... of the photos show students doing lessons in a secondary school.

2 In the first photo they're in a normal classroom with a whiteboard .... in the second photo they're in a laboratory.

3 Another important .... between the photos is that the students are all listening to the teacher in the first photo, but in the second photo they're working on their own.

4 One other .... between the photos is that in both photos the students look interested in the lesson.

4 **Complete the Speaking bank with the phrases in 3.**

💬 SPEAKING BANK

Useful expressions to compare and contrast photos

Comparing

- ....
- One thing that the photos have in common is that ....
- ....

Contrasting

- ....
- In the first photo … However, in the second photo … ....
- ....

PRACTICE MAKES PERFECT

5a [SPEAKING] **Work with a partner. Look at the photos and make a list of similarities and differences between them.**

5b **Work with another partner. Take it in turns to do this task. Use expressions from the Speaking bank.**

Compare and contrast the two photos below. How do you think the people feel and why?

Developing writing

A for-and-against essay

1 Work with a partner. Read the statement below and look at the three photos on this page. Make a list of arguments for and against.

> *We should all have the freedom to use our mobile phones where and when we like.*

2 READING **Read this essay. Does it contain any of your ideas from 1?**

Nowadays life seems almost impossible without a mobile phone. They are used in many different situations and we can now do almost everything on one device. But should we be able to use them where and when we like, or should there be some restrictions?

Mobile phones are small and easy to carry. You can turn the sound off on your mobile phone so, in theory, there is no reason why your phone should cause problems for other people. Furthermore, mobile phones can be essential in emergencies and accidents. If you have a mobile phone with you all the time, you could save lives.

However, there are times when using a mobile phone can create problems for other people. On the one hand, they are useful when there is an accident, as I mentioned before. On the other hand, they can actually cause accidents, for example if people use their phones when they are driving. What's more, in public places like cinemas, hospitals or schools, phones can disturb other people. Finally, they can interfere with other technology, for example inside a plane or in hospitals. This can be dangerous.

To sum up, I think mobile phones are necessary for our lives today, but there are times when people should not be able to use them. In my opinion, the problem is that some people can't switch their phones off and they forget that they are causing problems for others. This is why I think there should be some restrictions.

3 **Read the essay again. Write a title or short description of the content in each paragraph.**

Paragraph 1: ....

Paragraph 2: ....

Paragraph 3: ....

Paragraph 4: ....

4 **Complete the Writing bank with these linkers.**

> Furthermore, • However, • Secondly, To sum up, • What's more,

✏ WRITING BANK

Useful linkers in for-and-against essays

Sequencing arguments	Making contrasts
▪ Firstly,	▪ On the one hand,
▪ (a)	▪ On the other hand,
▪ Finally,	▪ In contrast,
Adding arguments	▪ (d) ....
▪ (b)	**Concluding**
▪ (c)	▪ In conclusion,
▪ In addition,	▪ (e) ....

PRACTICE MAKES PERFECT

5a **Work with a partner. Read the task and plan the essay. Remember to organise your ideas into paragraphs.**

'We depend too much on computers today.' Write an essay giving arguments for and against this statement and give your own opinion.

WRITING BANK ➤ PAGE 151

5b **Write your essay individually. Use expressions from the Writing bank.**

Grammar reference

The passive

FORM

Subject + *be* + past participle (+ *by* + agent)

The prizes are given at a ceremony. (present simple)

This invention is being used by millions of people. (present continuous)

These computers have been used by NASA. (present perfect)

The car wasn't invented in 1930. (past simple)

This type of energy will be used in the future. (will)

We make the passive with the correct tense and form of the verb *to be* and the past participle of the verb.

To make questions in the passive, we put the first auxiliary verb before the subject.

Is the ceremony being shown on TV?

Has the ceremony been filmed?

We use the preposition *by* to introduce the agent – the person or thing which does the action.

USE

We use **the passive** when:

1 we are more interested in the action than the people who do the action.

   English is spoken here.

2 we do not know who exactly does the action.

   My things have been moved.

3 it is obvious or understood who did the action.

   The criminal was arrested at 5.30 pm.

have something done

FORM

Subject + **have** or **get** + object + **past participle** (**by** + agent)

I get my eyes tested once a year. (present simple)

She is having a pizza delivered to her house. (present continuous)

He had his hair cut. (past simple)

We'll get our photo taken. (will)

USE

1 We use **have something done** to talk about actions which we don't do ourselves, somebody or something does them for us. We often pay them to do this action. **Get** is slightly more informal.

   We didn't paint the house ourselves. We had it painted by professionals.

2 We can use the preposition **by** to introduce the agent – the person or thing which does the action.

Gerunds and infinitives

USE

We use **the gerund**:

- as the subject or object of a sentence.
  Doing homework is useful.

- after prepositions.
  I'm worried about making mistakes.

- after verbs of liking or disliking, e.g. *like, love, enjoy, can't stand, don't mind, hate.*
  I don't like waiting.

- with *go* to talk about physical activities.
  go running, go swimming, go shopping …

We use **the infinitive**:

- to explain *why* somebody does something.
  Why did he go to the laboratory? To do an experiment.

- immediately after adjectives.
  It's easy to answer that question.

Vocabulary

Everyday inventions digital camera • dishwasher • e-reader • fridge-freezer • headphones home cinema system • laptop • microwave oven • mobile phone • MP3 player • music system • remote control satnav • speaker • vacuum cleaner • washing machine

Operating technology charge/recharge (a battery) • connect X to Y • insert • plug in • press a button (e.g. play/stop) • select (a network/a programme/a track/a function) • switch/turn on/off • tap (the screen)

Prepositional phrases with adjectives afraid of • aware of • bored with/of • different from/to • good at/for interested in • pleased with • ready for • responsible for • similar to • tired of • worried about

Other words and phrases ➤ page 140

Grammar revision

The passive / 8 points

1 Complete the sentences with the correct form of the passive of the verbs given.

1 His keys .... (steal) last week.

2 English .... (teach) all around the world.

3 This museum .... (visit) by thousands of people each week.

4 A new laboratory .... (build) next year.

5 The first successful software for MP3 players .... (invent) by Tomislav Uzelac in 1997.

6 I think next year's final .... (play) in Poland.

7 *The Hobbit* .... (translate) into over fifty languages.

8 Portuguese .... (speak) in Brazil.

have something done / 7 points

2 Complete the second sentences using the correct form of *have something done*.

1 She didn't decorate the house herself. She .... by professionals.

2 He won't fix the car. He .... at a garage.

3 She doesn't do her own hair. She .... at the hairdresser's.

4 We didn't paint the room. We ....

5 They didn't build the garage. They .... by an expert.

6 He didn't translate the email. He .... by a friend.

7 They haven't tested their son's eyesight. They .... by an optician.

Gerunds and infinitives / 5 points

3 Choose the correct alternative.

1 Do you enjoy *to listen/listening* to classical music?

2 It's interesting *to read/reading* about new technology.

3 I want to go to the cinema *to see/seeing* that new film.

4 I'm bored with *watch/watching* this match.

5 *To fix/Fixing* computers isn't easy.

Vocabulary revision

EVERYDAY INVENTIONS / 7 points

1 Complete the names of these everyday inventions. Is each one usually used for pleasure (P) or for housework (H)?

1 dish............................. ....

2 head............................. ....

3 vacuum ....

4 washing ....

5 MP3 ....

6 microwave ....

7 remote ....

OPERATING TECHNOLOGY / 6 points

2 Complete the text with these words.

insert • press • plug ... in • select • switch ... off • turn ... on

To play your favourite song from a CD

Your CD player doesn't have batteries so first you must
(a) .... it .... Then you (b) .... the CD player .... You (c) .... the disc in the machine. You (d) .... the song you want to hear. You (e) .... Play. When you finish listening, you (f) .... the CD player ....

PREPOSITIONAL PHRASES WITH ADJECTIVES / 7 points

3 Choose the correct alternative.

1 The teacher is pleased *of/with* my work.

2 She isn't worried *about/of* her marks.

3 People say I look similar *at/to* my father.

4 Are you aware *of/with* the situation?

5 Some people are afraid *with/of* flying.

6 Who is responsible *for/of* keeping the room tidy?

7 I'm good *at/in* writing essays.

Reading

1 READING **Read the text and match the pictures (1–4) to the Ig Nobel prize winners (A–D).**

2 Which paragraph (A–D) tells us about …

1 a discovery about human mental processes? ....
2 a work that solved a problem using mathematics? ....
3 a work that appeared in a magazine for doctors? ....
4 an experiment that didn't use humans? ....
5 a problem that somebody wanted to solve because it often happened to them? ....
6 an invention that tricks people? ....
7 a problem for new members of a profession? ....
8 research that may help language learners one day? ....

SOME MORE IG NOBEL PRIZE WINNERS

Do you remember reading about the Ig Nobel prizes? They are given annually to scientists whose work is funny, unusual and different.

A BRIAN WHITCOMBE AND DAN MEYER
PICTURE: ....

In 2007 an Ig Nobel Prize was won by Brian Whitcombe and Dan Meyer. They wrote an article which was published in the British Medical Journal. The article was an analysis of the problems suffered by professional sword-swallowers. To do his research, Whitcombe interviewed nearly 50 sword-swallowers. He discovered that swallowing swords doesn't usually cause anything more serious than sore throats. Generally, these sore throats only occur in one of these four situations: when someone is learning to swallow swords, when the act of swallowing the sword is repeated frequently, when the sword has an unusual shape, or when more than one sword is swallowed at the same time.

B JUAN MANUEL TORO PICTURE: ....

Another Ig Nobel Prize was won by neuroscientists at Barcelona University. Juan Manuel Toro and two other colleagues were interested in exploring the way in which languages are acquired by the brain. They discovered that rats cannot tell the difference between somebody speaking Dutch backwards and somebody speaking Japanese backwards. 64 rats were taught to press a button when they heard normal Dutch or Japanese. They could learn to do this. But when they heard the languages backwards they had no idea what was happening.

C DR BRIAN WANSINK PICTURE: ....

A food psychologist from New York called Dr Brian Wansink won his Ig Nobel Prize for an interesting experiment with soup. He invented a never-ending bowl. When people ate tomato soup from the bowl, the bowl was automatically filled again from a tube connected to the bottom of the bowl. He discovered that people ate 73% more than usual when they used this bowl. But they didn't feel full. The conclusion was that we decide how much to eat with our eyes, not with the way our stomach feels.

D NIC SVENSON AND PIERS BARNES
PICTURE: ....

Have you ever taken a photo of a large group of people? If you have, you've probably found that it's very difficult to take the photo with everybody's eyes open. Usually there are one or two people who blink just at the moment when you take the photo. An Australian, Nic Svenson, was tired of this always happening. So she asked a physicist, Dr Piers Barnes, to help her to calculate how many photos you need to take to be sure that nobody in a group has their eyes closed. After doing their complex calculations, they decided that for a group with a maximum of twenty people, you divide the number of people by three to decide how many photos you need to take. For groups of fifty or more, the scientists decided that it was almost impossible to be sure that everybody has their eyes open! For their hard work they won the Ig Nobel Prize in 2006.

Speaking

3 Look at the task. You have five minutes to prepare a presentation. Give your presentation to the class.

Prepare a presentation on this topic:

For scientists in the 21st century there is nothing new to invent. Everything important has already been invented.

Listening

➤ TIP FOR LISTENING EXAMS

In multiple-choice activities, remember …
Read the questions before you listen. The
questions are usually in the order that you hear
them in the recording.

➤ EXAM SUCCESS page 145

4 LISTENING ▶ 37 **Listen to a programme about
teenage students. Choose the best answers.**

1 Professor Foster discovered that teenage
   students …
   a prefer studying in the afternoon.
   b remember more in the afternoon.
   c have more lessons in the afternoon.

2 Professor Foster thinks that teenagers …
   a need more rest than young children.
   b need alarm clocks more than younger and
      older people.
   c should sleep longer at least two days a week.

3 At his school, Dr Kelley wants to …
   a change the school timetable.
   b have classes only in the afternoon.
   c have easy lessons between 9 and 11 am.

4 Most students …
   a like Dr Kelley's idea.
   b don't like Dr Kelley's idea.
   c don't mind getting up early.

5 Dr Kelley …
   a taught physical education.
   b didn't like interrupting his classes.
   c let students move at certain moments in his
      class.

5 SPEAKING **What about *you*?**

1 What do you think about Dr Kelley's idea?
2 When do you study better – in the morning,
   afternoon or evening?

Writing

➤ TIP FOR WRITING EXAMS

Before you start writing in an exam remember …
You should know who you are writing for. Write in the
correct style for that reader. You will usually get more
marks if you write in an appropriate way for the task.

➤ EXAM SUCCESS page 145

6 **Work with a partner. Read the task and plan the
   article. Remember to organise your ideas into
   paragraphs.**

Your school magazine wants to know what students think
about school uniform. Write an article for the magazine.
Give reasons **for** and **against** school uniform.
Finish the article with a conclusion giving your opinion.

7 **Write your essay individually.**

'CAN DO' PROGRESS CHECK UNITS 5–6   CEF

1 **How well can you do these things
   in English now? Give yourself a mark
   from 1 to 4.**

   > **1** = I can do it very well.
   > **2** = I can do it quite well.
   > **3** = I have some problems.
   > **4** = I can't do it.

   a I can talk about obligation, prohibition, advice
      and permission using modal verbs. ☐

   b I can talk about real, possible and imaginary
      situations and their consequences using the
      zero, first and second conditional. ☐

   c I can talk about different aspects of life at
      school and university. ☐

   d I can give simple oral presentations. ☐

   e I can write a formal letter applying for a
      scholarship. ☐

   f I can talk about processes using different forms
      of the passive and *have something done*. ☐

   g I know which prepositions to use with certain
      adjectives. ☐

   h I can understand written and spoken texts
      about inventions and technology. ☐

   i I can compare and contrast two photos
      orally. ☐

   j I can write for-and-against essays. ☐

2 **Now decide what you need to do to improve.**

   1 Look again at my book/notes.
   2 Do more practice exercises.
      ➤ WORKBOOK Units 5 and 6
   3 Ask for help.
   4 Other: ....

7 Play on!

Vocabulary

Sports and sports venues

1 **SPEAKING** Work with a partner. Try to match as many of the words as possible to each category. Check that you understand them.

> athletics • baseball • basketball • climbing
> cycling • diving • football • golf • gymnastics
> horse-riding • ice hockey • ice-skating • judo
> karate • rugby • sailing • skiing • snowboarding
> swimming • tennis • volleyball • weightlifting

1	team sports	
2	individual sports	
3	ball sports	
4	water sports	
5	winter sports	
6	combat sports	
7	indoor sports	

2a **PRONUNCIATION** Put the words in the correct column, according to the stress.

O	Oo	Ooo	oOo
golf			

2b ▶ 38 **Listen and check your answers. Practise saying the words with the correct stress.**

3 **Complete the sentences with these words.**

> course • court • gym • pitch • pool • rink
> slope • track

1 We go swimming and diving in a ....

2 We do gymnastics in a ....

3 You ski down a ....

4 You play tennis or basketball on a ....

5 You play football on a ....

6 You play ice hockey on a ....

7 You do athletics on a ....

8 You play golf on a ....

Sports equipment and scores

4 **Look at the photo. Which of these pieces of equipment can you see?**

> ball • bat • boots • club • goal/goal post
> goggles • net • racket • skates • skis • trainers

5 **Work with a partner. How many sports can you think of that use each piece of equipment in 4?**

You need a net to play tennis, volleyball …

6 **Name one sport where you can do these things with a ball.**

> bounce • catch • head • hit (with a bat)
> kick • pass • throw

7 **Choose the correct alternative. In one sentence, both are correct.**

1 Spain *beat/won* England 2–0 (two–nil).

2 Spain *beat/won* the match.

3 England lost *to Spain/the match*.

4 It was 1–1 (one all) so the teams *drew/lost*.

5 Messi *scored/shot* a great goal yesterday.

6 I don't know if Nadal will win the next *goal/point*.

8 **LISTENING** ▶ 39 **Listen. Which sport in 1 is the subject of each conversation?**

1 ....   3 ....

2 ....   4 ....

9 **SPEAKING** Work in groups. Play twenty questions. One person in your group thinks of a sport.

Is it a team sport?

No, it isn't.

1 Work with a partner. Discuss these questions.

1 What is a superstition?

2 What superstitions exist in your country?

2 READING **Read the text and complete the table.**

Footballer	Country	Most important superstition
1 Laurent Blanc		
2 Pelé		
3 Kolo Touré		
4 Pepe Reina		
5 Kim Little		

THE GAME BEFORE THE GAME

For the World Cup in Brazil there was focus in the media on 'the game before the game', the pre-match rituals of some of the world's top football players. Some of the rituals are quite normal things. For example, Neymar Jr. always speaks to his dad before each match. But some players have pre-match rituals that seem to be pure superstitions.

When does a routine become a superstition?

In the 1998 World Cup the French team had a strange habit. The defender Laurent Blanc kissed the goalkeeper's head at the start of every match! Sometimes other players joined in. But that wasn't the only superstition that the team had. Every time the team got on the coach to go to a match all the players always sat in exactly the same places. And in the changing room just before the match, they always listened to the same song – I Will Survive. Irrational? Yes. But France did win the World Cup that year! Maybe it helped that 1998 was the year when France hosted the World Cup.

Perhaps the greatest footballer of all time was the Brazilian, Edson Arantes do Nascimento, the player that is better known as Pelé. Pelé is the player who has the world record for scoring most goals in his career – an amazing 1,283 in 1,363 matches. After one great match, he gave away his favourite shirt to a fan. But then he started playing badly. He stopped scoring and started losing matches. Why? Pelé could think of only one reason – he needed the 'lucky' shirt which he had given away. He told a friend to find the fan and bring back the shirt. A week later, the friend gave Pelé his shirt and he started to score again! Pelé's friend thought it was better not to tell Pelé that he had never found where the fan lived and that the shirt was a completely different one!

There are players whose superstitions almost stop them from playing. Kolo Touré, from Ivory Coast, always has to be the last player to go out onto the pitch. In an important Champions League match, one of Touré's teammates was late. Touré refused to go onto the pitch and play until his teammate appeared. And, for some strange reason, Spanish goalkeeper Pepe Reina has to fill his car with petrol on his way to each match. He does this even when the tank is already almost full and there are lots of other cars in front of him! The night before a match he always eats the same cheese sandwich, too. His other superstitions include always touching the pitch, both goal posts and the crossbar after warming up at the start of each match.

So, when does a routine become a silly superstition, and why? Always eating the same food before a match is probably quite sensible. If you know that the food doesn't cause you any stomach problems, why change? But some routines are less logical. The Scottish women's player Kim Little always puts her left sock and boot on before her right … every match! This type of routine is irrational but psychologists believe that following a 'lucky' routine can make a player feel good, relaxed and in control. And not following the routine can have the opposite effect. So, maybe 'the game before the game' is important after all.

3 Are these sentences True (T) or False (F)? Write the number of the line(s) where you find the answer.

1 Neymar Jr. does something very unusual before each match.   T / F ....

2 In the 1998 World Cup France had one superstition on the pitch and two superstitions off the pitch.   T / F ....

3 Pelé started to play well again because he got his lucky shirt back.   T / F ....

4 Pepe Reina's car always needs petrol just before a match.   T / F ....

5 Eating the same food before each match is a silly superstition.   T / F ....

6 Psychologists don't believe that superstitions can help a player.   T / F ....

4 ⚙ **CRITICAL THINKING**

Think! Then compare ideas with your class.

■ What do you think is the author's opinion of sports superstitions? What is your opinion of their importance?

5 What do the underlined words in the text mean? Guess and then check in your dictionary.

6 SPEAKING **What about you?**

1 Which superstition or ritual in the text do you think is the funniest or most unusual?

2 Do you or anyone you know have superstitions? What are they?

Grammar in context

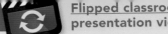

Defining relative clauses

1a Read the sentences. The words in blue are relative pronouns. Use them to complete the rules 1–5.

a He's the player **who** has the world record for scoring most goals.

b He needed the lucky shirt **which** he had given away.

c There are players **whose** superstitions almost stop them from playing.

d 1998 was the year **when** France hosted the World Cup.

e That wasn't the only superstition (**that**) the team had.

f Edson Arantes do Nascimento is the player **that** is better known as Pelé.

g He had never found the place **where** the fan lived.

1 We use .... and .... with people.

2 We use .... and .... with things.

3 We use .... to talk about possessions.

4 We use .... with places.

5 We use .... with times.

1b Answer these questions.

1 Why do you think we call these <u>defining</u> relative clauses? What do they define?

2 Why can we omit *that* in sentence e but not in sentence f?

GRAMMAR REFERENCE ➤ PAGE 94

2 Choose the correct alternative. If you think both are correct, choose both.

1 Football is a game *which/–* many people play.

2 A stadium is a place *that/where* you can watch sports like rugby and baseball.

3 The people *who/–* watch sports events are called spectators.

4 The leader of the Tour de France is the person *who/whose* shirt is yellow.

5 June is the month *when/which* Wimbledon starts.

6 A jockey is a person *who/that* rides a horse in a race.

7 Brazil is the country *where/which* has won the FIFA World Cup the most times.

✔ **EXAM SUCCESS**

The next activity is a cloze activity. You have a text with gaps, but you do not have the words to fill the gaps. What type of words do you think you will have to put in?

➤ EXAM SUCCESS page 145

3 Complete the text with the missing words.

Extreme ironing is an unusual sport (a) .... was invented in 1997 by an Englishman (b) .... name is Phil Shaw. He had to do the ironing at home, (c) .... he preferred to go rock climbing. So he decided (d) .... combine the two things. Of course, ironing and climbing are two activities (e) .... don't have a lot in common. But now people do it all over the world. When Phil was in New Zealand he started an organisation called Extreme Ironing International. Diving, skiing, skating and parachuting are some of (f) .... other sports which people have combined with ironing. Underwater, in the air and on the top of mountains are just some of the strange places (g) .... people have done this sport. Ben Gibbons and John Roberts are two Englishmen (h) .... adventure with extreme ironing became a short film, *Extreme Ironing to Mount Everest!*

Would you like to try extreme ironing?

4 Match the sentence halves and add a relative pronoun. Look up the words in *italics* in a dictionary if necessary.

1 The winner in a gymnastics competition is the person ....

2 A *referee* is the person ....

3 2024 is a year ....

4 A *tatami* is the place ....

5 *Time out* is a moment in a basketball match ....

6 A *black belt* is a thing you get ....

7 In football, *goalkeepers* are often the players ....

8 The *puck* is the thing ....

a you are really good at judo or karate.

b shirt has a number 1 on the back.

c you hit in an ice hockey match.

d mark is the highest.

e there will be Olympic Games.

f the players stop playing.

g job is to control football matches.

h you do judo.

5 Complete the sentences with a relative pronoun.

1 Maria Sharapova is a tennis player
Maria Sharapova is a tennis player who was born in Russia.

2 A net is something ....

3 Wimbledon is a place ....

4 Summer is the season ....

5 PE is a subject ....

6 The ice rink is a place ....

7 Swimming is an activity ....

8 2014 was the year ....

6a SPEAKING **Work with a partner. Read the definitions and identify the words.**

1 It's a person who teaches you a skill, like driving or skiing.

2 It's the place where you should put up a tent.

3 It's usually the first thing you do when you arrive at the airport to catch a plane.

6b Prepare definitions for at least six words that you have learnt so far this year. Read your definitions to other students. Can they identify your words?

> It's a person who teaches at a university.

Phrasal verbs connected with sport

1 Read the sentences. Match the phrasal verbs in red with their definitions (a–g).

1 She **took up** gymnastics when she was seven because she saw a competition and wanted to try it.

2 You should always **warm up** before a match so that your legs are ready.

3 Italy have **knocked out** England in the World Cup so England will be on the plane home tomorrow.

4 Hey, you! Don't just sit there watching. Come and **join in**.

5 It's impossible to beat you. I **give in**!

6 They really want to win so they're going to **go for** it.

7 She's really fit because she **works out** at the gym every day.

Phrasal verbs		Definitions	
1	take up	a	prepare for a sport or another activity by doing gentle exercises
2	warm up	b	stop competing and accept you can't win
3	knock out	c	try very hard to win or get something
4	join in	d	start participating in an activity with other people who are already doing it
5	give in	e	start a sport or hobby
6	go for	f	do physical exercise
7	work out	g	eliminate somebody from a competition by beating them/make somebody unconscious

2 Complete the sentences with the correct form of the phrasal verbs from 1.

1 I'm going to .... tennis. Tomorrow I'm going to buy a racket.

2 Yesterday we played in the semi-final. We aren't in the final because the other team .... us ....

3 A: Why don't you ....? B: Because I don't like team sports, I prefer individual ones.

4 She's got the right attitude to be a champion. When she's losing, she never ....

5 It'll be a hard race but she's going to .... the gold medal.

6 He's hurt his leg because he didn't .... before running.

7 They're really strong. They .... in the gym, doing weightlifting.

3 SPEAKING **Complete the sentences with the correct form of the phrasal verbs in 1. Ask your partner the questions.**

1 Do you ever .... out to keep fit? How often?

2 If there is a match or competition at school, do you .... in or do you just watch?

3 If something is difficult, do you usually .... for it and try hard to win, or do you .... in easily?

4 Have you ever been .... out of a competition?

5 When you do sport, do you usually .... up first or do you begin straight away?

6 What new sport or hobby would you like to .... up?

Looking after your heart

LIFE SKILLS OBJECTIVES

- To learn about risk factors contributing to heart disease.
- To find out how and why to calculate your resting and recovery heart rates.
- To consider practical ways to look after your heart.

KEY CONCEPTS

heart disease [n]: *Smoking can give you heart disease.* **blood pressure [n]:** *When you have high blood pressure, your heart is working too fast.*
pump [v]: *The heart pumps blood around the body.*
vessel, artery [n]: *Vessels and arteries are pipes which carry blood in your body.* **beat [n, v]:** *The heart usually beats between 60 and 100 times a minute.*
risk factor [n]: *Stress is a risk factor for heart disease.*

1a Look at the leaflet on the right. Work with a partner. Talk about what you can see. What is the message of the leaflet?

1b Apart from doing exercise, how do you think you can look after your heart? What should/shouldn't you do?

2 Match the numbers and information about the heart. Guess the answers.

1	100,000	a	the number of litres of blood in your body
2	5	b	the number of deaths caused by heart disease in the UK each year
3	23,000	c	the length of the blood vessels in your body
4	100,000 km	d	the number of times your heart beats in a day
5	74,000	e	the number of litres of blood that your heart pumps in a day

3 READING **Read the first part of the leaflet and answer the questions.**

1 What are the correct answers in 2?

2 Does the text mention any of your ideas in 1b? If so, which ones?

HEART ISSUES

1 Your amazing heart!

Your heart is a muscle which beats about 100,000 times each day. The body contains about five litres of blood, which your heart is continuously circulating. In total, it pumps about 23,000 litres of blood around your body daily! This blood delivers oxygen and nutrients to all parts of your body. It also carries away unwanted carbon dioxide and waste products. You have about 100,000 kilometres of blood vessels to do this!

Unfortunately, coronary heart disease is the biggest cause of death both in the UK and many other countries. It is responsible for around 74,000 deaths in the UK each year.

2 Risk factors contributing to heart disease

Here are some of the main factors which can increase the risk of developing heart disease:

A Family history of heart problems

B Smoking

C High blood pressure

D Being overweight

E Gender

F Age

G Physical inactivity

H High blood cholesterol

I Stress

4 Read the second part of the leaflet. Complete the activities. Check your answers on page 148.

3 Which factors can we do something about?

The good news is that by making simple changes to our lifestyle we can reduce some of those risk factors. Which factors in part 2 do you think we can change and which can't we change?

Things we can change	Things we can't change
1	1
2	2
3	3
4	
5	
6	

4 How can we reduce those risk factors?

Here are some simple ways that we can make a positive change to reduce the chances of developing heart disease. Match each one to one of the risk factors in part 2.

1 Eat a healthy, balanced diet and control how much you eat.

2 Reduce salt in your diet. Salt increases blood pressure. Your weight and fitness also affect your blood pressure, so eat sensibly and take exercise.

3 Be active every day.

4 Reduce the amount of saturated fat that you eat.

5 Never smoke.

6 Decide what is causing the stress and try to control the situation.

5 Look at the words and expressions below. Work with a partner. What do you think each one is?

Your heart rate ....
Beats per minute ....
A heart-rate monitor ....
The radial artery ....
The carotid artery ....

6 LISTENING ▶ 40 Watch or listen to two students presenting a PE assignment about calculating your recovery heart rate. Listen for the words and expressions in 5. Were your ideas correct?

7 ▶ 40 Watch or listen again and answer the questions.

1 How do you take your **resting** heart rate?
....
....

2 How do you find your **recovery** heart rate?
....
....

3 Why is your recovery heart rate important and useful to know?
....
....

LIFE TASK

In your school you want to create a campaign to raise awareness about taking care of your heart. Work in a small group and follow this plan:

1 *Choose one of the risk factors in part 2 of the text on page 88. Do some more research to find out more information about it.*

2 *Try to think of an original way to present the information you have discovered. It could be a poster, a leaflet, a computer presentation, a questionnaire or a physical activity/experiment.*

3 *Present your information to as many people as possible.*

✔ EXAM SUCCESS

You are going to do a True/False listening activity. What should you do if you miss the answer to a question?

➤ EXAM SUCCESS page 145

1 Read the sentences about the origin of basketball. Work with a partner. Do you think they are True (T) or False (F)?

1 Basketball was invented before 1900.   T / F
2 The inventor of basketball was born in the US.   T / F
3 The inventor of basketball was a PE teacher.   T / F
4 At first, basketball was an outdoor sport.   T / F
5 There were originally nine people in each basketball team.   T / F
6 Originally, they used a football to play basketball.   T / F
7 The inventor of basketball wrote 15 rules for the game.   T / F
8 Basketball became an Olympic sport in 1936.   T / F

2 LISTENING ▶ 41 **Listen and check your guesses in 1.**

3 ▶ 41 **Listen again and answer the questions.**

1 How long did James Naismith have to invent basketball?
2 Why did Naismith make basketball an indoor sport?
3 What was the problem with the first baskets that they used?
4 How long did a basketball match originally last in total, including the break?
5 After becoming popular in YMCA centres, where did basketball become popular?
6 What were Naismith's main objectives?

4 SPEAKING **What about you?**

1 Is basketball one of your favourite sports? Why/Why not?
2 Do you know the history behind any other sports? Which ones?

Non-defining relative clauses

1 Read sentences a–f and answer the questions.

a James Naismith, who was born in Canada, was working at a YMCA school.
b It needed to be a sport which would keep students fit.
c The man who invented it was James Naismith.
d Naismith went to Berlin, where the games took place that year.
e In 1936, when Naismith was 75 years old, basketball officially became part of the Olympic Games.
f Naismith was working in Massachusetts, which is really cold in the winter.

1 Which sentences do you think are non-defining relative clauses – giving extra, non-essential information?
2 Which clauses have commas, defining or non-defining relative clauses?
3 Can we omit the relative pronouns in sentences with non-defining clauses?
4 In sentence f, we cannot use *that* because of what comes just before the relative pronoun. What comes just before it?

GRAMMAR REFERENCE ➤ PAGE 94

2 Complete the sentences with non-defining relative clauses and the information given.

1 Golf balls, *which are usually white*, have a special surface so that they travel further.
(they are usually white)
2 Jenson Button, ..., failed his first driving test.
(he is a Formula 1 world champion)
3 Andy Murray, ..., has won the Wimbledon title.
(his brother Jamie also plays tennis)
4 In 2005, ..., the final was in Istanbul.
(Liverpool won the Champions League)
5 The San Siro Stadium, ..., is in Milan.
(two different teams play there)
6 Zara Philips, ..., won a gold medal for horse-riding.
(her grandmother is Queen Elizabeth II)

3 Read about Mo Farah. Choose the best answer (A, B, C or D) to complete the text.

Mohamed (Mo) Farah, **(1)** .... was born in Somalia, is now one of the most famous athletes in the world. When he arrived in London from Mogadishu with his family at the age of eight, he could hardly speak any English. His current fame was difficult to imagine!

He took **(2)** .... running when he was a schoolboy in London. His talent was spotted by a PE teacher, **(3)** .... encouraged him to train and compete. His first major success came in 2001 **(4)** .... he became the European junior champion at 5,000 metres. Five years later, he won a silver medal at the European Championships, **(5)** .... was at the time the high point of his adult career. 2011 was a great year for Mo: at the World Championships he won silver in the 10,000 metres, then a few days later added gold in the 5,000 metres. He was the first British athlete to ever do this.

(6) .... his success didn't end there. Mo, **(7)** .... personal motto is 'Go hard or go home', is not the sort of person to give **(8)** .... At the 2012 London Olympics, he became the first ever British gold medallist in the 10,000 metres, then a week later won a second gold in the 5,000. Suddenly he was a true sports superstar.

Mo now lives part of the year in Oregon (USA), **(9)** .... he trains with his coach. He and his wife also run the Mo Farah Foundation, a charity **(10)** .... raises money for the millions of people facing starvation and disease in East Africa.

1	A	when	B	that	C	whose	D	who
2	A	in	B	up	C	after	D	out
3	A	that	B	which	C	when	D	who
4	A	when	B	which	C	where	D	that
5	A	that	B	which	C	–	D	how
6	A	And	B	But	C	When	D	So
7	A	which	B	whose	C	who	D	that
8	A	him	B	surrender	C	in	D	on
9	A	that	B	–	C	which	D	where
10	A	what	B	that	C	–	D	and

4 Join the sentences with a relative clause.

1 The park is beautiful. I run there. (Defining)
The park where I run is beautiful.

2 Table tennis is easy to play. It's my favourite sport. (Non-defining)
Table tennis, which is my favourite sport, is easy to play.

3 Petra Kvitová is a great tennis player. She is from the Czech Republic. (Non-defining)

4 The athlete won the race. He broke the world record. (Defining)

5 Last Saturday was great. My team won the final. (Non-defining)

6 Anna is good at lots of sports. Her mum is a PE teacher. (Non-defining)

7 The swimming pool is great. I go there at the weekend. (Defining)

5a Prepare short sentences with information about people, places, things, activities and events in this book.

The Ig Nobel prizes are given every year.
Shanghai has lots of skyscrapers.
Pelé scored lots of goals.

5b SPEAKING **Work with a partner. Read your sentences. Your partner adds extra information to the sentences using non-defining relative clauses.**

The Ig Nobel prizes, which are really strange, are given every year.

Shanghai, where many people live, has lots of skyscrapers.

Pelé, who played for Brazil, scored lots of goals.

Developing speaking

A debate

1 [SPEAKING] **Work with a partner. Read this definition of 'role model' and make a list of people you think are good role models for young people.**

role model [n]: *someone whose behaviour is considered to be a good example for other people to copy*

2 [SPEAKING] **Read the statement below. Do you agree or disagree with it? Give reasons why.**

Today's top sports stars are good role models for young people.

3 [LISTENING] ▶ 42 **Listen to a boy and girl discussing the statement in 2. Whose opinion is closer to yours – the boy's or the girl's? Why?**

4 ▶ 42 **Look at the expressions in the Speaking bank. What word comes after the expressions for partially disagreeing? Listen again if necessary.**

💬 **SPEAKING BANK**

Useful expressions for agreeing or partially agreeing

- I (totally) agree (with you) (that …)
- I agree to an extent (that …)
- That's true.
- You're right.
- You've got a point.
- I take your point.
- I see what you mean.

Useful expressions for disagreeing or partially disagreeing

- I (totally) disagree (with you) (that …)
- I'm not sure that's true.
- I agree to an extent, ...
- That's true, ...
- You've got a point, ...
- I take your point, ...
- I see what you mean, ...

5 **Prepare six sentences about sport or sports stars. You don't have to agree with the statements.**

Football players are really good actors!

Women tennis players should be paid the same as men.

The Winter Olympics are more exciting than the Summer Olympics.

6 [SPEAKING] **Work in small groups. Listen to each other's statements. Give your honest opinion using expressions from the Speaking bank. You must say what you really think.**

Football players are really good actors!

I totally agree with you.

I agree to an extent, but sometimes when players say they're hurt it's true.

PRACTICE MAKES PERFECT

7a [SPEAKING] **Read the statement. Half of the class must agree with the statement. The other half must disagree. Prepare a list of points to support your opinion.**

Top football players are paid too much.

7b **Have a class debate using expressions from the Speaking bank.**

7c **Have a vote to see what the class really thinks about the statement.**

A magazine article

1 Imagine that you see this announcement in a magazine. Work with a partner and discuss your answers to the questions.

TEENAGERS *and* SPORT

- How important is sport in your life? Why?
- How would you encourage other teenagers to do more sport?

PLEASE WRITE AN ARTICLE FOR NEXT MONTH'S MAGAZINE!

2 READING **Read this student's article. Does it include any of your ideas in 1?**

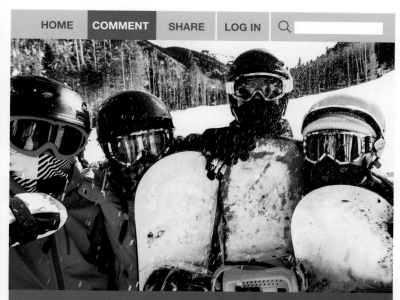

HOME | COMMENT | SHARE | LOG IN

1 Do you only do sport with a games console in your hand? Do you have a pair of trainers which have never been out of the box? Let me tell you about my passion for sport and that could change your mind!

2 (a) ...., I think I couldn't live without doing sport. At school I do PE and swimming. At the weekend, I play tennis and go cycling in the summer and I go snowboarding in the winter. Sport makes me feel strong, fit and healthy and I definitely feel that it helps me to concentrate. I'm (b) .... that if I didn't do sport, my marks at school would be worse.

3 Some people say they don't have time to do sport. As I (c) .... it, that's just an excuse. My (d) .... is that, if you can find time to watch TV, you can find time for sport. My advice is to get out into the fresh air. It doesn't matter if it's cycling, running or walking. Just being outside and doing something will immediately make you feel better than being indoors all day.

4 As (e) .... as I'm concerned, sport isn't a luxury, it's a necessity. Have you heard the expression 'a healthy mind in a healthy body'? I totally agree with that. So, go on. It's time to put your games console down and get your trainers out of the box!

3a Complete the text with these words.

> convinced • far • Personally, • see • view

3b Add the completed expressions from 3a to the other expressions in the Writing bank.

✎ WRITING BANK

Useful expressions of opinion
- I (don't) think (that) …
- I don't really know if …
- In my opinion,
- ....
- ....
- ....
- ....
- ....

4 Match the paragraphs with the descriptions of their content.

Paragraph 1	**a**	Talk about sport in your life
Paragraph 2	**b**	Get the readers' attention
Paragraph 3	**c**	Final overall opinion and recommendation
Paragraph 4	**d**	Give advice about sport

5 Work with a partner. Read the article in 2 again and answer the questions.

1 How does the first paragraph get the reader interested and involved?

2 How does the last paragraph end the article in a positive way?

PRACTICE MAKES PERFECT

6 Look at this announcement in a magazine. Write your article. Use the information in 4 and expressions from the Writing bank.

You and your favourite sport
- Which is your favourite sport and why?
- How and why would you encourage other teenagers to play or watch this sport?

Please write an article for next month's magazine!

WRITING BANK ➤ PAGE 151

Grammar reference

Defining relative clauses

FORM

James Naismith was the man **who/that** invented basketball.

That's the sport **which/that** I play.

That's the player **whose** team is top of the league.

London is the place **where** they celebrated the 2012 Olympics.

Sunday is the day **when** I play tennis.

We use **who** and **that** for people, **which** and **that** for things, **whose** for possessions, **where** for places, and **when** for times.

In defining relative clauses we can omit **who**, **which** or **that** when a noun or pronoun comes immediately after.

That's the sport **that** I play. = That's the sport I play.

She's the tennis player **that** I like. = She's the tennis player I like.

but

That's the sport **that** is popular. = ~~That's the sport is popular.~~

She's the tennis player **that** won the cup. = ~~She's the tennis player won the cup.~~

We do not use commas in defining relative clauses.

USE

We use **defining relative clauses** to give essential information about the person, thing, place or time in the first half of the sentence. The sentence does not usually make sense without the relative clause.

Germany is the country which won the World Cup in 2014.

~~Germany is the country.~~

Non-defining relative clauses

FORM

James Naismith, **who** was born in Canada, invented basketball.

Tennis, **which** is my favourite sport, is a very old game.

Jordan, **whose** team is top of the league, is a very good player.

London, **where** they celebrated the 2012 Olympics, is a great city.

Yesterday, **when** I played tennis, was a really warm day.

We use **who** for people, **which** for things, **whose** for possessions, **where** for places, and **when** for times.

We do not use **that** in non-defining relative clauses.

In non-defining relative clauses we cannot omit the relative pronoun.

We always use commas in non-defining relative clauses.

USE

We use **non-defining relative clauses** to give extra, non-essential information about the person, thing, place or time in the first half of the sentence. The commas work in a similar way to parentheses, showing that the information is not vital to the sentence.

Non-defining clauses are not so common in conversation and can seem formal.

Manchester, which is in north west England, is famous for its music.

Vocabulary

Sports and sports venues athletics • baseball • basketball • climbing • cycling • diving • football • golf gymnastics • horse-riding • ice hockey • ice-skating • judo • karate • rugby • sailing • skiing • snowboarding swimming • tennis • volleyball • weightlifting
course • court • gym • pitch • pool • rink • slope • track

Sports equipment and scores ball • bat • boots • club • goal/goal post • goggles • net • racket • skates skis • trainers • beat • bounce • catch • draw • goal • head • hit (with a bat) • kick • lose (a match/to somebody) nil • pass • point • score • shoot • throw • win

Phrasal verbs connected with sport give in • go for • join in • knock out • take up • warm up • work out

Other words and phrases ➤ page 141

Grammar revision

Defining relative clauses
/ 6 points

1 Complete the sentences with a relative pronoun. If you don't need a pronoun, put –.

1 The friends .... I made last weekend live near my house.

2 You're the teacher .... classes I like the most.

3 Jenny is the person .... has helped me the most.

4 Autumn is the time of year .... the leaves fall off the trees.

5 This is the town .... I lived in when I was small.

6 This is the country .... football began.

Non-defining relative clauses
/ 6 points

2 Are these sentences correct? If not, correct them.

1 The driver, which car wasn't very fast, never won a race.

2 This sport, that was invented two years ago, is becoming very popular.

3 Nadal, whose uncle was a football player, won Wimbledon in 2010.

4 That house, that I lived in when I was small, now belongs to my uncle.

5 Last summer, when we went to the beach, we had a brilliant holiday.

6 My neighbours, are really nice, have got a big garden.

Defining and non-defining relative clauses
/ 8 points

3 Write two sentences for each of these. One must contain a defining relative clause and the other a non-defining relative clause.

1 Football

   Football is a sport which is popular all over the world.

   Football, which I always play at the weekend, is my favourite sport.

2 Italy

3 Lewis Hamilton

4 Last year

5 Water

Vocabulary revision

SPORTS AND SPORTS VENUES
/ 7 points

1 Write one sport that you can play or do at each venue.

1 course ....

2 court ....

3 gym ....

4 pitch ....

5 rink ....

6 slope ....

7 track ....

SPORTS EQUIPMENT AND SCORES
/ 7 points

2 Write the words.

1 The thing you use to hit the ball in baseball:

   ....

2 The things football players wear on their feet in a match: ....

3 The things you wear to protect your eyes when you swim: ....

4 The thing you use to hit the ball in golf: ....

5 When you don't win or lose, you: ....

6 Mexico .... Italy 3–2.

7 0 in a football score: ....

PHRASAL VERBS CONNECTED WITH SPORTS
/ 6 points

3 Match the parts to make phrasal verbs, then find their meaning.

Phrasal verb Part 1	Phrasal verb Part 2	Meaning
1 warm	out	a do an activity with other people who are already doing it
2 knock	in	b eliminate somebody from a competition
3 join	up	c do gentle exercises before doing sport
4 give	up	d stop competing and accept that you can't win
5 go	for	e start a sport or hobby
6 take	in	f try very hard to win or get something

Vocabulary

Art, theatre, music

1 Use these words to talk about the photo.

> audience • cast • lighting
> performance • play • stage

2 Work with a partner. Read the sentences. Check that you understand the words in red. Use a dictionary if necessary.

1 Pass me the pencil. I haven't finished the drawing yet. This is just a sketch.

2 Do you think the painting looks like me? It's a self-portrait.

3 What is it? Is it a still life painting, with fruit and flowers? Ah! Now I understand. They aren't real objects. It's an abstract painting.

4 This song is OK. I love the tune but the lyrics aren't very good.

5 Let's go and see the exhibition at that new art gallery. There are some masterpieces in the collection, like one of Michelangelo's sculptures.

6 The British artist Constable was famous for his landscapes, the pictures he painted of the English countryside.

7 This is my favourite scene in the play. The main character appears for the first time.

8 A famous orchestra played a concert here once.

3 Put the words in 1 and 2 in the correct column. Some words can go in more than one column.

Art	Theatre	Music
	audience	audience
	cast	

Artists

4 Look at the sentences. Complete the words in red with -or, -er, -ian or -ist.

1 I think Robert Downey Jr. is the best paid act............... in Hollywood.

2 She's a great music............... She can play five instruments.

3 A conduct............... is responsible for the whole orchestra.

4 Who's the direct............... of this play?

5 She's a great perform............... She loves the stage.

6 In our band we've got a vocal............... and a guitar............... Now we need a good drumm...............

7 Mozart is my favourite compos...............

8 Ed Sheeran is a young sing...............-songwrit...............

9 Michelangelo was a great art............... He wasn't just a paint............... He was also a sculpt...............

5 SPEAKING Work with a partner. Take it in turns to give the name of a famous person and answer with their profession.

> Beethoven.

> He was a composer. Taylor Swift.

> She's a vocalist and a singer-songwriter, too.

6 LISTENING  43 Listen. Number these things or people in the order that you hear them.

> an actor performing • an audience
> a band on stage • the cast of a play • a conductor
> a composer • one musician • an orchestra
> a portrait painter • a sculptor

7 SPEAKING Work with a partner. Discuss these questions. Give details.

1 Do you ever go to the theatre or concerts?

2 Which plays have you seen or read?

3 Who are your favourite musicians or vocalists?

4 Do you ever go to art exhibitions?

5 Which artists or types of paintings do you like?

1 Work with a partner. Look at these photos. Take it in turns to describe what you can see.

2 READING Read the three texts. Match the photos in 1 with two of them.

3 What photo would you use to illustrate the remaining text?

4 Choose the best answer.

1 They call Liu Bolin the 'invisible man' because he …

   a doesn't appear in any of his photos.
   b makes it difficult for people to see him.
   c doesn't like speaking at conferences.

2 Liu Bolin …

   a prefers complicated backgrounds.
   b sometimes takes days to prepare for his photos.
   c needs a group of artists to help choose backgrounds.

3 Unfathomable Ruination's concerts in a cube …

   a were silent inside the box.
   b were seen by the audience.
   c were very difficult for the musicians to play.

4 James Blunt …

   a played the highest concert ever in 2010.
   b is the only person to have played a concert in a plane.
   c sang and flew a plane at the same time.

5 Stephen Wiltshire …

   a remembers what he sees very accurately.
   b spends a long time preparing each picture.
   c uses photos to help him draw cityscapes.

6 For Stephen Wiltshire …

   a it is impossible to talk to others.
   b art has always been more than a hobby.
   c exhibitions are the only reason he travels.

5 ⚙ **CRITICAL THINKING**

> **Think! Then compare ideas with your class.**
>
> ■ Do you think that knowing about the life of an artist can change how you look at their work? Why/Why not?

6 What do the underlined words in the text mean? Guess and then check in your dictionary.

7 SPEAKING What about *you*?

Which of the texts did you enjoy reading most? Why?

EXTREME ART!

Our weekly look at what's happening in the arts

1 The brilliant Chinese artist **Liu Bolin** has a fascinating new exhibition opening in London next week. Bolin is known as the 'invisible man'. That is because in his photos he 'disappears' into the background. The incredible thing is that the backgrounds are often very complicated. For example, in one photo he blends into supermarket shelves full of fruit and vegetables. In another he stands in front of a wall that is covered with hundreds of mobile phones. He has also disappeared outdoors in front of theatres, bus stops and museums. Passers-by have walked past him without seeing him at all! To help him disappear, his team of artists has to paint him carefully, from head to toe. This typically takes between three and ten hours, but some scenes have needed three or four days of preparation. At a conference, Bolin said that his photos made a statement about his place in society. He told the audience that he had chosen to become a part of his environment. The 41-year-old artist has certainly succeeded – it can often be almost impossible to separate him from it!

2 Recently, a British rock group called **Unfathomable Ruination** played a series of concerts inside a tiny cube. They went into the airtight cube and played until there was no oxygen left. Their first performance only lasted 14 minutes because inside it was uncomfortable and hot. "These are extreme conditions and we play extreme music," said their guitarist. It was impossible to hear the music outside the box, or to see anything happening. Unfathomable Ruination are not the only group to play gigs in unusual places. In 2010 British singer-songwriter James Blunt played a concert for 150 people in a plane at a record-breaking height of 13,000 metres. The previous record was 11,000 metres, set by the group Jamiroquai. Blunt is a licensed pilot, but luckily he wasn't flying at the time. Meanwhile, singer Katie Melua has the record for the deepest underwater concert, which she played 303 metres under the North Sea. Unsurprisingly, she said she would never forget the experience. But it's Lady Gaga who has plans for possibly the most unusual place yet. 'I'm going to be the first recording artist in space!' she told reporters.

3 The unique London-born landscape artist **Stephen Wiltshire** has just finished another of his amazing panoramas. This time the drawing is a cityscape of Singapore, and, as always, it's a masterpiece full of incredible detail. For this work he took a brief helicopter ride to see the city from the air. Then, without the aid of a camera, he drew the whole thing from memory in five days. And his memory serves him well as his sketches are always incredibly accurate. Wiltshire is autistic. He refused to speak when he was small, but communicated through his sketches and art. The first word he said was 'Paper!', when they took away his drawing materials at school. Now his art has taken him all over the world attending exhibitions of his work. His pencil is never far from his hand. After all, his motto is "Do the best you can and never stop."

Grammar in context

Reported speech – statements

1a Match the reported sentences (1–7) with the direct sentences (a–g).

1 He said that his photos made a statement.
2 He told them that he had chosen to do it.
3 He said that those were extreme conditions.
4 She told a reporter that she was going to be the first recording artist in space.
5 She said she would never forget the experience.
6 She told me that I had to look hard to find the artist.
7 He said that the message could depend on the background.

a 'I will never forget the experience.'
b 'These are extreme conditions.'
c 'My photos make a statement.'
d 'I'm going to be the first recording artist in space!'
e 'You must look hard to find the artist.'
f 'The message can depend on the background.'
g 'I chose to do it.'

1b Choose the correct alternative.

1 *Nouns/Pronouns* usually change when they go from direct to reported speech.
2 The tenses of most verbs *change/don't change* in reported speech.
3 With **say** we *need/don't need* to say the person we spoke to.
4 With **tell** we *need/don't need* to say the person we spoke to.
5 With **say** and **tell** we *always need/don't always need* to use *that*.

GRAMMAR REFERENCE ➤ PAGE 106

2 How do these tenses change in reported speech? Look at the Grammar reference for help.

Direct speech	Reported speech
1 present simple ➤	*past simple*
2 present continuous ➤	
3 present perfect ➤	
4 past simple ➤	
5 *will* ➤	
6 *can* ➤	
7 *may* ➤	
8 *must/have to* ➤	

3 Complete the table with these words.

a (week/month/year) ago • here • the day before
the following (week/month/year)
the previous (week/month/year) • that
that night • today • tomorrow

Direct speech	Reported speech
this	1 ....
2	there
3	that day
yesterday	4 ....
5	the next/following day
tonight	6 ....
next (week/month/year)	7 ....
last (week/month/year)	8 ....
9	a (week/month/year) before

4 Choose the correct alternative.

1 The pianist said *–/the audience* that he couldn't concentrate.
2 The musician told *–/reporters* that he was going to play a concert on the moon.
3 He *said/told* us that he had just finished a new picture of New York.
4 The critic *said/told* that he hoped they wouldn't let the band out of the box.
5 The reporter said *–/them* the actress was making a new film the following month.
6 The artist *said/told* the exhibition was going to be a great success.
7 He told *–/me* they had taken away his paper.

5 Put the reported speech in 4 into direct speech.

'I can't concentrate.'

Adjectives ending in *-ing* and *-ed*

1 **Read the sentences and answer the questions.**

   1   Stephen Wiltshire's picture was amazing.

   2   I was amazed when I saw Stephen Wiltshire's picture.

The words in red are adjectives. Which adjective describes how somebody feels? Which adjective explains why they feel this way?

2 **Look at these adjectives. Which are positive (+) and which are negative (–)? Which one word could be either?**

> amazed • bored • confused • depressed • disappointed
> disgusted • embarrassed • excited • fascinated
> frightened • inspired • interested • relaxed • surprised
> tired • uninspired • worried

3a PRONUNCIATION **Read the adjectives in 2 again. In which ones do we pronounce *-ed* as /ɪd/?**

3b ▶ 44 **Listen and check your answers. Which letter comes before *-ed* in those adjectives?**

3c **Practise saying the adjectives in 2.**

4 **Choose the correct alternative.**

   1   Artists are often *inspiring/inspired* by nature.

   2   Yuck! This soup is *disgusting/disgusted*.

   3   Drawing a whole city is *tiring/tired*.

   4   Many people are *confusing/confused* when they see modern art.

   5   Some people think opera is *boring/bored*.

   6   I would be *embarrassing/embarrassed* if I had to stand on a stage and sing.

   7   The band's new songs are very *disappointing/disappointed* – the lyrics are awful.

   8   We're really *exciting/excited* about going to see that play next week.

5a **Prepare things to say about the topics below.**

   1   Two people you think are inspiring.

   2   Two things you think are depressing.

   3   A moment in your life when you were very surprised.

   4   A time when something embarrassing happened to you.

   5   The most exciting thing you've ever done.

   6   Something that you are fascinated by.

5b SPEAKING **Work with a partner and discuss the topics. Ask questions to keep the conversation going.**

5c **Tell the class what your partner told you about one of the topics.**

> *Dana is inspired by her sister. Her sister works for a charity that helps children with learning difficulties.*

An artwork by the artist Banksy

6 **Read the statements made by famous people. Put them in reported speech.**

   1   Banksy: 'People either love me, or they hate me, or they don't really care.'

   2   James Dean: 'Being an actor is the loneliest thing in the world'

   3   Sylvia Plath: 'I write only because there is a voice within me that will not be still.'

   4   Andy Warhol: 'In the future everyone will be world-famous for 15 minutes.'

   5   Oscar Wilde: 'I am so clever that sometimes I don't understand a single word of what I'm saying.'

   6   Vincent Van Gogh: 'The only time I feel alive is when I'm painting.'

   7   Damien Hirst: 'I wanted to be stopped, but no one will stop me.'

   8   Sir Ian McKellen: 'I'm only an actor. All I've ever done is learn the lines and say them.'

7a **Write down things that your friends, family or teachers have said or told you recently.**

7b SPEAKING **Tell a partner what the people said. Can your partner guess who said them?**

> *Someone told me that they'd passed their driving test.*

> *Was it your brother?*

> *Yes!*

Appreciating ART

LIFE SKILLS OBJECTIVES	KEY CONCEPTS
■ To use different questions to help us appreciate different works of art. ■ To think about why art is important in our lives. ■ To investigate and analyse two different works of art.	**subject [n]:** *The subject of the painting is a white bird.* **theme [n]:** *This painting is all white and I think the theme is peace.* **symbolic [adj]:** *The colour white can be symbolic of peace.* **interpretation [n]:** *The artist doesn't tell you what the painting is about so you have to make your own interpretation of it.*

1 Work with a partner. Look at the three works of art. What are your first reactions to each painting?

1

2

3

1. ***Early Sunday Morning***, 1930, Realism, Oil on canvas 89.4cm x 153cm, Whitney Museum of American Art

    Edward Hopper, American realist painter, 1882–1967

2. ***Drowning Girl***, 1963, Popart, Oil and synthetic polymer paint on canvas 171.6cm x 169.5cm, Museum of Modern Art

    Roy Lichtenstein, American painter and sculptor 1923–1997

3. ***Camino Real (II)***, 2010, Abstract Impressionism, Acrylic on wood panel, 252.4cm x 185.1cm, Gagosian Gallery

    Cy Twombly, American painter of calligraphic and graffiti-like works, 1928–2011

Appreciating works of art

First reactions

1 What can you see in it? What is the subject of the painting?
2 What is the first word that comes to mind when you look at it?
3 Does it remind you of anything?
4 What do you think the artist wants to communicate?
5 How do you feel when you look at it?

Looking more closely

1 What materials and processes has the artist used to make the work?
2 How big is the work? What effect does that have?
3 Does the work have a title? Does this affect the way you see it?
4 Could the work have some symbolic meaning?
5 What do you think the theme of the painting is? Is the artist trying to 'tell' us something?
6 Do the paintings share any common themes?
7 Does the work make you think about your life or art in a new way?

Art in context

1 Who was the artist? When and where did they live?
2 Do you know anything about the life of the artist? Do you think this information can tell us more about how and why the work was created, or what it could be about?
3 Does the work have any connection with other artists or art of the past?
4 What, if anything, does the work tell us about the world?

---

2 SPEAKING The questions above are designed to help you look at any painting in more detail. Work with a partner and use the questions to discuss the paintings in 1.

3 Think about these questions, then say which of the three works you prefer and why.

4 LISTENING ▶ 45 Watch the video or listen to three students. Which painting in 1 does each one talk about?

Olivia: ....

Jack: ....

Luke: ....

5 ▶ 45 Read the reasons why the speakers like the paintings. Choose the correct speaker. Watch or listen again if necessary.

1 It has a connection with artists in the past. *Olivia/Jack/Luke*
2 It expresses positive and negative emotions. *Olivia/Jack/Luke*
3 It inspires me to paint something. *Olivia/Jack/Luke*
4 It makes me think about popular art and traditional art. *Olivia/Jack/Luke*
5 I like the colours. *Olivia/Jack/Luke*
6 It makes me think of the story behind the painting. *Olivia/Jack/Luke*
7 It's got energy and life. *Olivia/Jack/Luke*
8 I think it's funny. *Olivia/Jack/Luke*
9 The title of the painting is very appropriate. *Olivia/Jack/Luke*

6a Read the things that the speakers say about art in general. Decide if you agree or disagree with each statement and why.

1 You don't always have to understand art – sometimes you just feel it.
2 Art doesn't have to be perfect.
3 The aim of art is to inspire you to be creative in life.
4 Good art makes you think.
5 Art doesn't have to be serious and traditional.
6 Art is exciting because it doesn't always have to follow rules.
7 Art helps us to express and feel different emotions.
8 Art helps you to escape your world.

6b SPEAKING Compare your answers in small groups. Can you add any other reasons why art is important in our lives?

LIFE TASK

Follow this plan:

1 *Choose two paintings by two different artists. Use the questions above to think about the paintings and make notes.*

2 *Find out about the artists. When and where did they live? What themes were they interested in?*

3 *Use your notes to make a poster about your two paintings, include images of the paintings and include your personal response to them.*

4 *Turn your classroom into an art gallery with your posters. Walk round. Which are your favourite works and why?*

1 Work with a partner. Talk about the photo. What do you think it shows?

2 LISTENING ▶ 46 Listen and check your ideas in 1.

3 ▶ 46 Listen again and choose the best answers.

1 The creator of the duck …
   a is very tall.
   b lives in Asia.
   c is from the Netherlands.

2 Mr Hofman thinks people like the duck because …
   a it brings back childhood memories.
   b it has a happy and relaxed face.
   c they like the colour yellow.

3 In Taiwan there was a problem with the duck …
   a because somebody attacked it.
   b because the weather was always bad.
   c but nobody is certain what caused it.

4 Hofman doesn't want to use the duck for publicity because …
   a he wants people to think of it as an artistic object.
   b it's not easy for companies to do.
   c he thinks it should be in a museum.

5 The woman thinks that people …
   a never like the places they pass every day.
   b don't pay attention to the places they pass every day.
   c get bored of looking at the duck.

6 Hofman …
   a hated ducks when he was a child.
   b has only one rubber duck that he likes.
   c always gives ducks as presents.

4 SPEAKING **What about you?**

1 What do you think of the Giant Rubber Duck?

2 Would you go to see it if it was near where you live? Why/Why not?

Reported speech – questions

1 Look at the direct and reported questions. Then decide if rules 1–5 are True (T) or False (F).

   a 'Why do you think the duck is so popular?'
   b They asked him why he thought the duck was so popular.
   c 'Do you like rubber ducks?'
   d Somebody asked him if he liked rubber ducks.

   1 Tenses and pronouns change in reported questions in the same way as in reported statements. T / F
   2 We do not use the auxiliary verb *do* in reported questions. T / F
   3 We put the subject before the verb in reported questions. T / F
   4 We use question marks in reported questions. T / F
   5 We use **if** or **whether** when there is no question word. T / F

GRAMMAR REFERENCE ➤ PAGE 106

2 Choose the correct alternative.

1 'Where are you from?'
   They asked the artist *where was he/where he was* from.

2 'Do you travel a lot?'
   They asked the artist *where/if* he travelled a lot.

3 'Why did you make the duck so big?'
   They wanted to know why *he had/had he* made the duck so big.

4 'Do you work quickly?'
   They asked him whether *he did work/he worked* quickly.

5 'Have you done any other big sculptures?'
   They asked if he *has/had* done any other big sculptures.

6 'What will you do next?'
   The asked him what *he would do/would he do* next.

3 Complete the reported questions.

1 'Did you like the exhibition?'
She asked him ....

2 'Who is your favourite artist?'
She wanted to know ....

3 'Do you often visit art galleries?'
She asked him ....

4 'Will you recommend the exhibition to other people?'
She asked him ....

5 'Why did you decide to see the exhibition?'
She wanted to know ....

6 'Are you going to buy anything in the shop?'
She wanted to know ....

7 'Have you ever bought an original painting?'
She asked ....

4a SPEAKING **Write five questions to ask a partner about art, theatre or music.**

4b Work with a partner and ask your questions.

4c Change partners. Tell your new partner the five questions your first partner asked you, and your answers.

> She asked me if I liked going to art exhibitions. I told her that it depended.

Reported speech – commands

5 Read the direct and reported commands and answer the questions.

a 'Please be careful with the sculpture!'

b He asked them to be careful with the sculpture.

c 'Don't move the duck!'

d He told them not to move the duck.

1 Which verbs can we use to report commands? What is the difference between them?

2 In the reported command, do we change the tense of the verb from the direct command or do we use the infinitive?

3 Where does *not* come in reported commands that are negative?

GRAMMAR REFERENCE ➤ PAGE 106

6 Report these commands.

1 'Pay attention!' the teacher told the class.
The teacher ....
....

2 'Give me your tickets, please,' the man at the entrance asked them.
The man at the entrance ....
....

3 'Don't shout!' his mum told him.
His mum ....
....

4 'Please don't take photos inside the museum,' the guide asked the visitors.
The guide ....
....

5 'Don't come home late!' his dad told him.
His dad ....
....

6 'Use a bigger brush,' the art teacher told Jake.
The art teacher ....
....

7 'Please write a description of the painting for homework,' the teacher asked the students.
The teacher ....
....

7 SPEAKING **Play in two teams. Take it in turns to try and remember things that teachers asked or told you to do this week. You get one point for each correct sentence.**

> Our English teacher asked us to do this exercise.

> She told us not to speak in our own language.

Developing speaking

Describing a past event

1 [SPEAKING] **Work with a partner. Discuss these questions.**

1 Do you ever go on school trips? If so, what type of places do you usually go to?

2 Did you go on school trips when you were at primary school? Where did you go?

2 [SPEAKING] **Work with a partner. Look at the pictures. Take it in turns to describe what you can see.**

a

b

c

d

3 [LISTENING] ▶ **47 Listen to a teenager talking about a school trip that was special for her. Which photos are similar to her experience?**

4 ▶ **47 Look at the diagram. Make notes about what the teenager says. Listen again if necessary.**

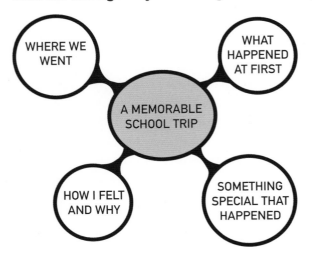

5 ▶ **47 Listen again and tick (✓) the words and expressions that you hear in the Speaking bank.**

💬 SPEAKING BANK

Useful words and expressions for reporting past events

- At first
- First
- Next
- Then
- Later
- Later on
- After that
- Afterwards

- A few seconds/minutes/ hours/days later
- After ten minutes/half an hour/a while
- Finally
- In the end
- At the end of (…)

✔ EXAM SUCCESS

What can you do to prepare for a speaking exam where you have to talk about a past event?

➤ EXAM SUCCESS page 146

6 **Think about a memorable school trip, or a trip to a concert, play or exhibition that you went on. Copy the diagram from 4 on a sheet of paper and make notes in the boxes.**

PRACTICE MAKES PERFECT

7a [SPEAKING] **Work with a partner. Use your diagram to tell your partner what happened in detail. Use words and expressions from the Speaking bank. Let your partner see your diagram. Answer any of your partner's questions about the trip.**

7b [SPEAKING] **Change partners and talk about your trip again.**

A film review

1 **SPEAKING** Work with a partner. Talk about the last film you saw. What was it about? Did you like it? Why/Why not?

2 **READING** Read the film review. What did the writer like about the film? Who would the writer recommend the film to?

FILM REVIEW

A CLASSIC! ★★★★★

THE FAULT IN OUR STARS
ONE SICK LOVE STORY
JUNE 6

1 *The fault in our stars* is a US film that was released in 2014. It stars the young new actors Shailene Woodley and Ansel Elgort. It's about the relationship between the two main characters.

2 The plot is beautiful and inspiring. Hazel Grace has cancer and she attends a cancer support group where she meets a boy called Augustus Waters. They become fascinated with one another because, apart from going through the same experience, they have a similar sense of humour. They both like a book written by a man who lives in Amsterdam and decide to go there to meet him. This is a really disappointing experience. But Hazel and Gus have many happy, funny and intense moments in the time they have together.

3 I really loved everything about this film. The story sounds a bit depressing and there's no typical happy ending, but the film is actually very inspiring because the two main characters' relationship is so strong. The acting is excellent, particularly Shailene Woodley, who plays the role of Hazel brilliantly.

4 To sum up, if you're looking for an action film with special effects, this film is definitely not for you. But if you like emotional stories about characters that you care for, I would definitely recommend you see this. But take some tissues because there are some incredibly sad scenes!

3 **Match the paragraphs with the descriptions of their content.**

Paragraph 1   a   a recommendation about the film
Paragraph 2   b   a summary of the plot or story
Paragraph 3   c   basic information about the film
Paragraph 4   d   the writer's opinion of the film

4 **Read the review again and answer these questions.**

1 What tense does the writer use to summarise the plot?

2 Does the writer mix present and past tenses to write the summary of the plot?

3 Is the text only a summary of the plot of the film?

4 Does the writer give reasons and examples for his/her opinions?

5 **Put these headings in the correct place in the Writing bank and check that you understand all the words and expressions in the box.**

1 Positive adjectives to describe films

2 Negative adjectives to describe films

3 Types of film

4 Other words to talk about films

✎ WRITING BANK

Useful words and expressions in film reviews

(a) ....

action and adventure • animated film • comedy
drama • fantasy • horror • musical • science fiction
thriller

(b) ....

amazing • emotional • exciting • fascinating
funny • great • inspiring • spectacular

(c) ....

awful • boring • confusing • depressing
disappointing • sentimental • stupid • uninspiring

(d) ....

happy ending • main character • play the role of
plot • scene • screenplay • soundtrack
special effects • (the film) stars

PRACTICE MAKES PERFECT

6 **Look at the task. Write your review. Use the words and expressions in the Writing bank and the paragraph plan in 3.**

School Film Club

We want you to send us a review of a film that you think other students at school will enjoy. Tell us what the film is about, why you liked it, and who you would recommend it to. Reviews must be between 100 and 150 words!

We need your reviews!

WRITING BANK ➤ PAGE 151

✔ EXAM SUCCESS

Why is it so important to read the instructions very carefully in a writing exam?

➤ EXAM SUCCESS page 146

Grammar reference

Reported speech – statements

In reported speech, when the reporting verb (**say**, **tell**) is in the past, the tense of the verb in reported speech usually changes, going one tense 'back'.

Direct speech – tenses	Reported speech – tenses
'I walk home.' *Present simple*	She said she **walked** home. *Past simple*
'I'm walking.' *Present continuous*	She said she **was walking**. *Past continuous*
'I have walked.' *Present perfect*	She said she **had walked**. *Past perfect*
'I walked.' *Past simple*	She said she **had walked**. *Past perfect*
'I had walked.' *Past perfect*	She said she **had walked**. *Past perfect*
'I will walk.' *will*	She said she **would walk**. *would*
'I can walk.' *can*	She said she **could walk**. *could*
'I may walk.' *may*	She said she **might walk**. *might*
'I must/have to walk.' *must/have to*	She said she **had to walk**. *had to*

Could, **would**, **should** and **might** do not change.

In reported speech, pronouns and possessive adjectives also change.
'I watched your concert.' ➤ Joe said he had watched my concert.

With **say** you do not need to use a personal object to say who you are saying something to.
She said she needed help.

With **tell** you must use a personal object to say who you are saying something to.
She told Jamie she needed help.

Reported speech – questions

We do not use the auxiliary verb **do** in reported questions.
'Do you like art?' ➤ She asked me if I liked art.

There is no inversion of subject and verb in reported questions.
'Where is the exhibition?' ➤ He asked me where the exhibition was.

Reported questions are not real questions so they do not need question marks.
When there is no question word (who, what, how, why, etc.), we use **if** or **whether**.
'Are you listening?' ➤ She asked me if I was listening.

Reported speech – commands

Direct speech	Reported speech
'Stand up!'	She told them **to stand up**.
'Don't write on the table!'	They told him **not to write** on the table.
'Please write your name here.'	He asked me **to write** my name there.

For reported commands we use *to* + **infinitive** or *not to* + **infinitive**.
If necessary we change pronouns and other words in the same way as in reported statements.
We use *told* to report stronger commands and *asked* for more polite requests.

Vocabulary

Art, theatre, music abstract painting • audience • cast • concert • drawing • exhibition • gallery • landscape lighting • lyrics • main character • masterpiece • orchestra • performance • play • scene • sculpture (self-)portrait • sketch • stage • still life • tune

Artists actor • artist • composer • conductor • director • drummer • guitarist • musician • painter • performer pianist • sculptor • singer-songwriter • vocalist

Adjectives ending in -ing and -ed amazed/amazing • bored/boring • confused/confusing • depressed/depressing • disappointed/disappointing • disgusted/disgusting • embarrassed/embarrassing • excited/exciting fascinated/fascinating • frightened/frightening • inspired/inspiring • interested/interesting • relaxed/relaxing surprised/surprising • tired/tiring • uninspired/uninspiring • worried/worrying

Other words and phrases ➤ page 142

Grammar revision

Reported speech – statements

1 Rewrite the sentences in reported speech.

1 I'm happy to be here today.   She said ....
2 I'm writing a play.   She told ....
3 I've never written a play before.   She said ....
4 When I finish, I'll choose the actors myself.   She said ....
5 I was inspired by a trip to California last year.   She told ....
6 I may go to the US again next year.   She said ....
7 I must go now because my manager's waiting for me.   She said ....

Reported speech – questions
/ 7 points

2 Rewrite these reported questions in direct speech.

1 She asked me what I was doing there.
'...?'

2 They asked me when I had arrived.
'...?'

3 The teacher asked him if he knew what the answer was.
'...?'

4 He wanted to know if she had ever written a poem.
'...?'

5 I asked him what he would do with the money.
'...?'

6 I asked him how many pages the book had.
'...?'

7 I asked her if that bag was hers.
'...?'

Reported speech – commands
/ 7 points

3 Write the direct commands.

1 The police told him to get out of the car.
'...'

2 They told me not to panic.
'...'

3 She told him to do the exercise carefully.
'...'

4 I asked her not to sing that song.
'...'

5 They told me to get ready.
'...'

6 She asked him not to interrupt her.
'...'

7 He asked me to give him the bag.
'...'

Vocabulary revision

ARTISTS
/ 6 points

1 Who are these people?

1 The person in charge of an orchestra: c..........................
2 Someone who plays the drums: d..........................
3 Someone who writes and sings their own songs: s..........................
4 Someone who writes classical music: c..........................
5 Someone who makes sculptures: s..........................
6 A singer who performs in a group: v..........................

ART, THEATRE, MUSIC
/ 7 points

2 Complete the definitions.

1 A landscape is a painting of ....
2 The lyrics are the part of the song which ....
3 The cast are the people who ....
4 A sketch is a picture which ....
5 The audience are ....
6 A portrait is a picture of ....
7 The stage is the place where ....

ADJECTIVES ENDING IN -ING AND -ED
/ 6 points

3 Complete the sentences with the -ing or -ed form of the words given.

1 Aren't you ....?
You've been studying all day. **TIRE**

2 It's .... when you forget somebody's name. **EMBARRASS**

3 I'm .... I don't know what to think. **CONFUSE**

4 The result of the match was .... We lost 6–0. **DISAPPOINT**

5 We were .... We thought we were going to win. **SURPRISE**

6 This meal is really bad. In fact, it's .... **DISGUST**

Use of English

1 Work with a partner. Look at the photo. What do you think this sport is? What do you think the rules are?

2a Read the text and answer the questions in 1. Ignore the gaps.

Chess Boxing was invented (a) .... a Dutch artist (b) .... name is Iepe Rubingh. If you've never heard of the sport before, the name Chess Boxing tells you what you need to know. Yes, that's right. It's a mixture of chess and boxing. The Dutch man (c) .... invented the sport thinks that chess and boxing are two sports that have a lot in common. The rules are easy. First, you play a round of chess, and then there is a round of boxing. And then more chess and more boxing. The sport (d) .... always played in a boxing ring. They bring (e) .... table and chairs into the boxing ring after each round of boxing. The players can take off their gloves to move the chess pieces. The winner is the person who gets checkmate or knocks (f) .... their opponent first. Berlin was the place (g) .... they had the first ever Chess Boxing World Championship in 2007. An American (h) .... a German were in the final. The German won. Now there (i) .... a school in Berlin where people can take (j) .... the sport. Some people once asked Rubingh what the aim of the sport was. He told (k) .... that he didn't like separating things or classifying sports in only one way. It's certainly true that if you want to win Chess Boxing, you have (l) .... be strong *and* intelligent!

2b Complete the text with the correct words.

3 SPEAKING What about *you*?
1 What do you think of this sport?
2 Would you like to try it? Why/Why not?

Listening

4 Work with a partner. Take it in turns to describe the photo. What do you think it shows?

5 LISTENING ▶ 48 Listen to two people who are at the scene of the photo. What is happening?

6 ▶ 48 Listen again. Are these sentences True (T) or False (F)?

1	The title of the work is a number.	T/F
2	The runners participate for money.	T/F
3	The runners bring their own sports equipment.	T/F
4	The work of art has a message.	T/F
5	The athletes can choose which speed they run at.	T/F
6	The inspiration for the work came from an experience which the artist had in Italy.	T/F
7	Visitors can participate in the work of art.	T/F
8	The artist designed the work, but he didn't run in it.	T/F

7 SPEAKING What about *you*?

What do you think of this work of art?

Speaking

➤ TIP FOR SPEAKING EXAMS

In activities where you have to describe a past event, remember …
Before the exam, make sure you know as many regular and irregular past simple forms as possible. Check that you know when and how to use the past simple, past continuous and past perfect. Revise words and expressions to explain the order of events, e.g. *First, Then, Next, In the end.*

➤ EXAM SUCCESS page 146

8 Read these three sentences. Which tense is used in each one and why?

1 We were all waiting for the start of the match.

2 They had already won the match.

3 We put our trainers on and went outside.

9 Look at the task and prepare what you are going to say.

Tell an English-speaking friend about a sports event that you took part in or watched and that was special to you for some reason. Say:

■ what the event was

■ where and when the event took place

■ what happened first

■ what happened in the end

■ why it was special

10 SPEAKING Work with a partner. Take it in turns to do the task.

Writing

➤ TIP FOR WRITING EXAMS

In writing exams, remember …
Always read the instructions carefully. Check that you know how many words you need to write, how much time you have, and what information you need to include.

➤ EXAM SUCCESS page 146

11 SPEAKING You see this announcement in a magazine. Work with a partner and discuss your answers to the questions.

YOU AND THE
WORLD OF CINEMA!

● How often do you watch films? Who with?
● Where do you prefer to watch films and why?
● What films do you love? Which do you hate? Why?

Write an article for next month's magazine with your answers to these questions. Write between 100 and 120 words.

12 Write your magazine article using between 100 and 120 words.

'CAN DO' PROGRESS CHECK UNITS 7–8   CEF

1 How well can you do these things in English now? Give yourself a mark from 1 to 4.

> **1** = I can do it very well.   **3** = I have some problems.
> **2** = I can do it quite well. **4** = I can't do it.

a I can describe or give extra information about people, things or places using defining or non-defining relative clauses. ☐

b I can talk about sports and use phrasal verbs connected with sport. ☐

c I can understand written and spoken texts about sports. ☐

d I can take part in a debate expressing agreement and disagreement. ☐

e I can write an article on a topic related to my life. ☐

f I can report what other people have said, asked or commanded using reported speech. ☐

g I can discuss art, theatre and music. ☐

h I can describe people and things using adjectives ending in *-ing* and *-ed*. ☐

i I can describe past events and explain what order they happened in. ☐

j I can write a simple film review. ☐

2 Now decide what you need to do next to improve.

1 Look again at my book/notes.

2 Do more practice exercises.
   ➤ WORKBOOK Units 7 and 8

3 Ask for help.

4 Other: ....

Vocabulary

Nations

1 Work with a partner. Match these words to the photos of the United Kingdom.

> capital city • currency • flag • national anthem
> prime minister/president • royal family

a
b
c

d
e
f

2 SPEAKING Work with a partner. Talk about the US using the words from 1.

> *They don't have a royal family.*

> *They have a president, not a prime minister.*

State and politics

3 Match these types of government with the definitions below.

> constitutional monarchy • democracy • monarchy • republic

1 A country that is ruled by a president or other leader, not by a king or queen.
2 A system of government where people vote in elections to choose the people who will govern them.
3 A type of government where a country is ruled by a king or queen.
4 A country ruled by a king or queen whose powers are limited by a set of basic laws.

4 Work with a partner. Can you think of a country for each different type of government?

5 Read the text about the United Kingdom. Match the <u>underlined</u> words with the definitions 1–8.

The United Kingdom is a constitutional monarchy. The head of state is the King or Queen, but power is in the hands of the Prime Minister. They have <u>general elections</u> at least every five years. You have to be 18 to <u>vote</u> in a general election.

Historically, the three biggest <u>political parties</u> have been the Conservative Party, the Labour Party, and the Liberal Democrat Party. The different parties organise <u>campaigns</u> before the elections. In these campaigns they explain what their <u>policies</u> are – what they plan to do about health, education, etc.

The Prime Minister and his or her government <u>run</u> the country. For example, they suggest new <u>laws</u>. The United Kingdom is a <u>member</u> of the European Union and so some laws also come from Europe.

1 Occasions when you can vote for a government: ....
2 A part of an organisation or group: ....
3 Groups of people with similar ideas about politics: ....
4 Control, organise: ....
5 Official rules that people must obey: ....
6 Plans or actions agreed on by a government, political party or other group: ....
7 Formally express an opinion by choosing between two or more people or parties: ....
8 Series of things that a political party does to try to win an election: ....

6 SPEAKING Work with a partner. Discuss the questions.

1 How often do you have general elections in your country?
2 What political parties do you know in your country?

1 Work with a partner and answer the questions.

1 Which famous English kings or queens do you know? What do you know about them?

2 What do you think a conspiracy theory is? What conspiracy theories do you know?

2 READING Read the article quickly and explain the title.

QUEEN ELIZABETH I
AND THE BOY FROM BISLEY

Elizabeth I (1533–1603) was a famous and fascinating member of the English monarchy. She reigned for almost 50 years. During this time, the government
5 was relatively stable, and under her rule England became a major international power. It was also during Elizabeth's reign that Shakespeare wrote many of his famous plays.

10 But there were some mysterious things about Elizabeth. Firstly, she never got married. This was strange at the time. Kings and queens usually married members of other royal or aristocratic families to form links between nations. Secondly,
15 she became bald at a young age. Thirdly, she gave strict instructions that no one should examine her body when she died. Over the years, a conspiracy theory has formed to explain these curious facts.

20 Elizabeth was the daughter of King Henry VIII. In the summer of 1542 she was staying at a house called Over Court in the village of Bisley. The king had sent the 9-year-old princess there from the
25 capital to avoid the plague. Two people were looking after her at Over Court – Lady Kat Ashley and Thomas Parry.

According to the conspiracy theory, this is what could have happened. The king
30 was about to visit Elizabeth at Over Court when suddenly she became very ill. She had a terrible fever and died just before the king arrived. Ashley and Parry were too frightened to tell the king that Elizabeth had died. So they decided to find another girl of Elizabeth's age in the village to take the
35 place of the princess.

However, there was a problem. There were no other girls of the same age in the village. But there was a boy from a local family

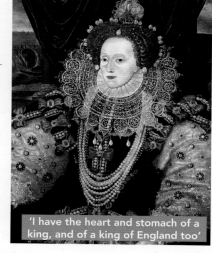

'I have the heart and stomach of a king, and of a king of England too'

who had played and studied with Elizabeth. He had red hair and pale skin, just like the princess. Ashley and Parry thought
40 that, with a bit of luck, the king may believe the 'Bisley Boy' was his daughter if he dressed up in Elizabeth's robes. Henry did not visit his daughter often and Elizabeth had always been very quiet and uncomfortable in front of him. And so, according to the story, the plan worked.

45 After Henry's visit, Ashley and Parry started training the new Elizabeth to take the role of the princess. It can't have been easy, but time passed and the 'Bisley Boy' became Queen Elizabeth I. This may explain why Elizabeth always refused to get married. It might also explain the words in her most
50 famous speech. Just as the Spanish Armada approached the English coast, she said to her soldiers: 'I have the heart and stomach of a king, and of a king of England too'. This may have been literally true – she had the heart
55 of a king, not of a queen. It could also explain why she was always careful to wear lots of make-up and wigs in public. Meanwhile, Ashley and Parry remained very close to Elizabeth and she always protected them.
60 One or two other senior ministers might have known the secret but perhaps kept silent for the good of the nation.

To add to the mystery, there have been frequent stories about a coffin being
65 discovered in Bisley. Inside was a young girl dressed in very fine, expensive clothes. Some say that this must have been the princess because nobody in the village could have had such good clothes.

70 Was Elizabeth really the Bisley Boy? Historians say the story can't be true because it is just too improbable. But some people say that the only way to really know is by scientific examination of the queen's bones. Only then will we be certain whether Queen Elizabeth I was really the boy from
75 Bisley or not.

3 Read the text again and answer the questions.

1 What do we know about Elizabeth I's reign?

2 Why was it important for kings and queens to marry?

3 Where was Elizabeth in the summer of 1542 and why?

4 What do we know about the relationship between Elizabeth and her father?

5 According to the conspiracy theory, who took Elizabeth's place? How and why?

6 According to the story, why were Elizabeth's words to her soldiers significant?

7 What do we know about Elizabeth's physical appearance?

8 Which discovery makes the story of the Bisley Boy seem possible and why?

4 ⚙ CRITICAL THINKING

Think! Then compare ideas with your class.

- Why do you think conspiracy theories like this exist? Why do you think there are so many conspiracy theories?

5 What do the underlined words in the text mean? Guess and then check in your dictionary.

6 SPEAKING What about *you*?

What do you think? Is it possible that Queen Elizabeth I was really the boy from Bisley? Why/Why not?

Grammar in context

Modal verbs of speculation and deduction – present

1 Read the sentences and answer the questions.

1 This **must** be a conspiracy theory.
2 It **might** explain the words in her most famous speech.
3 It **could** explain why she always wore lots of make-up
4 Serious historians say the story **can't** be true.
5 Some people think it **may** be true.
6 It **might not** be just a story.

a Which verb do we use when we are 90% certain that something is true?
b Which verb do we use when we are 90% certain that something is NOT true?
c Which verbs do we use when there is a 50% possibility that something is true (or not)?
d What form of the verb comes after the verbs in **blue**?

GRAMMAR REFERENCE ➤ PAGE 120

2 Choose the correct alternatives.

Country 1

1 It's a republic.
It _must/can't_ be the UK because they have a royal family.
2 They speak Spanish there.
It _must/might_ be Mexico because they speak Spanish there.
3 The capital city is Lima.
It _must/may_ be Peru.

Country 2

1 The currency is the Euro.
It _could/can't_ be lots of countries because 18 countries or more use Euros.
2 It's a republic which has a president and a prime minister.
It _may/can't_ be France or Italy because they both have a president and a prime minister.
3 Their national anthem is sometimes called 'Fratelli d'Italia'.
It _could/must_ be Italy.

3 Complete the sentences with _may_, _might_, _must_ and _can't_.

Flag 1

1 This flag is green, white and red.
It .... be the Italian flag because that has the same colours.
2 It has a picture in the middle of the flag.
It .... be the Italian flag because that doesn't have a picture on it.
3 The picture includes a Mexican eagle, a snake and a cactus.
It .... be the Mexican flag.

Flag 2

1 This flag has only two colours, white and red.
It .... be the British flag because that is blue, white and red.
2 There is a red cross on the flag.
It .... be the English flag, or it ....
be the Georgian flag because they both have red crosses.
3 There are four small red crosses, one in each corner of the flag.
It .... be the Georgian flag because that has one big red cross and four small red crosses.

4 [SPEAKING] **Work with a partner. Look at the photo and talk about where you think this place is. Use _can't_, _may_, _might_, _could_ and _must_ to make speculations and deductions.**

It must be a big city like New York or Paris.

Modal verbs of speculation and deduction – past

5 Read the sentences and answer the questions.

1 Some senior ministers **might have known** the secret.
2 This girl **must have been** the princess.
3 She **may have died**.
4 This **could have happened**.
5 It **can't have been** easy.
6 They **may not have realised** the truth.
7 The king **couldn't have known**.

a Which verb do we use when we are 90% certain that something was true?
b Which verbs do we use when we are 90% certain that something was NOT true?
c Which verbs do we use when there is a 50% possibility that something was true (or not)?
d What comes after the modal verbs –
have + ...?

GRAMMAR REFERENCE ➤ PAGE 120

6a PRONUNCIATION ▶ 49 **Listen to the two sentences. Do we pronounce** *have* **in the same way in both sentences?**

1 You have to go now.

2 You must have known.

6b ▶ 50 **Listen to these sentences. Do you hear** /hæv/ **or** /əv/?

1 She might have gone.

2 They can't have done it.

3 It couldn't have been me.

4 You must have heard it.

5 We may have lost.

6 They must have known.

6c ▶ 50 **Listen again and repeat the sentences.**

7 Complete the sentences with past modal verbs and the verbs given.

King Arthur – myth or fact?

1 King Arthur .... (exist) but nobody really knows.

2 If he really existed, he .... (be) an amazing person because many stories were written about him.

3 Merlin .... (use) magic because magic doesn't exist.

4 The British poet Alfred Lord Tennyson .... (like) the stories about Arthur because he wrote poems about him.

5 Arthur's popularity .... (disappear) because people are still making films and TV series about him now.

6 Some people think that if there was a real King Arthur, he .... (live) at a place called Tintagel Castle in Cornwall, but there is no real evidence for this.

7 Arthur .... (believe) that all his knights were equal. That was why he had a round table where each place was equally important.

8 According to the legends, Arthur .... (take) his sword Excalibur from a stone or he .... (receive) it from a mysterious hand in a lake.

Adjective suffixes

1 Write these words in two columns: noun or adjective.

> aristocracy • aristocratic • care • careful • careless comfort • comfortable • fame • famous • luck • lucky science • scientific • terrible • terror • uncomfortable

2 For each word in 1, underline the suffix which makes it an adjective.

aristocratic

3 Turn these words into adjectives and write them in the correct column.

> artist • danger • enjoy • help • hunger • mystery nature • office • sense • use

-y	-ic	-able	-ible
	artistic		

-ful	-less	-al	-ous

✔ **EXAM SUCCESS**

You are going to do a word formation cloze activity. Read the instructions for the activity. How do you know if you need to add a suffix, a prefix or both to the word given?

➤ EXAM SUCCESS page 146

4 Complete the text with adjectives formed from the word given.

There are many ghost stories connected to the **(a)** .... (OFFICE) residences of the British Royal Family. In Balmoral Castle in Scotland, Queen Elizabeth II herself felt the **(b)** .... (MYSTERY) presence of an old servant to her great great grandmother, Queen Victoria. In Holyrood Palace, also in Scotland, some **(c)** .... (TERROR) events took place, including murder. Perhaps it's not surprising that some people feel **(d)** .... (COMFORT) when they visit the palace. At Windsor Castle in England, some say there are 25 different ghosts, including the ghost of Elizabeth I. They say that visitors should be **(e)** .... (CARE) in the park. They say that it's very **(f)** .... (DANGER) if you see the ghost of a servant of King Richard III riding a horse. Apparently, anybody who sees the ghost is **(g)** .... (LUCK) for the rest of their lives. Of course, there must be **(h)** .... (SENSE) explanations for all these ghost stories.

Considering SOCIAL ISSUES

LIFE SKILLS OBJECTIVES	KEY CONCEPTS
■ To learn about the United Kingdom Youth Parliament. ■ To think about important issues that affect young people today. ■ To give a brief presentation about a current social issue and what we can do about it.	**issue [n]:** *Unemployment is an important issue for young people and we need to discuss it.* **youth [n]:** *This problem affects our youth and older people, too.* **stand for election [phrase]:** *In the US the President can only stand for election twice.* **manifesto [n]:** *The party explained what it wanted to do in its manifesto.* **speak up for [phrase]:** *Somebody needs to speak up for all the people who are suffering and help them.* **represent [v]:** *This politician represents the Labour Party.*

1 Work with a partner. Look at the advert and answer the questions.

1 What do you think the UK Youth Parliament is?

2 What type of people are they looking for?

3 Do you think you have the qualities that they are looking for? Why/Why not?

2 READING **Read the information about the UK Youth Parliament and answer the questions.**

1 What does the UK Youth Parliament do?

2 What are MYPs and what do they do?

UK Youth Parliament

VOTE FOR US

WHAT IS THE UK YOUTH PARLIAMENT?

The UK Youth Parliament is run by young people for young people. It provides opportunities for 11–18-year-olds to express their views in creative ways to bring about social change. The Youth Parliament aims to give the young people of the UK a voice, which will be heard and listened to by local, regional and national government.

WHO CAN STAND FOR ELECTION?

The UK Youth Parliament has over 600 representatives, all aged 11–18. Members of the Youth Parliament (MYPs) are usually elected in annual youth elections throughout the UK. Any person aged 11–18 can stand for election or vote. In the past two years one million young people have voted in UK Youth Parliament elections. There are no political parties in The Youth Parliament.

WHAT DO MYPS DO?

After they are elected, MYPs organise different events and projects. They run campaigns to try to influence decision makers on the issues which matter most to young people. The government has occasionally changed its policies as a direct result of Youth Parliament campaigns.

WHAT DO PEOPLE VOTE ON?

Each year young people can vote to decide the most important things that the Youth Parliament should campaign for. One year, over 850,000 young people voted to choose the topics! Recent popular topics include:

- Letting 16- and 17-year-olds vote in general elections
- Fighting youth unemployment
- Zero tolerance to bullying in schools
- Changing the school curriculum to prepare students better for life
- Spending more money, not less, on youth services
- Giving all young people a week of work experience

WHAT HAPPENS NEXT?

Five topics are chosen from a list of ten. Then there is a debate in the House of Commons. This is where the most important British politicians actually work and discuss new laws. After the debate, the MYPs choose the two most important topics and the Youth Parliament then campaigns for those two things all year.

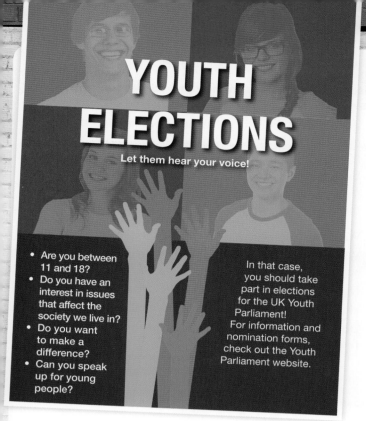

YOUTH ELECTIONS

Let them hear your voice!

- Are you between 11 and 18?
- Do you have an interest in issues that affect the society we live in?
- Do you want to make a difference?
- Can you speak up for young people?

In that case, you should take part in elections for the UK Youth Parliament! For information and nomination forms, check out the Youth Parliament website.

3 Read the text again. Are these sentences True (T) or False (F)?

1 Young people between 11 and 18 control the Youth Parliament. **T / F**

2 Above all, the Youth Parliament lets young people say what they think. **T / F**

3 They have elections for the Youth Parliament once every four years. **T / F**

4 Each member of the Youth Parliament must belong to a political party. **T / F**

5 The Youth Parliament never actually influences the government. **T / F**

6 Trying to stop bullying at school is an important question for young people in the UK. **T / F**

7 The Youth Parliament can only campaign for topics connected with school. **T / F**

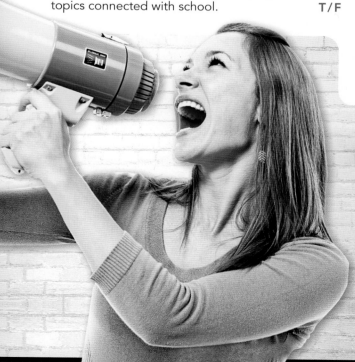

4 LISTENING ▶ 51 Watch or listen to four teenagers explaining why they are standing for election as Young Mayor. Which issue from the text in 2 does each speaker talk about?

Olivia: ....

Jack: ....

Luke: ....

Chloe: ....

5 ▶ 51 Watch or listen again. Match the sentences (a–h) with the speakers.

Olivia: .... , ...

Jack: .... , ...

Luke: .... , ...

Chloe: .... , ...

a Young people aren't totally prepared for adult life.

b I want to help with a problem because people in general have told me it's one of the biggest problems for young people.

c I want to stop a problem which worries my friends.

d I believe that experts can help to solve a big problem for young people.

e Young people need to be able to participate in general decisions about the future.

f 16-year-olds have a number of responsibilities.

g Young people are very active and creative.

h I can help to change what you do each day.

6a SPEAKING Work with a partner. Talk about each of the issues that appear at the end of the text in 2. How important do you think each one is and why? Give a mark from 1 (not very important) to 5 (extremely important).

6b What do you think we can do about these issues?

6c What other issues do you think are important to people of your age? What positive action can we take to solve each one?

LIFE TASK

Work with a partner. Follow this plan.

1 *Decide what you think the most important issue is today for people of your age.*

2 *Prepare a short manifesto explaining what the issue is and what you would do about it.*

3 *Present your manifesto to the class. When you all finish, have a class vote to choose the best three manifestos.*

Listening

1 Work with a partner. Describe the photo. Do you know what this event was and why it was important?

✓ **EXAM SUCCESS**

You are going to do an activity where you listen and complete gaps in some notes with the word(s) you hear. How can it help you to read the notes before you listen?

➤ EXAM SUCCESS page 146

2 LISTENING ▶ 52 **Listen to two people talking about the event and complete the notes with one to three words or numbers.**

Notepad

The event was the Rugby World Cup, which took place in South Africa in **(1)** ....

Nelson Mandela had spent **(2)** .... in prison, but then became the President.

Most of the players in the South African rugby team were **(3)** .... at that time.

At a match between England and South Africa before the World Cup, many black South Africans had wanted **(4)** .... to win.

For the World Cup there was a new slogan for the South African rugby team: 'One Team, **(5)** ....'

For the World Cup the South African team learnt to sing the **(6)** ....

Thanks to the final of the World Cup, Nelson Mandela became a hero for **(7)** ....

Some people think South Africa won the final because many of the New Zealand players were **(8)** .... during the match. The New Zealand players had eaten at **(9)** ....

3 SPEAKING **What about you?**

Have you seen the film, *Invictus*, about this historical sports event? If so, what was your opinion of the film? If not, would you like to see it? Why/Why not?

Grammar in context

Third conditional

1 **Read these sentences in the third conditional and answer the questions.**

a If you**'d seen** the film, you **would have learned** a lot about South Africa.

b Perhaps the country **wouldn't have united** if it **hadn't been** for the Rugby World Cup.

c If they **hadn't been** ill, perhaps they **would have won** the final.

1 What tense do we use in the half of the sentence with **if**?

2 What form of the verb do we use in the other half of the sentence?

3 Does the half of the sentence with **if** always come first?

4 How do we know when **'d** is **had** or **would**?

5 Do we use the third conditional for imaginary situations in the present or the past?

GRAMMAR REFERENCE ➤ PAGE 120

2 **Choose the correct alternative.**

1 If the Roman Empire had never *end/ended*, Latin would *has/have* remained the universal language.

2 If aliens *land/had landed* on the Earth, somebody would *had/have* some physical evidence to prove it by now.

3 Perhaps dinosaurs would *survive/have survived* if an asteroid *didn't/hadn't* hit the Earth.

4 Perhaps Sir Isaac Newton wouldn't have *think/thought* about gravity if an apple *hadn't fallen/wouldn't fall* on his head.

5 The world would *has/have* evolved in a totally different way if somebody *has/had* invented the computer two hundred years ago.

6 If the Titanic *hadn't/didn't* hit an iceberg, it *had/would have* arrived in New York safely.

3 **Read the text and complete the sentences with the correct form of the verb given.**

In the 17th century England and Holland were terrible rivals. They both competed for exotic spices around the world. A spice called nutmeg was one of the most valuable in the world. People thought it cured the plague. In 1616 England found a tiny island called Run in South East Asia which produced nutmeg. The Dutch wanted the island and so they attacked it. One Englishman (Nathaniel Courthope) and a group of natives protected the island for five years. But in the end the Dutch won and took the island. The English were very angry and decided to steal a Dutch colony. They took a poor, unattractive island called New Amsterdam in North America. In 1667 a peace agreement was signed. In this agreement, the Dutch 'won' the island of Run. Today it has almost no value. The English were given New Amsterdam. They renamed it New York!

1 If, in the past, people .... (not think) nutmeg cured the plague, nutmeg .... (not be) so valuable.

2 Holland .... (take) the island of Run if they .... (find) it first.

3 If Nathaniel Courthope .... (not defend) the island, it .... (become) Dutch much sooner.

4 If the English .... (not be) so angry, they .... (not take) a Dutch colony.

5 If New Amsterdam .... (be) richer and more attractive at the time, the Dutch .... (keep) it.

6 Maybe the whole of North America .... (speak) Dutch, not English, if New Amsterdam .... (remain) Dutch.

7 If nutmeg .... (not be) so valuable in the past, probably the history of the world .... (be) very different.

4 **Read the situations and write sentences in the third conditional.**

1 It was raining and we got wet because we didn't take an umbrella.
If we had taken an umbrella, we wouldn't have got wet.

2 I got ten in the exam because I studied a lot.

3 The road was wet because it was raining.

4 I didn't buy you a present because I didn't have any money.

5 I only knew her secret because you told me.

6 We didn't know they were such horrible people when we became their friends.

7 He did really badly in the race because he hadn't trained.

8 She arrived on time because she got up early that morning.

9 My brother had enough money to buy the tickets because my dad gave him £20.

5 **Complete each sentence in the third conditional.**

1 If I had never learnt to read,
....

2 If I had appeared on TV yesterday,
....

3 If I'd gone to primary school in Australia,
....

4 If I hadn't come to school this morning,
....

5 If the sun hadn't come up this morning,
....

6 If I'd lived in a palace when I was five,
....

6a SPEAKING **Work with a partner. Ask and answer these questions.**

What would you have done if …
1 you had met the President or Prime Minister of your country yesterday?
2 a dog had eaten your homework last night?
3 you had been born into a royal family?
4 the teacher had given you just one day to do a long assignment?
5 you had broken your laptop/tablet/mobile phone yesterday?

6b **Individually, write five similar questions. Then ask your partner your questions.**

What would you have done if you had lost your mobile phone and you had found it in your friend's bag?

I would have asked my friend why it was there!

Developing speaking

Describing photos – 2

1 [SPEAKING] **Work with a partner. Look at the photo. Write questions to ask about it.**

What can you see in the background?
Where do you think they are?

2 [LISTENING] ▶ **53 Listen to a student talking about the photo. Does she answer any of your questions? Do you agree with what she says? Why/Why not?**

3 ▶ **53 Listen again. Tick (✓) expressions in the Speaking bank that you hear.**

💬 **SPEAKING BANK**

Making speculations and deductions
- I imagine …
- I'm not sure but …
- (He/It) must be …
- (She) may/might/could be …
- (They) can't be …
- (It) is/are probably …
- It seems that …
- (It/They) looks/look as if/like …
- (She) must have been …
- (They) may/might/could have been …
- (It) can't have been …

PRACTICE MAKES PERFECT

4a Read and prepare the task below.

Choose one of the photos. Spend three minutes preparing to talk about it.
- Say where you think it is and what you think is happening.
- How do you think the people in the photo are feeling?

4b [SPEAKING] **Work with a partner. Take it in turns to describe your photo. Use the expressions in the Speaking bank to help you. If your partner stops, ask questions to help them.**

A story

1 READING **Read the story and answer the questions.**

   1 What did Amy win and how?

   2 Where exactly did Amy have to go and how?

   3 How do you think Amy felt at the end of the story?

2 **Read the story again and <u>underline</u> any words or expressions which help you to understand when or in what order the events in the story happened.**

3 **Look at the Writing bank. Match the tenses and verbs (1–5) with their uses in the story.**

> ✎ **WRITING BANK**
>
> **Narrative tenses**
> 1 past simple
> 2 past continuous
> 3 past perfect
> 4 *used to*
> 5 *must/may/might/can't have*
>
> **a** We use it for the background of the story, to talk about actions that happened before other actions in the past.
>
> **b** We use it to talk about past habits.
>
> **c** We use these to make speculations or deductions about what happened.
>
> **d** We use it to tell the main events and actions in the story.
>
> **e** We use it to describe scenes and talk about activities in progress.
>
> WRITING BANK ➤ PAGE 151

4 **Read the story again. Find an example of each of the narrative tenses in the Writing bank.**

5 PRACTICE MAKES PERFECT **Read the task and write your story. Use the Writing bank for help.**

> Write a story which begins:
> *When Amy finished reading the email, she thought 'It can't be true!'*
> Use narrative tenses carefully and include words that explain when or in what order events happened.

When Amy finished reading the email, she thought 'It can't be true!' She had just received an invitation to meet the Prime Minister!

A few months ago, Amy had entered a competition. In the competition she had to say ten things that she would do if she were the Prime Minister. The prize was the chance to meet the actual Prime Minister at his official residence at 10 Downing Street and discuss her ideas. Amy had always wanted to share her ideas with somebody important so she wrote them down carefully and sent them off.

At first Amy didn't believe that she had won. She thought the email must have been a mistake or a joke. But an hour later she received an official telephone call giving her details about her visit to 10 Downing Street, which was next Wednesday. Surely this wasn't a joke now!

On Wednesday, after school, Amy was waiting nervously at home when a big black car arrived. Excitedly, all of her neighbours were watching and wondering what was happening and where she was going. Amy jumped in the car and off she went.

After about 40 minutes, they arrived at 10 Downing Street. Suddenly the Prime Minister came out to meet Amy, as if she was an important head of state! They spoke for two hours. By the end, Amy had convinced the Prime Minister to put into practice some of her ideas to help young people. Amy used to dream of a moment like this, and now it had actually come true!

Grammar reference

Modal verbs of speculation and deduction – present

FORM

She **must** be good at maths because she always gets a 10.
She **may/might/could/may not/mightn't (might not)** be good at maths, but I don't really know.
She **can't** be good at maths because her marks are always bad.
After these modal verbs we use an infinitive without **to**.

USE

We use **must** when we are 90% certain something is true.
We use **may, might, could, may not, mightn't** when there is a 50% possibility that something is true (or not).
We use **can't** when we are 90% certain that something is not true.
When we are 100% certain that something is or isn't true, we do not use modal verbs of speculation and deduction.
I know she's good at maths.

Modal verbs of speculation and deduction – past

FORM

She **must have done** well in her last exam because she was really happy afterwards.
She **may/might/could/may not/mightn't (might not) have passed** her exam, but I don't really know.
She **can't/couldn't have passed** her exam because she was really sad afterwards.
To make sentences in the past using modal verbs we use this form:
must/may/might/can't/couldn't + have + past participle

USE

We use **must have** when we are 90% certain that something was true.
We use **may have, might have, could have, may not have, mightn't have** when there is a 50% possibility that something was true (or not).
We use **can't have, couldn't have** when we are 90% certain that something was not true.
When we are 100% certain that something was or wasn't true, we do not use modal verbs of speculation and deduction.
She didn't pass her exam.

Third conditional

FORM

If + **past perfect**, ... **would/wouldn't have** + past participle
*If I **had seen** him, I'd **have spoken** to him.*
*We **wouldn't have passed** our exams if we **hadn't studied**.*
If can go at the start of the sentence or in the middle. If it goes at the start, we must use a comma before the second half of the sentence.

USE

We use the **third conditional** to talk about imaginary or impossible situations in the past and their consequences. The situations are impossible because we cannot change them now that they have happened.
If I had done my homework last night (imaginary past situation – it didn't happen), *the teacher wouldn't have been angry with me.* (the consequence)

Vocabulary

Nations capital city • currency • flag • national anthem • prime minister/president • royal family (king/queen/prince/princess)

State and politics campaign • constitutional • monarchy • democracy • general election • law • member monarchy • policy • political party • republic • run (the country) • vote

Adjective suffixes aristocratic • artistic • careful • careless • comfortable • dangerous • enjoyable famous • helpful • helpless • hungry • lucky • mysterious • natural • official • scientific • sensible • terrible uncomfortable • unlucky • useful • useless

Other words and phrases ➤ page 143

Grammar revision

Modal verbs of speculation and deduction – present

/ 6 points

1 Complete the sentences with *must*, *may* or *can't*.

1 Sarah _____ be Toby's sister because she looks totally different.

2 She _____ be German because she's got a German passport.

3 They _____ like cats – they've got ten!

4 He _____ play tennis well – I don't know.

5 That _____ be my notebook because it's red and mine's yellow.

6 I don't know when Joe is coming. It _____ be soon.

Modal verbs of speculation and deduction – past

/ 7 points

2 Complete the sentences with *must*, *might* or *can't* and the correct form of the verb given.

1 You _____ (see) Mike yesterday because he wasn't here.

2 Somebody called before. It _____ (be) Jack, but I didn't recognise the voice.

3 The postman _____ (come) early because the letters are already here.

4 It _____ (rain) last night – the road is wet!

5 It _____ (snow) last night because it isn't cold enough for snow.

6 Somebody broke a window. Josh _____ (do) it, but I can't be sure.

7 Ben _____ (eat) the brownies because he hates chocolate.

Third conditional

/ 7 points

3 Complete the third conditional sentences with the correct form of these verbs.

> buy • cook • die • pass • play • send • shine

1 If I _____ my driving test, my parents would have bought me a car.

2 They _____ her a present if they had known she was getting married.

3 If her cat _____, she would have been sad.

4 The meal would have been better if my mum _____ it.

5 If the sun _____ yesterday, we would have gone out.

6 She _____ him an email if she had known his address.

7 They would have won if they _____ a bit better.

Vocabulary revision

NATIONS

/ 7 points

1 Complete the sentences with the correct words.

1 The _____ is Paris.

2 The _____ is 'La Marseillaise'.

3 The _____ has three colours, blue, white and red.

4 The _____ in 2014 was François Hollande.

5 There is no _____ because France is a republic. But the last _____ was Louis XVI.

6 The _____ is the Euro.

STATE AND POLITICS

/ 5 points

2 Match the words and write a simple definition.

1 general   a minister
2 run   b party
3 political   c monarchy
4 prime   d a country
5 constitutional   e elections

ADJECTIVE SUFFIXES

/ 8 points

3 Complete the sentences with the adjective form of these words.

> artist • care • comfort • enjoy • hunger
> mystery • nature • sense

1 I'm really _____. I need to eat.

2 He's a very _____ writer. He makes lots of mistakes.

3 Becky's very _____. She loves drawing.

4 It isn't very _____ to go out in the rain without a coat.

5 I love this sofa. It's so _____.

6 Bears should live in their _____ habitat.

7 We spent a very _____ day in the country. I loved it.

8 He just disappeared. It was all very _____.

10 The material world

Vocabulary

Shops

1 SPEAKING **Work with a partner. Play 'vocabulary tennis' with these words.**

Choose one of the shops. Take it in turns to say things you can buy there. If you can't think of anything, if you say an incorrect word, or if you repeat a word, you lose the point.

> bakery • bookshop • butcher's • chemist's
> clothes shop • department store
> electrical goods shop • greengrocer's • jeweller's
> newsagent's • post office • shoe shop
> sports shop • stationery shop • supermarket

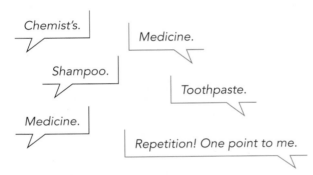

Chemist's.

Medicine.

Shampoo.

Toothpaste.

Medicine.

Repetition! One point to me.

2 LISTENING ▶ 54 **Listen to four dialogues. Where are the people? What do they want to buy?**

1 .... 3 ....

2 .... 4 ....

Shopping

3 **Look at the photo. Which of these words can you use to talk about it?**

> afford • bargain • cash • cashier
> changing room • checkout • debit card
> discount • queue • receipt • refund • trolley

4 **Match the words in 3 with the definitions. Use a dictionary if necessary.**

1 A plastic card that you use to pay for things.
2 The person who takes the money in a shop.
3 Money in the form of notes and coins.
4 The place where you pay in a supermarket or a big shop.
5 A line of people waiting, for example to pay in a shop.
6 Have enough money to buy something.
7 A reduction in the price of something.
8 Something that you buy which is much cheaper than usual.
9 A piece of paper that the cashier gives you to show that you've paid for something.
10 The money that a shop gives you when you take a product back.
11 A large container with wheels that you use to put products in when shopping, especially in a supermarket.
12 A place where you can try clothes on before you buy them.

5 **Complete the text with words from 3.**

The other day I was in my local supermarket, pushing the **(a)** .... and filling it with food for the week. I was bored with looking at the food, so I went to see if they had any DVDs. I saw that they had a new one with Ryan Gosling. There was a 50% **(b)** .... on the DVD. It was a real **(c)** .... so I bought it. There was a really long **(d)** .... with people waiting to pay at the **(e)** .... That was because the **(f)** .... (he was new, I think) was really slow. Anyway, I didn't have any money with me so when it was finally my turn I paid for everything with my **(g)** .... When I got home I put the DVD on but it didn't work. I went straight back to the supermarket with the DVD and asked for a **(h)** .... I wanted my money back, obviously. They asked if I'd paid by **(i)** .... and I told them I hadn't. I had to show them my card to get my money back. But then they asked me for the **(j)** .... too, to show them that I'd bought it at that shop. I didn't have it. I'd thrown it away. In the end, the DVD was a total waste of money!

6 SPEAKING **Work with a partner. Discuss these questions.**

1 Do you enjoy going shopping? How often do you go?
2 Which type of shops do you like or hate? Why?
3 Which is your favourite shop and why?

Title: ....

You need some bread and milk. You pop into the supermarket for two minutes. Half an hour later, you leave the supermarket with a trolley
5 full of food and a big hole in your bank account. What games do supermarkets play to make us spend so much money?

The tricks usually start before you walk in. Outside the supermarket entrance,
10 anybody who walks past can smell warm, freshly-baked bread. That makes us hungry and ready to buy lots of food, not just bread. Even if you never planned on going into the supermarket or buying
15 anything, it's such a great smell that nobody can resist!

Now you're inside and, of course, you need somewhere to put your shopping. A small basket would be fine, but all
20 they have are trolleys. And of course the problem with a trolley is that it looks sad and lonely with just one or two items inside. So our tendency is to fill it with something. In fact, supermarket trolleys
25 are actually getting bigger so that we buy more. In one experiment, researchers deliberately made the trolleys double the size and customers bought 19% more!

Of course, many people shop in
30 supermarkets because they think everything is cheaper than in other shops. But most people only know the price of a few essential products – milk, bread, eggs, etc. So
35 supermarkets offer very cheap prices on these things but then have higher prices for other products. One new trick is to put red stickers on products. Customers usually associate red
40 stickers with discounts so the red sticker attracts them, even when there is no reduction! Interestingly, this trick appears to work more with men than with women.

45 There is a story behind the position of everything in the supermarket. For example, customers often go only to buy milk. So they put it right at the back, forcing you to go past hundreds
50 of shelves full of other products. The position of products on each shelf is also significant. The most expensive items are usually at eye-level so you see these immediately. In fact,
55 companies often pay supermarkets to put their products in this important space. The exception is anything that

might attract children. These products are on lower shelves so that kids see them.

60 Apart from what you see and smell in a supermarket, what about what you listen to? In most supermarkets they have soft, slow music. It's so relaxing that you slow down and spend more time (and money!)
65 in the store. You also move more slowly when the supermarket is busy. Experts suggest it's better to shop when it's quieter, on a Monday or a Tuesday for example. And be careful with queues at the
70 checkout. These are sometimes deliberate, to make you buy something from the checkout shelves while you wait.

So, next time you go into your local supermarket, pick up a small basket, put
75 some dance music on your headphones, ignore the red stickers and see if you can come out with just the things you went for.

---

1 READING Read the magazine article and think of a good title. Give your reasons.

✓ EXAM SUCCESS

The next exercise is a multiple-choice activity. First you should read the text quickly to get a general understanding. What should you do next?

➤ EXAM SUCCESS page 146

2 Read the text again and choose the best answers.

1 Smells from the supermarket bakery …

   a persuade people to go inside the supermarket.
   b are more effective with people who are already hungry.
   c make us buy more bread than we need.

2 Supermarkets prefer us not to use baskets because …

   a they don't usually have many.
   b they're too small.
   c people use them to hide things.

3 The text talks about supermarkets which use red stickers …

   a only for bargains.
   b to mark products that are mainly for men.
   c so people think they're saving money.

4 According to the text, you would usually find a cheap breakfast cereal for adults …

   a on a shelf at eye-level so that everyone can see it easily.
   b on a low shelf so that children can see them more easily.
   c on a low shelf so that you don't notice them immediately.

5 According to the text, it's better for supermarkets if …

   a customers shop without hurrying.
   b the people who work at the checkouts are fast and efficient to avoid queues.
   c you shop at the start of the week.

3 Make a list of the techniques used by supermarkets to make us buy things.

Using the smell of freshly-baked bread

4 ⚙ CRITICAL THINKING

Think! Then compare ideas with your class.

■ Do you think knowing about the tricks in the text would change the way people shop? How?

5 What do the underlined words in the text mean? Guess and then check in your dictionary.

6 SPEAKING What about you?

How often do you shop in supermarkets? Who do you go with and what do you usually buy?

Grammar in context

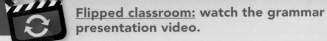

Flipped classroom: watch the grammar presentation video.

Indeterminate pronouns: some-, any-, no-, every-

1a Read the sentences.

1 You never planned on buying **anything**.
2 **Anybody** who walks past can smell freshly baked bread.
3 **Nobody** can resist it!
4 You need **somewhere** to put your shopping.
5 Our tendency is to fill it with **something**.
6 **Everybody** goes shopping at the weekend.

1b Match the sentence halves to make rules.

1 We use pronouns with **some** ....
2 We use pronouns with **any** ....
3 We use pronouns with **no** ....
4 We use pronouns with **every** ....

a in negative sentences, questions, and in affirmative sentences when it means *it doesn't matter who, what, where.*
b with affirmative verbs because the meaning of the pronoun is already negative.
c in affirmative sentences and in offers and requests.
d in all types of sentences and in questions.

1c Complete the table.

some-	any-	no-	every-
something	anything		
	anybody/ anyone	nobody/ no-one	everybody/ everyone
somewhere			

GRAMMAR REFERENCE ➤ PAGE 132

2 Choose the correct alternative.

1 I've finished my homework. I've done *anything/everything*.
2 Who's upstairs? I can hear *somebody/anybody*.
3 Where are my keys? I can't find them *somewhere/anywhere*.
4 The teacher's really angry. *No-one/Anyone* knows the answer.
5 Why are you so serious? Is *nothing/anything* wrong?
6 The concert is a real success. *Everybody/Anybody* is having a great time.
7 Excuse me *everyone/no-one*! Does *anyone/everyone* know where Joe is?
8 That's strange. There isn't *nobody/anybody* here.

3 Complete the dialogue with the indeterminate pronouns in 1c.

Holly: Would you like to do (a) .... this weekend?

Megan: OK, but what?

Holly: (b) .... I don't mind.

Megan: Well, how about going shopping? I have to buy (c) .... for my sister. It's her birthday next week.

Holly: What are you going to buy her?

Megan: A nice top to wear at parties. She always says she can't go out because she hasn't got (d) .... to wear. So then she wears all my clothes – (e) ....! And she never returns them so in the end I've got (f) .... to wear and I can't go out!

Holly: (g) .... should speak to her.

Megan: Who? Me? My mum? My sister never listens to (h) ....!

4a Complete the questions with *anybody*, *anywhere*, *anything*.

1 If you could go .... in the world for your holidays, where would you go?
2 If you could have .... you liked for dinner, what would you ask for?
3 If you could meet .... in the world, who would you meet?
4 If you could be .... in the world apart from yourself, who would you be?
5 If you could live .... in the world, where would you live?
6 If you could change .... in the world, what would you change?

4b SPEAKING Work with a partner. Ask and answer the questions. Are any of your answers similar?

so and such

5 **Read the sentences and choose the correct alternative.**

a   It looks **so** sad and lonely.

b   They do it **so** well.

c   It's **so** relaxing that you slow down.

d   It was **such** a bargain.

e   It's **such** a great smell that nobody can resist it.

1 We use *so* to intensify the meaning of *adjectives and adverbs/nouns*.

2 We use *such* to intensify the meaning of *adjectives only/nouns (with or without adjectives)*.

3 After sentences with *so* or *such* we can continue the sentence with *that/than*.

GRAMMAR REFERENCE ➤ PAGE 132

6a PRONUNCIATION ▶ 55 **Listen to these sentences. What do you notice about the pronunciation of *so* and *such*?**

1   That dress is so expensive.

2   It's such an amazing shop.

3   I'm so happy that you're here.

4   It's such a pity that you can't come.

6b ▶ 55 **Listen again and repeat.**

7 **Complete the sentences with *so* or *such*.**

1   That's .... a good shop.

2   I find shopping .... tiring.

3   It was .... a problem to get here.

4   You and I are .... good friends.

5   We did .... well in that competition.

6   I was .... sorry to hear the news.

7   The queue at the checkout was .... long.

8a **Complete these sentences in a logical way.**

1   Everything was so expensive in the shop that ....

2   The customer was so angry that ....

3   I was so late for school that ....

4   It was such a rainy day that ....

5   The TV programme was so bad that ....

6   She was such a clever student that ....

7   The music was so loud that ....

8b SPEAKING **Work with a partner. Compare your sentences in 8a.**

Collocations with *money*

1 **Look at these verbs that frequently go with the word *money*. Use them to complete the definitions below.**

> borrow • donate • earn • lend • make • owe
> raise • save • spend • waste • win

When you:

1   .... money, you get it in a competition.

2   .... money, you use more than you should, or you use it in a silly way.

3   .... money, somebody gives it to you, but you have to pay it back later.

4   .... money, you give it as a present to a charity, organisation or institution.

5   .... money, you get it for working.

6   .... money, you give it to somebody, but they have to pay you back later.

7   .... money, you use it to buy something.

8   .... money, you don't spend it, you put it in a bank for example.

9   .... money, you get it for working or by investing it or through a business plan or transaction.

10   .... money, you collect it for a particular use, e.g. for a charity.

11   .... money, you have to give it back to somebody.

2 **Complete the sentences with the correct form of the verbs in 1.**

1   How much money do shop assistants usually .... when they work full time?

2   She .... £30 a month on CDs, DVDs and books.

3   Can I .... some money? I forgot to bring any when I left home this morning.

4   My uncle .... £100 on the lottery today.

5   Every year Bill Gates .... a lot of money to charity.

6   Hey, where's my money? I .... you £10 last week and you still haven't given it back.

7   Thomas Edison .... a lot of money from his inventions.

8   I'm .... £20 a week because next year I want to buy a new computer.

9   You .... your money when you bought that exercise bike. You never use it!

10   You lent me £10 this week and £10 last week, so I .... you £20.

11   Last year our school .... £1,000 to repair the gym.

Managing your MONEY

LIFE SKILLS OBJECTIVES	KEY CONCEPTS
<ul><li>To reflect on how you spend or save money.</li><li>To learn about how other people manage their money.</li><li>To consider tips for spending less and saving more.</li></ul>	**have something left [v]:** *I bought a DVD for £8. I had £10 so now I've got £2 left.* **pocket money/allowance [n]:** *My parents give me pocket money/an allowance once a week, to buy small things I want.* **budget [n, v]:** *To plan a budget you need to know how much money is coming in and how much you can spend.* **luxury [n]:** *That product is a luxury. You don't really need it.* **make your money go further [v]:** *If you spent less on expensive clothes that you don't need, you could make your money go further.* **interest [n]:** *The bank is giving me 2% interest on the money that I have in my savings account there.*

1 READING **Read the quiz about managing money and tick (✓) your answers.**

How smart are you with MONEY?

1 Which is the most common situation for you?

a You never have any money.

b Sometimes you have some money, but sometimes you owe money to a friend or family member.

c You usually have money.

2 What do you usually do with your allowance?

a You usually spend it as soon as you get it.

b You have a basic plan in your head for how you will spend it so that it goes further and hopefully lasts the week.

c You plan your budget carefully and write down what you spend.

3 Where do you keep your savings?

a What savings??

b In the bank account that I've had since I was little.

c I opened a bank account with a high interest rate so my savings can make me more money.

4 You get a surprise gift of £50 from one of your relatives. What do you do?

a Spend it all on some computer games/DVDs/books that you want.

b Spend half on computer games/DVDs/books and save the rest.

c Put it all in the bank. You don't want to waste it.

5 You want a new bicycle. What do you do?

a Ask for one as a present.

b Discuss the idea with your parents and see if they can help you out a little.

c Start earning the cash yourself.

6 You hear that the local newsagent's wants someone to do a few hours work for them early on Saturday morning. What do you do?

a Say you aren't interested because you don't like getting up early.

b Say you'll take the job.

c Go and ask about the pay and conditions and then decide if you are going to apply or not.

7 You need to buy a present for your mum soon. What do you do?

a Hope the rest of your family will give you enough money to buy something.

b Start saving money quickly by spending less and hope you have enough to buy something.

c Take out money from the bank that you had already planned to spend on the present.

8 You're going away on holiday with your family in a few weeks and will need some spending money. What do you do?

a Hope your parents give you some.

b Hope you can save a little from what you get each week.

c See if you can find some extra jobs to earn some extra money.

9 You want a new pair of expensive trainers, but your parents say you can only have a less expensive pair. What do you do?

a Keep asking them until they get tired and give you the money.

b Ask a grandparent to lend you some money to make up the difference and arrange to pay them back when you can.

c Consider buying the less expensive trainers – you don't really need the expensive ones.

10 You see some jeans in the sales. They're a real bargain, but you just bought a new pair last week. What do you do?

a Buy three pairs. You can never have too many pairs of jeans!

b Buy one pair because they're such a bargain.

c Don't buy them. You don't need them at the moment and there'll be other sales in the future.

11 You want to buy a new MP3 player. What do you do?

a Go into the nearest shop and buy the first one you see.

b Get one like your friend's because she seemed to pay a reasonable price.

c Check out the prices yourself and see where you can find a bargain.

12 A friend really needs some cash to buy a new jumper she wants. What do you do?

a Tell her it's her problem and you can't help.

b Offer to lend her some money from the money you're saving.

c Discuss ways of helping her to raise the money.

2a Look at your answers. Which do you have most – a, b or c?

2b Look at what the quiz says about you and your attitude to money. Do you agree with it? Why/Why not?

3a LISTENING ▶ 56 Watch the video or listen to four British teenagers talking about how they manage money. Mark the speakers' answers to questions 1 and 2 with a tick or a cross.

	Toby	Rachel	Naomi	Callum
1) Do you get an allowance?				
2) Do you ever borrow money from others?				

3b ▶ 56 Make notes about what each speaker does to make their money go further.

Mostly A
It probably seems to you that you never have any money. That's because you're not very good at managing it! You need to think more carefully before you spend your money and start taking more responsibility for spending it by planning a budget. Also, you tend to rely on your parents to give you money instead of either saving or earning some extra money yourself.

Mostly B
You are beginning to understand how to manage money. You make some sensible decisions, but sometimes you may find yourself without enough money. You need to make sure you always think ahead and save something so that you don't have to depend on others when you want to buy presents or have cash to spend on holidays.

Mostly C
You're careful with your money and already good at managing it. You realise that you need to plan ahead by saving for things. When you haven't got enough money for what you want, you are prepared to do something to try to earn the money yourself. But make sure you keep a balanced attitude towards your money and don't just save it all!

4 ▶ 56 Watch or listen again. Who says these things? There may be more than one answer.

1 I do work outside my house to make some money. *Toby/Rachel/Naomi/Callum*

2 I'd like to be more independent in terms of money. *Toby/Rachel/Naomi/Callum*

3 I prefer not to buy something than to borrow money. *Toby/Rachel/Naomi/Callum*

4 I borrowed money because of an accident at home. *Toby/Rachel/Naomi/Callum*

5 I divide my money so that I don't immediately spend it all. *Toby/Rachel/Naomi/Callum*

6 I save money by comparing different prices for the same product. *Toby/Rachel/Naomi/Callum*

7 I save money by not buying the most expensive designer clothes. *Toby/Rachel/Naomi/Callum*

8 I save money by deciding what my priorities are. *Toby/Rachel/Naomi/Callum*

5 SPEAKING Work with a partner. Which of the speakers are you similar to? In what ways?

LIFE TASK 👤

You are going to make a leaflet or poster which gives advice to teenagers about how to make their money go further. Follow this plan:

1 *Work in a group. Apart from the ideas in 3 and 4, think of other ways that you can save money, spend less, or generally make your money go further.*

2 *Organise your ideas in a logical way and decide how you are going to illustrate your ideas.*

3 *Make your leaflet or poster and display it.*

4 *Look at all the leaflets and posters and discuss what you think are the five best ideas.*

Grammar in context

Listening

1 **SPEAKING** Work with a partner. Describe the photo.

2 **LISTENING** ▶ 57 **Listen to four dialogues. Which one is about somebody who …**

a doesn't like shopping?

b needs help to buy something?

c bought too many things?

d found a bargain for somebody else?

3 ▶ 57 **Listen again and tick (✓) the correct column.**

Who …	A speaker in			
	1	2	3	4
1 has been lying to their friend to avoid going shopping with them?				
2 spent more time and money shopping than they had planned?				
3 thinks they made a mistake by spending less money on a product?				
4 needs somebody else to pay for what they want to buy?				
5 doesn't like going shopping at all?				
6 can't find what they want to buy?				
7 writes down what they need to buy to save money?				
8 has a friend who doesn't mind going shopping with them?				

4 **SPEAKING** **What about you?**

1 Do you prefer shopping alone or with somebody else? Why?

2 If you prefer going with somebody else, who do you like going with?

Grammar in context

I wish and If only

1 **Read the sentences and choose the correct alternative.**

a I wish I **had** enough money to buy it.

b If only my feet **were** smaller!

c I wish I**'d bought** a better one.

d If only I**'d had** my lunch before going to the supermarket.

e I wish you **wouldn't** do that!

1 Sentences a and b use **I wish/if only** + the *present simple/past simple* to talk about *present/past* situations. They express imaginary wishes.

2 Sentences c and d use **I wish/if only** + the *past simple/past perfect* to talk about *present/past* situations that we would like to be different. They express regrets.

3 Sentence e uses **I wish/If only** with the *past simple/would* to talk about habitual behaviour that the speaker *wants/doesn't want* to criticise and change.

GRAMMAR REFERENCE ➤ PAGE 132

2 **Read the situations. Write what you think the people wish was different using the word(s) given.**

1 Joe's office is 10 kilometres away and there is no public transport to get there. (car)
He wishes he had a car.

2 Ryan is short but he wants to be a basketball player. (taller)

3 Layla really loves animals, but her parents won't let her have a pet. (cat)

4 It's a cold winter's day, but Lisa is thinking of the summer holidays. (on a beach)

5 My dad is bald and he doesn't like it. (long hair)

6 This is Connor's first skiing lesson and he keeps falling over. (ski well)

3 **SPEAKING** Work with a partner. Say if you wish these things were true for you or not. Give reasons why.

1 be a millionaire

2 be famous

3 know what people are thinking

4 have X-ray vision

5 speak five languages

I wish I was a millionaire because I'd be able to travel around the world.

4 Complete the regrets with the correct form of the verb given.

1 If only I .... (not tell) him my secrets yesterday.

2 I wish I .... (choose) to study something different last year.

3 I wish I .... (treat) my little sister better when we were younger.

4 If only I .... (study) more for our last exam.

5 I wish I .... (learn) to play the guitar when I was younger.

6 If only I .... (not listen) to my friend yesterday.

7 I wish I .... (not say) that to my friend yesterday.

8 If only I .... (pay) more attention to my last maths teacher.

5 Look at the pictures. What do you think the people are saying? Use *I wish you would/wouldn't*.

1 ....

2 ....

3 ....

6a **SPEAKING** **Work with a partner. What do you think these people and animals wish? You can use *wish/if only + past simple, past perfect* or *would*.**

a

b

c

d   e

6b Read out your ideas. Can other students match them to the correct pictures?

If only I had a friend in here to help pass the time.

I think it's photo d.

Developing speaking

At a clothes shop

1 [SPEAKING] Work with a partner. Describe the photo.

2 [LISTENING] ▶ 58 Listen to a dialogue in a clothes shop. What does the girl buy? What colour and size?

3 Put these lines in order to make a logical conversation.

1 __e__   4 _____   6 _____
2 _____   5 _____   7 _____
3 _____

a I'm looking for **a shirt**. It's for **my brother**.

b No problem. Just remember to bring the receipt.

c What size is he?

d These are new. We've got them in **black** or **grey**.

e Can I help you?

f I like the **black** one. I'll take it. Can I bring it back if it doesn't fit or if he doesn't like it?

g Medium.

4 [SPEAKING] Practise the dialogue in 3 in the correct order. Change the words in bold to make your dialogue different.

5 [LISTENING] ▶ 59 Read and listen to the same customer in the shop a week later. Answer the questions.

1 What is the customer's problem?

2 What does the shop assistant offer her?

3 What does the customer take?

Shop assistant:	Good morning. Can I help you?
Lily:	Yes, I'd like to make a complaint.
Shop assistant:	Oh dear. What seems to be the problem?
Lily:	I bought this hoodie here last week as a present for a friend. It shrank the first time he washed it! It was a large, but now it's more like a small.
Shop assistant:	I'm sorry. We haven't had anybody else with that problem. Are you sure he followed the washing instructions?
Lily:	Yes!
Shop assistant:	I see. Well, we can either replace it for you straight away, or we could give you a refund. Which would you prefer?
Lily:	I'll take the refund.
Shop assistant:	Fine. Have you got the receipt?
Lily:	Yes, here it is.
Shop assistant:	Thank you. £40. There you are. Sorry about that.

6 Look at the expressions in the Speaking bank. Use a dictionary to check any new words. Which expressions can be used for:

1 making a complaint?

2 apologising?

3 offering help?

4 responding to help?

5 asking for information or an opinion?

6 giving information or an opinion?

💬 SPEAKING BANK

Useful expressions in a shop

Shop assistant
- Can I help you?
- What size are you?
- How about this/these?
- What seems to be the problem?
- We can replace it.
- Sorry about that.

Customer
- Yes, I'm looking for …
- No, thanks. I'm just looking.

- Have you got anything in blue/green/medium/large?
- I like it/them
- I'll take this one/these.
- Can I bring it back?
- I'd like to make a complaint.
- It shrank the first time I washed it.
- It's the wrong size.
- It's faulty.
- Can I have a refund?

PRACTICE MAKES PERFECT

7a [SPEAKING] Work with a partner. Prepare a dialogue. Use the expressions in the Speaking bank and the dialogue in 5 to help you.

Imagine that you are in a clothes shop.

Student A: You are a customer. Choose a type of clothing that you bought last week, a problem with it, and the solution you would like.

Student B: You are the shop assistant. Find out what the customer wants and try to keep him/her happy.

7b Practise your dialogue and then act it out for the class.

✔ EXAM SUCCESS

What do you need to do to get a good mark in a speaking exam? Think of good advice.

➤ EXAM SUCCESS page 146

Developing writing

A formal email of complaint

1 Have you ever bought anything that didn't work or was faulty? What happened?

2 READING **Read the email and answer the questions.**

1 What did Oliver buy?
2 What was the problem with it?
3 What did he do?
4 What happened next?
5 What solution does he want?

Dear Sir or Madam,

I am writing to complain about the goods and service in your store.

On 19th August I bought an e-reader at your store in Guildford. When I arrived home, I removed the e-reader from its box and discovered that the screen was broken. As a result, I took it back to the store the following day. However, the shop assistant told me that I could only have a refund if I returned the e-reader in its original box.

The next day I went back again with the e-reader in its original packaging. This time a different shop assistant told me that I could not have a refund because he said I had broken the screen myself. This was not true. In the end, I had to leave the store with the original, faulty e-reader and without my refund.

I will not go back again to the store in Guildford since the shop assistants there are so rude. I demand a full refund for the faulty e-reader. Furthermore, I would like a written apology for the bad treatment I have received. If I do not hear from you in the next two weeks I will take my complaint to a Consumer Advice Centre.

I look forward to hearing from you soon.

Yours faithfully,
Oliver Lucas

---

3 **Put the information in the order that they appear in Oliver's email.**

a Details of the complaint.
b Action to be taken if there is no solution.
c A brief explanation of the reason for writing.
d A demand for a solution.
e Where and when the problem began.

1 .... 2 .... 3 .... 4 .... 5 ....

4 **Read the email again and <u>underline</u> any expressions that you think are useful for an email of complaint.**

5 **Put these words from the email in the correct list in the Writing bank.**

> As a result • Furthermore
> However • In the end • since

WRITING BANK

Useful linkers in formal emails and letters.

- Consequence: *Therefore, and so,*
  (a) ....
- Time and sequence: *Next, Then,*
  (b) ....
- Contrast: *but, although,*
  (c) ....
- Reason: *because, as,*
  (d) ....
- Addition: *In addition, What is more,*
  (e) ....

WRITING BANK ➤ PAGE 150

6 **Complete these sentences in a logical way.**

1 I am very disappointed with your shop. As a result, …
2 The shop assistant was very unhelpful. Furthermore, …
3 I am usually very happy with the service in your store. However, …
4 I would like a full refund since …
5 I went back to the shop three times. In the end, …

PRACTICE MAKES PERFECT

7a **Look at the task, then write your email of complaint. Use the email in 2 and words from the Writing bank to help you.**

In March you ordered two tickets for a concert by your favourite band on the Internet. The tickets were very expensive. The concert was on 1st April, but the tickets only arrived two days later so you couldn't go. You rang the ticket company three times before 1st April, but they promised the tickets would arrive on time. Write a letter of complaint to the manager of the ticket company.

- Explain what the problem is.
- Ask for a solution and explain what you will do if there is no solution.

7b **Give your email to another student. Now write a short reply to the letter you receive.**

Grammar reference

Indeterminate pronouns: some-, any-, no-, every-

FORM

some-	any-	no-	every-
something	anything	nothing	everything
somebody/someone	anybody/anyone	nobody/no-one	everybody/everyone
somewhere	anywhere	nowhere	everywhere

USE

We use -thing for objects, -body and -one for people, and -where for places.

We use pronouns with some- in affirmative sentences and in offers and requests.

Somebody called you an hour ago.

Would you like something to drink?

We use pronouns with any- in negative sentences, questions, and in affirmative sentences when it means it doesn't matter who, what, where.

I haven't got anything to do tomorrow.

Is there anybody in the library?

Anybody can come tonight. You're all invited.

We use pronouns with no- with affirmative verbs because the meaning of the pronoun is already negative.

Nobody called you yesterday.

Is there nothing on the table?

We use pronouns with every- in all types of sentences and in questions.

I've got everything I need.

He's travelled everywhere!

Is everybody here now?

so and such

USE

We use so to intensify the meaning of adjectives and adverbs.

That painting is so beautiful.

They ran so fast.

We use such to intensify the meaning of nouns, with or without adjectives. We use a/an after such when we continue with a singular countable noun, but not with uncountable or plural nouns.

It's such a lovely morning.

It's such a pity.

She paints such beautiful pictures.

This is such fresh air.

After sentences with so or such we can continue the sentence with that.

The music is so loud that I can't concentrate.

I wish and If only

USE

We use I wish/If only + the past to talk about imaginary situations in the present. It expresses wishes for things to be different in the present.

I wish I was on holiday right now.

If only I had a brother or sister.

We use I wish/If only + the past perfect to talk about past situations that we regret or would like to be different.

I wish I had listened to the teacher last year.

If only I hadn't told her my secret.

We use I wish/If only with would/wouldn't + infinitive to talk about somebody's habitual behaviour that we want to criticise and change.

My sister takes my clothes. I wish she wouldn't do it.

I wish you would arrive on time.

Vocabulary

Shops bakery • bookshop • butcher's • chemist's • clothes shop • department store • electrical goods shop • greengrocer's • jeweller's • newsagent's • post office • shoe shop • sports shop • stationery shop • supermarket

Shopping afford • bargain • cash • cashier • changing room • checkout • debit card • discount • queue • receipt • refund • trolley

Collocations with *money* borrow • donate • earn • lend • make • owe • raise • save • spend • waste • win

Other words and phrases ➤ page 143

Grammar revision

1 Complete these sentences with the correct indeterminate pronoun.

1 I haven't got .... in my pocket.

2 Homeless people haven't got .... to go at night.

3 She's got .... important to tell you.

4 Can you come to the phone, Sam? .... wants to talk to you.

5 .... needs to drink water to survive.

6 I can hear people talking, but there isn't .... there.

---

so and such / 8 points

2 Rewrite the *so* sentences with *such* and vice-versa.

1 This country is so big. ....

2 They're such good students. ....

3 The exam was so difficult. ....

4 The weather was so bad that we stayed in. ....

5 It was such a loud film that my ears hurt. ....

6 I've got such a bad headache. ....

7 That road is so dangerous. ....

8 The experience was so painful. ....

I wish and If only / 6 points

3 Choose the correct alternative.

1 I wish I *have/had* a pen with me now.

2 If only you *had/would* pay more attention in class.

3 If only I *understood/had understood* what you're saying.

4 I wish I *met/had met* you last year.

5 I wish you *would stop/had stopped* interrupting me when I'm talking.

6 If only I *didn't fail/hadn't failed* my driving test last week.

Vocabulary revision

SHOPS / 6 points

1 In which shops can you buy these things?

1 meat: b ....' ...

2 fruit and vegetables: g ....' ...

3 MP3 players, vacuum cleaners, dishwashers: e .... g .... s ....

4 almost anything, not just food: d .... s ....

5 paper and pens: s .... s ....

6 bread and cakes: b ....

SHOPPING / 8 points

2 Complete the sentences with words connected to shopping.

1 I haven't got a debit card. I'll have to pay by ....

2 You pay by giving the money to the ....

3 Mum's in the .... waiting to pay.

4 I can't .... that tablet. It's too expensive for me.

5 That shirt was a real .... – £20 instead of £60!

6 I have a .... which proves that I bought the DVD here.

7 Where are the ....? I'd like to try this dress on.

8 This week we have 10% .... on jeans. Yes, they're all 10% cheaper than usual!

COLLOCATIONS WITH *MONEY* / 6 points

3 Are these sentences correct or not? If not, change the word in italics.

When you …

1 *lend* money, you get money, but then you have to give it back.

2 *win* money, you do professional work.

3 *donate* money, you give it to a charity or an organisation.

4 *save* money, you use it to buy things you don't need.

5 *make* money, you get money by working, selling things, or making investments.

6 *spend* money, you give it to somebody, but then they have to give it back to you.

Reading

1 **Work with a partner. Look at these Frequently Asked Questions (FAQs) from a website. Can you answer any of them?**

1 What is the Commonwealth?
2 How does the Commonwealth work?
3 Which countries are in the Commonwealth?
4 What are the Commonwealth Games?

2 **Read the text to check your answers. Match the questions to the paragraphs.**

A ....

There is no fixed constitution for the Commonwealth. There are some basic principles, for example the use of the English language, democracy and human rights. The King or Queen of England is the head of the Commonwealth, but the monarch is a symbol. They have no power to tell countries what to do. The heads of government of the Commonwealth countries meet once every two years to discuss matters of common interest. If a country stops being democratic, it has to leave the Commonwealth. This is why the Commonwealth often sends observers to different countries, to check that their elections are fair and democratic.

B ....

It is a group of 53 countries. Almost all of the countries were once part of the British Empire. Queen Victoria (1819–1901) was once in charge of the biggest empire in the world. It covered a quarter of the world's land mass and a quarter of the world's population. Today Britain is just another member of the Commonwealth, with no special powers or extra responsibilities. The main office for the Commonwealth is in London, but the people who work there are from all over the Commonwealth.

C ....

Generally they are former British colonies which later became independent countries. They include the United Kingdom, Australia, Canada, New Zealand, India, Jamaica, Pakistan, Bangladesh, and Malaysia. At the moment three members are in Europe, twelve in North America, one in South America, eighteen in Africa, eight in Asia, and eleven in Oceania. Nearly one third of the world's population lives in Commonwealth countries.

D ....

They began in 1930 and the idea was to be similar to the Olympic Games. There is a spirit of unity and friendship at these games, and their unofficial name is 'the friendly games'. They happen every four years, the same as the Olympics. There are between ten and 20 sports in the Commonwealth Games. Another interesting difference between the Olympics and the Commonwealth Games is that at the Olympics the United Kingdom has just one team, but for the Commonwealth Games there is an English team, a Scottish team, a Welsh team and a Northern Irish team.

3 **Read the text again and choose the best answers.**

1 The King or Queen of England ...
   a decides what happens in Commonwealth countries.
   b does not take decisions in Commonwealth countries.
   c is just one of the heads of the Commonwealth.

2 The Commonwealth heads of state ...
   a meet twice a year.
   b meet to discuss human rights.
   c don't meet every year.

3 Today the population of the Commonwealth ...
   a is 25% of the world's population.
   b is more than a quarter of the world's population.
   c lives in an area that covers a third of the world's land mass.

4 In the Commonwealth Games ...
   a there are more different sports than in the Olympic Games.
   b the competitions are friendly but not official.
   c there is no team called 'United Kingdom'.

Speaking

4 **Work with a partner.**

Student A: Look at the photo on page 147.
Student B: Look at the photo on page 148. Spend three minutes preparing to talk about it.

5 SPEAKING **Work with a partner. Take it in turns to talk about your photo.**

- Say what you can see. Make speculations about where it is, who the people are, what they are doing, etc.
- Have you ever been in a situation like the one in the photo? If so, what happened? If not, would you like to be? Why/Why not?

Listening

> **TIP FOR LISTENING EXAMS**

In listening activities where you complete notes, remember …
Check how many words or numbers you can write in each space. Write the actual words you hear and be careful with spelling.

➤ EXAM SUCCESS page 146

6 **LISTENING** ▶ **60 Listen to a history programme on the radio and answer the questions.**

1 What was the SS Empire Windrush?

2 Why was it so important in modern British history?

7 ▶ **60 Listen again and complete the notes with one or two words or numbers.**

Notepad ✎

SS Empire Windrush sailed
from **(a)** .... to
(b) .... It carried
(c) .... men and
women. Most of these people wanted to
(d) .... in Britain. The biggest
surprise at first was **(e)** ....
In the 1950s and 1960s many people came
to Britain from **(f)** .... ,
particularly **(g)** .... ,
Pakistan and Bangladesh. Approximately
(h) .... of the British population
are from different ethnic backgrounds. They have
brought their customs, **(i)** .... ,
clothes and **(j)** ....

Use of English

> **TIP FOR USE OF ENGLISH**

In word formation cloze activities, remember …
Look at the words just before and after the gap and make sure you understand the whole sentence. To change the **type** of word you will usually need a **suffix** (e.g. *-ion* to make a noun, *-ly* to make an adverb). To change the **meaning** of the word you will usually need a **prefix** (e.g. *im-*, *re-*).

➤ EXAM SUCCESS page 146

8 **Complete the text with the correct form of the word in capitals.**

When he was young, my brother always
wanted to have a **(a)** ....
job, like being an explorer. Then, when he
was older he was **(b)** .... in
becoming a professional **(c)** ....
because he loved reading about the past.
But now that he's started working, he doesn't
think his job is very **(d)** ....
He's an **(e)** .... at a local
department store where he has to work
long hours. It's a **(f)** .... job
and he doesn't earn much. Sometimes he
works in **(g)** .... conditions,
for example standing for hours and hours
in the same position. But my brother is very
(h) .... and kind to the customers
and he **(i)** .... with his boss so
they have promised him promotion. The store
he works for is part of a big **(j)** ....
group so he might be able to work abroad.
My brother studies English in the evenings
and he wants to get some type of
(k) .... certificate in English. So
he's **(l)** .... about the idea of going
to an English-speaking country. My brother
is clever and ambitious. It wouldn't be so
(m) .... if one day he became the
(n) .... of the company!

DANGER

INTEREST
HISTORY

INSPIRE
EMPLOY

TIRE

COMFORT

HELP
OPERATE

NATION

OFFICE
EXCITE

SURPRISE
DIRECT

'CAN DO' PROGRESS CHECK UNITS 9–10 · CEF

1 How well can you do these things in English now? Give yourself a mark from 1 to 4.

| **1** = I can do it very well. | **2** = I can do it quite well. | **3** = I have some problems. | **4** = I can't do it. |

a I can make speculations and deductions in the present and past using modal verbs. ☐

b I can talk about imaginary situations in the past and their consequences using the third conditional. ☐

c I can make adjectives by adding suffixes. ☐

d I can describe photos and make speculations and deductions about them. ☐

e I can write a story using narrative tenses. ☐

f I can use indeterminate pronouns (*some-*, *any-*, *every-*, *no-*) correctly. ☐

g I can talk about wishes using *I wish* and *If only*. ☐

h I can understand written and spoken texts about shopping and money. ☐

i I can ask for things and explain problems in a clothes shop. ☐

j I can write a formal letter of complaint. ☐

2 Now decide what you need to do next to improve.

1 Look again at my book/notes.

2 Do more practice exercises. ➤ WORKBOOK Units 9 and 10

3 Ask for help.

4 Other: ....

(adj) = adjective
(adv) = adverb
(conj) = conjuction
(det) = determiner
(n/n pl) = noun/noun plural
(phr) = phrase
(prep) = preposition
(pron) = pronoun
(v) = verb

The most common and useful words in English are marked according to the Macmillan Dictionary 'star rating'. This is so you can easily recognise the vocabulary you need to know especially well.

★★★ = very common words ★★ = common words ★ = fairly common words

If there is no star next to the word, this means that it is not very common.
In the Macmillan Dictionary, (r) is used to indicate where the sound /r/ is pronounced in American English and some other regional varieties of English. In a standard British accent, (r) is only pronounced if it occurs at the end of a word which is followed by another word starting with a vowel sound, for example *far away* /fɑːr əˈweɪ/.

Unit 1

Appearance

attractive (adj) ★★★ /əˈtræktɪv/
bald (adj) ★ /bɔːld/
blonde (adj) ★ /blɒnd/
curly (adj) ★ /ˈkɜː(r)li/
cute (adj) /kjuːt/
dark (adj) ★★★ /dɑː(r)k/
fair (adj) ★★★ /feə(r)/
good-looking (adj) ★★ /ˌɡʊd ˈlʊkɪŋ/
long (adj) ★★★ /lɒŋ/
medium-height (adj) /ˌmiːdiəm ˈhaɪt/
medium-length (adj) /ˌmiːdiəm ˈleŋθ/
overweight (adj) /ˌəʊvə(r)ˈweɪt/
pretty (adj) ★★★ /ˈprɪti/
short (adj) ★★★ /ʃɔː(r)t/
spiky (adj) /ˈspaɪki/
straight (adj) ★★★ /streɪt/
strong (adj) ★★★ /strɒŋ/
tall (adj) ★★★ /tɔːl/
thin (adj) ★★★ /θɪn/
wavy (adj) /ˈweɪvi/
well-built (adj) /ˌwel ˈbɪlt/

Personality

arrogant (adj) ★ /ˈærəɡənt/
bossy (adj) /ˈbɒsi/
calm (adj) ★★ /kɑːm/
cheerful (adj) ★ /ˈtʃɪə(r)f(ə)l/
clever (adj) ★★ /ˈklevə(r)/
confident (adj) ★★ /ˈkɒnfɪd(ə)nt/
friendly (adj) ★★★ /ˈfren(d)li/
funny (adj) ★★★ /ˈfʌni/
hard-working (adj) ★ /ˌhɑː(r)d ˈwɜː(r)kɪŋ/
impatient (adj) ★ /ɪmˈpeɪʃ(ə)nt/
lazy (adj) ★★ /ˈleɪzi/
nervous (adj) ★★ /ˈnɜː(r)vəs/
nice (adj) ★★★ /naɪs/
patient (adj) ★★★ /ˈpeɪʃ(ə)nt/
quiet (adj) ★★★ /ˈkwaɪət/

reliable (adj) ★★ /rɪˈlaɪəb(ə)l/
selfish (adj) ★ /ˈselfɪʃ/
serious (adj) ★★★ /ˈsɪəriəs/
shy (adj) ★ /ʃaɪ/
talkative (adj) /ˈtɔːkətɪv/
tidy (adj) ★ /ˈtaɪdi/
unfriendly (adj) ★ /ʌnˈfren(d)li/
untidy (adj) ★ /ʌnˈtaɪdi/

Synonyms and partial synonyms

beautiful (adj) ★★★ /ˈbjuːtəf(ə)l/
bright (adj) ★★★ /braɪt/
difficult (adj) ★★★ /ˈdɪfɪk(ə)lt/
elderly (adj) ★★★ /ˈeldə(r)li/
glad (adj) ★★★ /ɡlæd/
happy (adj) ★★★ /ˈhæpi/
handsome (adj) ★★ /ˈhæns(ə)m/
hard (adj) ★★★ /hɑː(r)d/
intelligent (adj) ★★ /ɪnˈtelɪdʒ(ə)nt/
old (adj) ★★★ /əʊld/
outgoing (adj) /ˈaʊtɡəʊɪŋ/
slim (adj) ★★ /slɪm/
sociable (adj) /ˈsəʊʃəb(ə)l/

Other words and phrases

ability (n) ★★★ /əˈbɪləti/
achievement (n) ★★★ /əˈtʃiːvmənt/
active (adj) ★★★ /ˈæktɪv/
apparently (adv) ★★★ /əˈpærəntli/
attempt (n) ★★★ /əˈtempt/
capable (adj) ★★★ /ˈkeɪpəb(ə)l/
celebrate (v) ★★★ /ˈseləˌbreɪt/
champion (n) ★★★ /ˈtʃæmpiən/
characteristic (n) ★★ /ˌkærɪktəˈrɪstɪk/
coast (n) ★★★ /kəʊst/
competitive (adj) ★★ /kəmˈpetətɪv/
contribution (n) ★★★ /ˌkɒntrɪˈbjuːʃ(ə)n/
control (v) ★★★ /kənˈtrəʊl/
detail (n) ★★★ /ˈdiːteɪl/
exist (v) ★★★ /ɪɡˈzɪst/
genius (n) ★ /ˈdʒiːniəs/
goal (n) ★★★ /ɡəʊl/

gradually (adv) ★★★ /ˈɡrædʒuəli/
human (n) ★★★ /ˈhjuːmən/
interrupt (v) ★★ /ˌɪntəˈrʌpt/
justify (v) ★★ /ˈdʒʌstɪfaɪ/
lung (n) ★★ /lʌŋ/
main (adj) ★★★ /meɪn/
mind (n) ★★★ /maɪnd/
natural (adj) ★★★ /ˈnætʃ(ə)rəl/
objective (n) ★★★ /əbˈdʒektɪv/
oxygen (n) ★★ /ˈɒksɪdʒ(ə)n/
particularly (adv) ★★★ /pə(r)ˈtɪkjʊlə(r)li/
positively (adv) ★★ /ˈpɒzətɪvli/
progress (n) ★★★ /ˈprəʊɡres/
proud (of) (adj) ★★ /praʊd (ɒv)/
prove (v) ★★★ /pruːv/
reduce (v) ★★★ /rɪˈdjuːs/
solution (n) ★★★ /səˈluːʃ(ə)n/
strategy (n) ★★★ /ˈstrætədʒi/
talent (n) ★★ /ˈtælənt/
theory (n) ★★★ /ˈθɪəri/
train (v) ★★★ /treɪn/
valuable (adj) ★★★ /ˈvæljʊb(ə)l/
victory (n) ★★★ /ˈvɪkt(ə)ri/

Unit 2

Transport and travel

bike (n) ★★ /baɪk/
arrivals (n) /əˈraɪv(ə)lz/
cancel (v) /ˈkæns(ə)l/
catch (v) ★★★ /kætʃ/
coach (n) ★★ /kəʊtʃ/
delay (n) ★★ /dɪˈleɪ/
departures (n) /dɪˈpɑː(r)tʃə(r)z/
fare (n) ★★ /feə(r)/
ferry (n) ★ /ˈferi/
hot-air balloon (n) /hɒt ˌeə(r) bəˈluːn/
lorry (n) ★★ /ˈlɒri/
luggage (n) ★ /ˈlʌɡɪdʒ/
miss (v) ★★★ /mɪs/
motorbike (n) ★ /ˈməʊtə(r)ˌbaɪk/
platform (n) ★★ /ˈplætˌfɔː(r)m/

return (n) ★★★ /rɪˈtɜː(r)n/
rocket (n) ★ /ˈrɒkɪt/
single (n) ★★★ /ˈsɪŋɡ(ə)l/
spaceship (n) /ˈspeɪsˌʃɪp/
subway (n) /ˈsʌbˌweɪ/
tram (n) /træm/
ticket office (n) /ˈtɪkɪt ˌɒfɪs/
van (n) ★★ /væn/
yacht (n) ★ /jɒt/
underground (n) ★ /ˈʌndə(r)ˌɡraʊnd/

Accommodation

bed and breakfast (n) /ˌbed ən(d) ˈbrekfəst/
campsite (n) /ˈkæmpˌsaɪt/
caravan (n) /ˈkærəvæn/
hostel (n) /ˈhɒst(ə)l/
hotel (n) ★★★ /həʊˈtel/
motel (n) /məʊˈtel/
tent (n) ★★ /tent/

Phrasal verbs connected with travel

break down (v phr) /ˌbreɪk ˈdaʊn/
check in (v phr) /ˌtʃek ˈɪn/
get away (v phr) /ˌɡet əˈweɪ/
get into (v phr) /ˌɡet ˈɪntuː/
get off (v phr) /ˌɡet ˈɒf/
get on (v phr) /ˌɡet ˈɒn/
get out of (v phr) /ˌɡet ˈaʊt ɒv/
set off (v phr) /ˌset ˈɒf/
take off (v phr) /ˌteɪk ˈɒf/

Other words and phrases

acceptable (adj) ★★ /əkˈseptəb(ə)l/
alternative (n) ★★★ /ɔːlˈtɜː(r)nətɪv/
announcement (n) ★★★ /əˈnaʊnsmənt/
approximately (adv) ★★ /əˈprɒksɪmətli/
capital (n) ★★★ /ˈkæpɪt(ə)l/
carbon footprint (n) /ˌkɑː(r)bən ˈfʊtprɪnt/
collect (v) ★★★ /kəˈlekt/
conductor (n) ★ /kənˈdʌktə(r)/
conserve (v) /kənˈsɜː(r)v/
consume (v) ★★ /kənˈsjuːm/
contaminate (v) /kənˈtæmɪneɪt/
continually (adv) /kənˈtɪnjʊəli/
culture (n) ★★★ /ˈkʌltʃə(r)/
damage (v) ★★★ /ˈdæmɪdʒ/
destination (n) ★★ /ˌdestɪˈneɪʃ(ə)n/
energy (n) ★★★ /ˈenə(r)dʒi/
energy efficient (adj) /ˌenə(r)dʒi ɪˈfɪʃ(ə)nt/

exactly (adv) ★★★ /ɪɡˈzæk(t)li/
expedition (n) ★★ /ˌekspəˈdɪʃ(ə)n/
feed (v) ★★★ /fiːd/
foreign (adj) ★★★ /ˈfɒrɪn/
fragile (adj) ★ /ˈfrædʒaɪl/
harm (v) ★★ /hɑː(r)m/
historical (adj) ★★★ /hɪˈstɒrɪk(ə)l/
hole (n) ★★★ /həʊl/
honestly (adv) ★★ /ˈɒnɪs(t)li/
impact (n) ★★★ /ˈɪmpækt/
indoor (adj) ★ /ˈɪndɔː(r)/
inspiration (n) ★★ /ˌɪnspəˈreɪʃ(ə)n/
journey (n) ★★★ /ˈdʒɜː(r)ni/
label (n) ★★ /ˈleɪb(ə)l/
law (n) ★★★ /lɔː/
limit (v) ★★★ /ˈlɪmɪt/
local (adj) ★★★ /ˈləʊk(ə)l/
marine (adj) ★ /məˈriːn/
meal (n) ★★★ /miːl/
object (n) ★★★ /ˈɒbdʒekt/
order (v) ★★★ /ˈɔː(r)də(r)/
organic (adj) ★ /ɔː(r)ˈɡænɪk/
original (adj) ★★★ /əˈrɪdʒ(ə)nəl/
path (n) ★★★ /pɑːθ/
pick (v) ★★★ /pɪk/
principal (n) ★★★ /ˈprɪnsəp(ə)l/
recycling bin (n) /riːˈsaɪklɪŋ ˌbɪn/
reservation (n) ★★ /ˌrezə(r)ˈveɪʃ(ə)n/
responsible (adj) ★★★ /rɪˈspɒnsəb(ə)l/
ritual (n) ★★ /ˈrɪtʃuəl/
rock (n) ★★★ /rɒk/
route (n) ★★★ /ruːt/
sail (v) ★★ /seɪl/
sailor (n) ★ /ˈseɪlə(r)/
sensitive (adj) ★★★ /ˈsensətɪv/
spectacular (adj) ★★ /spekˈtækjʊlə(r)/
standard class (n) /ˈstændə(r)d ˌklɑːs/
station (n) ★★★ /ˈsteɪʃ(ə)n/
stone (n) ★★★ /stəʊn/
timetable (n) ★★ /ˈtaɪmˌteɪb(ə)l/
tourist (n) ★★★ /ˈtʊərɪst/
towel (n) ★★ /ˈtaʊəl/
upstairs (n) ★★ /ʌpˈsteə(r)z/
vacancy (n) ★ /ˈveɪkənsi/

Gateway to exams: Units 1-2

adventure (n) ★★ /ədˈventʃə(r)/
basic (adj) ★★★ /ˈbeɪsɪk/
command (v) ★★★ /kəˈmɑːnd/
companion (n) ★★ /kəmˈpænjən/
east (adj) ★★★ /iːst/

hill (n) ★★★ /hɪl/
ideal (adj) ★★★ /aɪˈdɪəl/
introductory (adj) /ˌɪntrəˈdʌkt(ə)ri/
lifelong (adj) /ˈlaɪfˌlɒŋ/
luxury (n) ★ /ˈlʌkʃəri/
memory (n) ★★★ /ˈmem(ə)ri/
prehistoric (adj) /ˌpriːhɪˈstɒrɪk/
rapid (adj) ★★★ /ˈræpɪd/
resolve (v) ★ /rɪˈzɒlv/
ruin (v) ★★ /ˈruːɪn/
scuba diving (n) /ˈskuːbə ˌdaɪvɪŋ/
sense (n) ★★★ /sens/
similarity (n) ★★ /ˌsɪməˈlærəti/
south (adj) ★★★ /saʊθ/
space (n) ★★★ /speɪs/
strict (adj) ★★ /strɪkt/
tremendous (adj) ★★ /trəˈmendəs/
trip (n) ★★★ /trɪp/
unplanned (adj) /ʌnˈplænd/
west (adj) ★★★ /west/

Unit 3

Cities and houses

block of flats (n) /ˌblɒk əv ˈflæts/
bungalow (n) ★ /ˈbʌŋɡəˌləʊ/
city centre (n) /ˌsɪti ˈsentə(r)/
cottage (n) ★★ /ˈkɒtɪdʒ/
detached house (n) /dɪˌtætʃt ˈhaʊs/
factory (n) ★★★ /ˈfæktri/
flat (n) ★★★ /flæt/
inner city (n) /ˌɪnə(r) ˈsɪti/
port (n) ★★★ /pɔː(r)t/
outskirts (n) /ˈaʊtˌskɜː(r)ts/
semi-detached house (n) /ˌsemiˌdɪˌtætʃt ˈhaʊs/
skyscraper (n) /ˈskaɪˌskreɪpə(r)/
square (n) ★★★ /skweə(r)/
suburbs (n) /ˈsʌbɜː(r)bs/
terraced house (n) /ˌterəst ˈhaʊs/
town hall (n) /ˌtaʊn ˈhɔːl/

Adjectives describing cities

busy (adj) ★★★ /ˈbɪzi/
clean (adj) ★★★ /kliːn/
crowded (adj) ★ /ˈkraʊdɪd/
dirty (adj) ★★ /ˈdɜː(r)ti/
historic (adj) ★★ /hɪˈstɒrɪk/
lively (adj) ★★ /ˈlaɪvli/
modern (adj) ★★★ /ˈmɒdə(r)n/
noisy (adj) ★ /ˈnɔɪzi/
quiet (adj) ★★★ /ˈkwaɪət/

Extreme adjectives

ancient (adj) ★★★ /'eɪnʃ(ə)nt/
boiling (adj) ★ /'bɔɪlɪŋ/
dreadful (adj) ★★ /'dredf(ə)l/
enormous (adj) ★★★ /ɪ'nɔː(r)məs/
filthy (adj) ★ /'fɪlθi/
freezing (adj) ★ /'friːzɪŋ/
packed (adj) ★ /pækt/
silent (adj) ★★★ /'saɪlənt/
stunning (adj) ★ /'stʌnɪŋ/
tiny (adj) ★★★ /'taɪni/

Other words and phrases

absolutely (adv) ★★★ /'æbsəluːtli/
accommodate (v) ★ /ə'kɒmədeɪt/
according to (phr) /ə'kɔː(r)dɪŋ tuː/
appear (v) ★★★ /ə'pɪə(r)/
architect (n) ★★★ /'ɑː(r)kɪ,tekt/
average (n) ★★★ /'æv(ə)rɪdʒ/
build (v) ★★★ /bɪld/
calculate (v) ★★ /'kælkjʊleɪt/
canal (n) ★★ /kə'næl/
central (adj) ★★★ /'sentrəl/
completely (adv) ★★★ /kəm'pliːtli/
conditions (n pl) /kən'dɪʃ(ə)nz/
consequence (n) ★★★ /'kɒnsɪkwəns/
decrease (v) ★★ /diː'kriːs/
demonstration (n) ★★
  /,demən'streɪʃ(ə)n/
dramatically (adv) /drə'mætɪkli/
electricity (n) ★★★ /ɪ,lek'trɪsəti/
entire (adj) ★★★ /ɪn'taɪə(r)/
exhibition (n) ★★★ /,eksɪ'bɪʃ(ə)n/
expert (n) ★★★ /'ekspɜː(r)t/
extremely (adv) ★★★ /ɪk'striːmli/
fall (v) ★★★ /fɔːl/
frequent (adj) ★★ /'friːkwənt/
green (adj) ★★★ /griːn/
grow (v) ★★★ /grəʊ/
growth (n) ★★★ /grəʊθ/
half (n) ★★★ /hɑːf/
iconic (adj) /aɪ'kɒnɪk/
increase (v/n) ★★★ /ɪn'kriːs/
inhabitant (n) ★★ /ɪn'hæbɪtənt/
invade (v) ★ /ɪn'veɪd/
lift (n) ★★★ /lɪft/
majority (n) ★★★ /mə'dʒɒrəti/
medicine (n) ★★ /'med(ə)s(ə)n/
megacity (n) /'megə,sɪti/
nearby (adv) ★★ /,nɪə(r)'baɪ/
obvious (adj) ★★★ /'ɒbviəs/
per cent (n) ★★★ /pə(r)'sent/

planet (n) ★★ /'plænɪt/
population (n) ★★★ /,pɒpjʊ'leɪʃ(ə)n/
predict (v) ★★★ /prɪ'dɪkt/
private (adj) ★★★ /'praɪvət/
quarter (n) ★★★ /'kwɔː(r)tə(r)/
rainwater (n) /'reɪn,wɔːtə(r)/
recently (adv) ★★★ /'riːs(ə)ntli/
renewable energy (n) /rɪ,njuːəb(ə)l
  'enə(r)dʒi/
residential (adj) ★★ /,rezɪ'denʃ(ə)l/
rise (v) ★★★ /raɪz/
show (n) ★★★ /ʃəʊ/
situation (n) ★★★ /,sɪtʃu'eɪʃ(ə)n/
slightly (adv) ★★★ /'slaɪtli/
social media (n) ★ /,səʊʃəl 'miːdiə/
social networking (n) /,səʊʃəl
  'netwɜː(r)kɪŋ/
solar power (n) /,səʊlə(r) 'paʊə(r)/
statistic (n) /stə'tɪstɪk/
steadily (adv) /'stedəli/
support (v) ★★★ /sə'pɔː(r)t/
table (n) ★★★ /'teɪb(ə)l/
totally (adv) ★★★ /'təʊt(ə)li/
transformation (n) ★★
  /,trænsfə(r)'meɪʃ(ə)n/
urgent (adj) /'ɜː(r)dʒ(ə)nt/

Unit 4

Food and meals

carrot (n) ★ /'kærət/
chicken (n) ★★ /'tʃɪkɪn/
cream (n) ★★ /kriːm/
dessert (n) ★ /dɪ'zɜː(r)t/
dish (n) ★★ /dɪʃ/
lamb (n) ★★ /læm/
lettuce (n) ★ /'letɪs/
main course (n) /'meɪn ,kɔː(r)s/
oil (n) ★★★ /ɔɪl/
olive (n) /'ɒlɪv/
pancake (n) /'pæn,keɪk/
pea (n) ★ /piː/
peach (n) ★ /piːtʃ/
pie (n) ★ /paɪ/
plum (n) ★ /plʌm/
rice (n) ★★ /raɪs/
snack (n) ★ /snæk/
starter (n) ★ /'stɑː(r)tə(r)/
sweetcorn (n) /'swiːt,kɔː(r)n/
tuna (n) /'tjuːnə/
turkey (n) ★ /'tɜː(r)ki/

Describing food

baked (adj) /beɪkt/
boiled (adj) /bɔɪld/
fast (adj) ★★★ /fɑːst/
fresh (adj) ★★★ /freʃ/
fried (adj) ★★ /fraɪd/
frozen (adj) ★ /'frəʊz(ə)n/
healthy ★★★ /'helθi/
unhealthy (adj) /ʌn'helθi/
raw (adj) ★★ /rɔː/
roast (adj) /rəʊst/
spicy (adj) /'spaɪsi/
stale (adj) ★ /steɪl/
tasty (adj) ★ /'teɪsti/

Prefixes

cooperate (v) ★ /kəʊ'ɒpəreɪt/
disadvantage (n) ★★ /,dɪsəd'vɑːntɪdʒ/
international (adj) ★★★
  /,ɪntə(r)'næʃ(ə)nəl/
misunderstood (adj)
  /,mɪsʌndə(r)'stʊd/
overbooked (adj) /,əʊvə(r)'bʊkt/
overcooked (adj) /,əʊvə(r)'kʊkt/
precooked (adj) /,priː'kʊkt/
recooked (adj) /,riː'kʊkt/
redo (v) /,riː'duː/
undercooked (adj) /,ʌndə(r)'kʊkt/
underestimate (v) ★ /,ʌndər'estɪ,meɪt/

Other words and phrases

agriculture (n) ★★ /'ægrɪ,kʌltʃə(r)/
attend (v) ★★★ /ə'tend/
attitude (n) ★★★ /'ætɪ,tjuːd/
bacteria (n) ★★ /bæk'tɪəriə/
blogger (n) /'blɒgə(r)/
burn (v) ★★★ /bɜː(r)n/
carbohydrate (n) /,kɑː(r)bəʊ'haɪdreɪt/
contain (v) ★★★ /kən'teɪn/
crisis (n) ★★★ /'kraɪsɪs/
critic (n) ★★★ /'krɪtɪk/
cure (n) ★★ /kjʊə(r)/
detailed (adj) ★★★ /'diːteɪld/
developing country (n) /dɪ,veləpɪŋ
  'kʌntri/
diet (n) ★★★ /'daɪət/
drop (v) ★★★ /drɒp/
entertainment (n) ★★
  /,entə(r)'teɪnmənt/
essential (adj) ★★★ /ɪ'senʃ(ə)l/
event (n) ★★★ /ɪ'vent/
flavour (n) ★★ /'fleɪvə(r)/
genetically-modified (adj) /dʒə,netɪkli
  'mɒdɪfaɪd/

global warming (n) ★ /ˌgləʊb(ə)l ˈwɔː(r)mɪŋ/

hygiene (n) ★ /ˈhaɪdʒiːn/

ingredient (n) ★★ /ɪnˈɡriːdiənt/

invent (v) ★★ /ɪnˈvent/

invisible (adj) ★★ /ɪnˈvɪzəb(ə)l/

laboratory (n) ★★ /ləˈbɒrət(ə)ri/

mineral (n) ★ /ˈmɪn(ə)rəl/

mixture (n) ★★★ /ˈmɪkstʃə(r)/

nutrient (n) /ˈnjuːtriənt/

nutrition (n) ★ /njuːˈtrɪʃ(ə)n/

powder (n) ★★ /ˈpaʊdə(r)/

pre-packaged (adj) /ˌpriː ˈpækɪdʒd/

prepare (v) ★★★ /prɪˈpeə(r)/

preserve (v) ★★★ /prɪˈzɜː(r)v/

processed (adj) /ˈprəʊsest/

protein (n) ★★ /ˈprəʊtiːn/

quality (adj) ★★★ /ˈkwɒləti/

quantity (n) ★★ /ˈkwɒntəti/

slippery (adj) /ˈslɪpəri/

soft drink (n) /ˌsɒft ˈdrɪŋk/

vitamin (n) ★★ /ˈvɪtəmɪn/

waste (v) ★★★ /weɪst/

weight (n) ★★★ /weɪt/

worldwide (adj) ★ /ˌwɜː(r)ldˈwaɪd/

Gateway to exams: Units 3–4

Earth (n) ★★★ /ɜː(r)θ/

fog (n) ★ /fɒg/

freezing (adj) ★ /ˈfriːzɪŋ/

genetic engineering (n) /dʒəˌnetɪk endʒɪˈnɪərɪŋ/

indoors (adv) ★ /ɪnˈdɔː(r)z/

mosquito (n) /mɒˈskiːtəʊ/

organism (n) ★★ /ˈɔː(r)ɡəˌnɪz(ə)m/

outdoors (adv) /ˌaʊtˈdɔː(r)z/

painful (adj) ★★ /ˈpeɪnf(ə)l/

penetrate (v) ★★ /ˈpenəˌtreɪt/

remote (adj) ★★ /rɪˈməʊt/

resident (n) ★★★ /ˈrezɪd(ə)nt/

suggest (v) ★★★ /səˈdʒest/

underwear (n) ★ /ˈʌndə(r)ˌweə(r)/

Unit 5

School and university subjects

architecture (n) ★★ /ˈɑː(r)kɪˌtektʃə(r)/

art (n) ★★★ /ɑː(r)t/

biology (n) ★ /baɪˈɒlədʒi/

business studies (n) /ˈbɪznəs ˌstʌdis/

chemistry (n) ★★ /ˈkemɪstri/

computer science (n) /kəmˌpjuːtə(r) ˈsaɪəns/

drama (n) ★★★ /ˈdrɑːmə/

engineering (n) ★★★ /ˌendʒɪˈnɪərɪŋ/

English (n) /ˈɪŋɡlɪʃ/

geography (n) ★★ /dʒiːˈɒɡrəfi/

history (n) ★★★ /ˈhɪst(ə)ri/

literature (n) ★★★ /ˈlɪtrətʃə(r)/

maths (n) ★ /mæθs/

media studies (n) /ˈmiːdiə ˌstʌdiz/

medicine (n) ★★ /ˈmed(ə)s(ə)n/

music (n) ★★★ /ˈmjuːzɪk/

PE (physical education) (n) /ˌpiː ˈiː/

physics (n) ★★ /ˈfɪzɪks/

psychology (n) ★★ /saɪˈkɒlədʒi/

Words connected with studying

assessment (n) ★★ /əˈsesmənt/

assignment (n) ★★ /əˈsaɪnmənt/

coursework (n) /ˈkɔː(r)s,wɜː(r)k/

essay (n) ★★ /ˈeseɪ/

fail (n) ★★★ /feɪl/

grade (n) ★★ /ɡreɪd/

mark (n) ★★★ /mɑː(r)k/

resit (v) /ˌriːˈsɪt/

scholarship (n) ★ /ˈskɒlə(r)ʃɪp/

term (n) ★★★ /tɜː(r)m/

timetable (n) ★★ /ˈtaɪmˌteɪb(ə)l/

Noun suffixes

electrician (n) /ɪˌlekˈtrɪʃ(ə)n/

employee (n) ★★★ /ɪmˈplɔɪiː/

employer ★★★ /ɪmˈplɔɪə(r)/

farmer (n) ★★★ /ˈfɑː(r)mə(r)/

instructor (n) /ɪnˈstrʌktə(r)/

journalist (n) ★★ /ˈdʒɜː(r)nəlɪst/

librarian (n) ★ /laɪˈbreəriən/

photographer (n) ★★ /fəˈtɒɡrəfə(r)/

physicist (n) /ˈfɪzɪsɪst/

professor (n) /prəˈfesə(r)/

scientist (n) ★★★ /ˈsaɪəntɪst/

technician (n) ★ /tekˈnɪʃ(ə)n/

trainee (n) /ˌtreɪˈniː/

Other words and phrases

academic institution (n) /ˌækəˌdemɪk ˌɪnstɪˈtjuːʃ(ə)n/

affect (v) ★★★ /əˈfekt/

attendance (n) ★★ /əˈtendəns/

bulb (n) ★ /bʌlb/

community (n) ★★★ /kəˈmjuːnəti/

company director (n) /ˌkʌmp(ə)ni dəˈrektə(r)/

computer technician (n) /kəmˌpjuːtə(r) tekˈnɪʃ(ə)n/

country (n) ★★★ /ˈkʌntri/

creator (n) ★ /kriˈeɪtə(r)/

data (n) ★★★ /ˈdeɪtə/

detect (v) ★★ /dɪˈtekt/

educational (adj) ★★★ /ˌedjʊˈkeɪʃ(ə)nəl/

evaluate (v) ★★ /ɪˈvæljueɪt/

force (v) ★★★ /fɔː(r)s/

format (n) ★★ /ˈfɔː(r)mæt/

freedom (n) ★★★ /ˈfriːdəm/

general election (n) /ˌdʒen(ə)rəl ɪˈlekʃ(ə)n/

grow (v) ★★★ /ɡrəʊ/

homeless (adj) ★ /ˈhəʊmləs/

implication (n) ★★★ /ˌɪmplɪˈkeɪʃ(ə)n/

initial (adj) ★★★ /ɪˈnɪʃ(ə)l/

inspirational (adj) /ˌɪnspəˈreɪʃ(ə)n(ə)l/

local (adj) ★★★ /ˈləʊk(ə)l/

massive (adj) ★★★ /ˈmæsɪv/

navigate (v) /ˈnævɪɡeɪt/

neighbourhood (n) /ˈneɪbə(r)ˌhʊd/

nursery (n) ★★ /ˈnɜː(r)s(ə)ri/

obligatory (adj) /əˈblɪɡət(ə)ri/

participate (v) ★★ /pɑː(r)ˈtɪsɪpeɪt/

permission (n) ★★ /pə(r)ˈmɪʃ(ə)n/

persuade (v) ★★★ /pə(r)ˈsweɪd/

pick up (v phr) /ˌpɪk ˈʌp/

plagiarism (n) /ˈpleɪdʒəˌrɪz(ə)m/

primary school (n) /ˈpraɪməri ˌskuːl/

radiator (n) ★ /ˈreɪdiˌeɪtə(r)/

report (v) ★★★ /rɪˈpɔː(r)t/

secondary school (n) /ˈsekənd(ə)ri ˌskuːl/

society (n) ★★★ /səˈsaɪəti/

source (n) ★★★ /sɔː(r)s/

statement (n) ★★★ /ˈsteɪtmənt/

straightaway (adv) /ˌstreɪtəˈweɪ/

transform (v) ★★ /trænsˈfɔː(r)m/

university professor (n) /ˌjuːnɪˈvɜː(r)səti prəˌfesə(r)/

update (v) ★★ /ʌpˈdeɪt/

Unit 6

Everyday inventions

digital camera (n) /ˌdɪdʒɪt(ə)l ˈkæm(ə)rə/

dishwasher (n) /ˈdɪʃˌwɒʃə(r)/

e-reader (n) /ˈiː ˌriːdə(r)/

fridge-freezer (n) /ˌfrɪdʒ ˈfriːzə(r)/

headphones (n pl) /ˈhedˌfəʊnz/

Wordlist: Units 6–7

home cinema system (n) /ˌhəʊm ˈsɪnəmə ˌsɪstəm/

laptop (n) /ˈlæp,tɒp/

microwave oven (n) /ˌmaɪkrəweɪv ˈʌv(ə)n/

mobile phone (n) ★★ /ˌməʊbaɪl ˈfəʊn/

MP3 player (n) /ˌem piː ˈθriː ˈpleɪə(r)/

music system (n) /ˈmjuːzɪk ˌsɪstəm/

remote control (n) ★ /rɪˌməʊt kənˈtrəʊl/

satnav (n) /ˈsæt,næv/

speaker (n) ★★★ /ˈspiːkə(r)/

vacuum cleaner (n) /ˈvækjʊəm ˌkliːnə(r)/

washing machine (n) ★ /ˈwɒʃɪŋ məˌʃiːn/

Operating technology

charge (v) ★★★ /tʃɑː(r)dʒ/

recharge (v) /riːˈtʃɑː(r)dʒ/

connect (v) ★★★ /kəˈnekt/

insert (v) ★★★ /ɪnˈsɜː(r)t/

plug in (v phr) /,plʌg ˈɪn/

plug (n) ★ /plʌg/

press a button (phr) /ˌpres ə ˈbʌt(ə)n/

select (v) ★★★ /sɪˈlekt/

switch on (v phr) /ˌswɪtʃ ˈɒn/

switch off (v phr) /ˌswɪtʃ ˈɒf/

tap (the screen) (v) ★★ /tæp/

turn on (v phr) /ˌtɜː(r)n ˈɒn/

turn off (v phr) /ˌtɜː(r)n ˈɒf/

Prepositional phrases with adjectives

afraid of (phr) /əˈfreɪd ɒv/

aware of (phr) /əˈweə(r) ɒv/

bored of (phr) /ˈbɔː(r)d ɒv/

bored with (phr) /ˈbɔː(r)d wɪð/

different from (phr) /ˈdɪfrənt frɒm/

good at (phr) /ˈgʊd æt/

interested in (phr) /ˈɪntrəstɪd ɪn/

pleased with (phr) /ˈpliːzd wɪð/

ready for (phr) /ˈredi fɔː(r)/

responsible for (phr) /rɪˈspɒnsəb(ə)l fɔː(r)/

similar to (phr) /ˈsɪmɪlə(r) tuː/

tired of (phr) /ˈtaɪə(r)d ɒv/

worried about (phr) /ˈwʌrid əˌbaʊt/

Other words and phrases

adapt (v) ★★ /əˈdæpt/

adhesive (adj) /ədˈhiːsɪv/

analysed (adj) /ˈænəlaɪzd/

annually (adv) /ˈænjuəli/

autonomy (n) ★ /ɔːˈtɒnəmi/

aware (adj) ★★★ /əˈweə(r)/

brainstorming (n) /ˈbreɪn,stɔː(r)mɪŋ/

ceremony (n) ★★ /ˈserəməni/

comment (n) ★★★ /ˈkɒment/

compose (v) ★★ /kəmˈpəʊz/

contribute (v) ★★★ /kənˈtrɪbjuːt/

copper (n) ★★ /ˈkɒpə(r)/

define (v) ★★★ /dɪˈfaɪn/

device (n) ★★★ /dɪˈvaɪs/

discover (v) ★★★ /dɪˈskʌvə(r)/

distance (n) ★★★ /ˈdɪstəns/

emergency (n) ★★★ /ɪˈmɜː(r)dʒ(ə)nsi/

experiment (n) ★★★ /ɪkˈsperɪmənt/

fix (v) ★★★ /fɪks/

function (n) ★★★ /ˈfʌŋkʃ(ə)n/

gadget (n) /ˈgædʒɪt/

generate (v) ★★★ /ˈdʒenəreɪt/

humorous (adj) /ˈhjuːmərəs/

improbable (adj) /ɪmˈprɒbəb(ə)l/

individual (adj) ★★★ /ˌɪndɪˈvɪdʒuəl/

innovative (adj) ★ /ˈɪnəveɪtɪv/

inspire (v) ★★ /ɪnˈspaɪə(r)/

invention (n) ★★ /ɪnˈvenʃ(ə)n/

investigation (n) ★★★ /ɪn,vestɪˈgeɪʃ(ə)n/

journal (n) ★★ /ˈdʒɜː(r)n(ə)l/

leader (n) ★★★ /ˈliːdə(r)/

logical (adj) ★★ /ˈlɒdʒɪk(ə)l/

millisecond (n) /ˈmɪlɪ,sekənd/

motion (n) ★★★ /ˈməʊʃ(ə)n/

network (n) ★★★ /ˈnet,wɜː(r)k/

Nobel prize (n) /nəʊ,bel ˈpraɪz/

online shopping (n) /ˌɒnlaɪn ˈʃɒpɪŋ/

overall (adj) ★★★ /ˌəʊvərˈɔːl/

permanent (adj) ★★★ /ˈpɜː(r)mənənt/

philosophy (n) ★★★ /fɪˈlɒsəfi/

pipe (n) ★★ /paɪp/

procedure (n) ★★★ /prəˈsiːdʒə(r)/

process (n) ★★★ /ˈprəʊses/

psychologist (n) ★★ /saɪˈkɒlədʒɪst/

publish (v) ★★★ /ˈpʌblɪʃ/

reach (v) ★★★ /riːtʃ/

react with (v phr) /riˈækt wɪð/

record (v) ★★★ /rɪˈkɔː(r)d/

research (n) ★★★ /rɪˈsɜː(r)tʃ/

secretary (n) ★★★ /ˈsekrətri/

solve (v) ★★★ /sɒlv/

specialist (n) ★★ /ˈspeʃəlɪst/

tap (n) ★★ /tæp/

technique (n) ★★★ /tekˈniːk/

track (n) ★★★ /træk/

translation (n) ★★ /trænsˈleɪʃ(ə)n/

turn (v) ★★★ /tɜː(r)n/

winner (n) ★★★ /ˈwɪnə(r)/

acquire (v) ★★ /əˈkwaɪə(r)/

backwards (adv) ★★ /ˈbækwə(r)dz/

blink (v) ★ /blɪŋk/

calculation (n) ★★ /ˌkælkjʊˈleɪʃ(ə)n/

colleague (n) ★★★ /ˈkɒliːg/

complex (adj) ★★★ /ˈkɒmpleks/

fill (v) ★★★ /fɪl/

full (adj) ★★★ /fʊl/

interview (v) ★★★ /ˈɪntə(r),vjuː/

never-ending (adj) /ˌnevə(r) ˈendɪŋ/

tube (n) ★★ /tjuːb/

Unit 7

Sports and sports venues

athletics (n) ★ /æθˈletɪks/

ball sports (n pl) /ˈbɔːl ,spɔː(r)ts/

baseball (n) ★ /ˈbeɪs,bɔːl/

basketball (n) ★ /ˈbɑːskɪt,bɔːl/

climbing (n) /ˈklaɪmɪŋ/

course (n) ★★★ /kɔː(r)s/

court (n) ★★★ /kɔː(r)t/

cycling (n) ★ /ˈsaɪk(ə)lɪŋ/

diving (n) /ˈdaɪvɪŋ/

football (n) ★★★ /ˈfʊt,bɔːl/

golf (n) ★★★ /gɒlf/

gym (n) ★ /dʒɪm/

gymnastics (n) /dʒɪmˈnæstɪks/

horse-riding (n) /ˈhɔː(r)s ,raɪdɪŋ/

ice hockey (n) /ˈaɪs ,hɒki/

ice-skating (n) /ˈaɪs ,skeɪtɪŋ/

individual sports (n pl) /ˌɪndɪˈvɪdʒuəl ,spɔː(r)ts/

indoor sports (n pl) /ˈɪndɔː(r) ,spɔː(r)ts/

judo (n) /ˈdʒuːdəʊ/

karate (n) /kəˈrɑːti/

martial arts (n pl) ★ /ˌmɑː(r)ʃ(ə)l ˈɑː(r)ts/

pitch (n) ★★ /pɪtʃ/

pool (n) ★★★ /puːl/

rink (n) /rɪŋk/

rugby (n) ★ /ˈrʌgbi/

sailing (n) /ˈseɪlɪŋ/

skiing (n) /ˈskiːɪŋ/

slope (n) ★★ /sləʊp/

snowboarding (n) /ˈsnəʊ,bɔː(r)dɪŋ/

swimming (n) ★ /ˈswɪmɪŋ/

team sports (n pl) /ˈtiːm ,spɔː(r)ts/

tennis (n) ★★ /ˈtenɪs/

volleyball (n) /ˈvɒli,bɔːl/

water sports (n pl) /'wɔːtə(r) ,spɔː(r)ts/

weightlifting (n) /'weɪt,lɪftɪŋ/

winter sports (n pl) /'wɪntə(r) ,spɔː(r)ts/

Sports equipment and scores

ball (n) ★★★ /bɔːl/

bat (n) ★★ /bæt/

beat (v) ★★★ /biːt/

boots (n pl) /buːts/

bounce (v) ★★ /baʊns/

catch (v) ★★★ /kætʃ/

club (n) ★★★ /klʌb/

draw (v) ★★★ /drɔː/

goal post (n) /'gəʊl ,pəʊst/

goggles (n pl) /'gɒg(ə)lz/

head (v) ★★★ /hed/

hit (v) ★★★ /hɪt/

kick (v) ★★★ /kɪk/

lose a match (v phr) /,luːz ə 'mætʃ/

lose to someone (v phr) /'luːz tə ,sʌmwʌn/

net (n) ★★★ /net/

nil (n) /nɪl/

pass (v) ★★★ /pɑːs/

point (n) ★★★ /pɔɪnt/

racket (n) ★ /'rækɪt/

score (v) /skɔː(r)/

shoot (v) ★★★ /ʃuːt/

skates (n pl) /skeɪts/

skis (n pl) /skiːz/

throw (v) ★★★ /θrəʊ/

trainers (n pl) ★ /'treɪnə(r)z/

win (v) ★★★ /wɪn/

Phrasal verbs connected with sport

give in (v phr) /,gɪv 'ɪn/

go for (v phr) /'gəʊ fɔː(r)/

join in (v phr) /,dʒɔɪn 'ɪn/

knock out (v phr) /,nɒk 'aʊt/

take up (v phr) /,teɪk 'ʌp/

warm up (v phr) /,wɔː(r)m 'ʌp/

work out (v phr) /,wɜː(r)k 'aʊt/

Other words and phrases

artery (n) /'ɑː(r)təri/

carbon dioxide (n) ★ /,kɑː(r)bən daɪ'ɒksaɪd/

cause (v) ★★★ /kɔːz/

championship (n) ★★★ /'tʃæmpiənʃɪp/

changing room (n) /'tʃeɪndʒɪŋ ,ruːm/

cholesterol (n) ★ /kə'lestərɒl/

circulate (v) ★★ /'sɜː(r)kjʊleɪt/

combine (v) ★★★ /kəm'baɪn/

defender (n) ★★ /dɪ'fendə(r)/

deliver (v) ★★★ /dɪ'lɪvə(r)/

extreme (adj) ★★ /ɪk'striːm/

fan (n) ★★ /fæn/

fit (adj) ★★★ /fɪt/

fitness (n) ★★ /'fɪtnəs/

foundation (n) ★★★ /faʊn'deɪʃ(ə)n/

give away (v phr) /,gɪv ə'weɪ/

goalkeeper (n) ★ /'gəʊl,kiːpə(r)/

gold medallist (n) /,gəʊld 'med(ə)lɪst/

habit (n) ★★★ /'hæbɪt/

host (v) ★★ /həʊst/

in control (phr) /,ɪn kən'trəʊl/

inactivity (n) /,ɪnæk'tɪvəti/

index finger (n) /'ɪndeks ,fɪŋgə(r)/

intensity (n) /ɪn'tensɪti/

interfere (v) ★★ /,ɪntə(r)'fɪə(r)/

irrational (adj) /ɪ'ræʃ(ə)nəl/

jockey (n) ★ /'dʒɒki/

ladder (n) ★★ /'lædə(r)/

leaflet (n) ★★ /'liːflət/

medal (n) ★★ /'med(ə)l/

moderate (adj) ★★ /'mɒd(ə)rət/

monitor (n) ★★ /'mɒnɪtə(r)/

motto (n) /'mɒtəʊ/

muscle (n) ★★★ /'mʌs(ə)l/

parachuting (n) /'pærə,ʃuːtɪŋ/

petrol (n) ★★ /'petrəl/

practical (adj) ★★★ /'præktɪk(ə)l/

puck (n) /pʌk/

pulse (n) ★★ /pʌls/

pump (v) ★★ /pʌmp/

race (n) ★★★ /reɪs/

recovery (n) ★★★ /rɪ'kʌvəri/

reduce (v) ★★★ /rɪ'djuːs/

referee (n) ★★ /,refə'riː/

refuse (v) ★★★ /rɪ'fjuːz/

ritual (n) ★★ /'rɪtʃuəl/

routine (n) ★★ /ruː'tiːn/

spectator (n) ★ /spek'teɪtə(r)/

spot (v) ★★★ /spɒt/

starvation (n) /stɑː(r)'veɪʃ(ə)n/

strange (adj) ★★★ /streɪndʒ/

superstition (n) /,suːpə(r)'stɪʃ(ə)n/

teammate (n) /'tiːm,meɪt/

thumb (n) ★★ /θʌm/

top (adj) ★★★ /tɒp/

underwater (adj) /,ʌndə(r)'wɔːtə(r)/

vessel (n) ★★ /'ves(ə)l/

Unit 8

Art, theatre, music

abstract painting (n) /,æbstrækt 'peɪntɪŋ/

audience (n) ★★★ /'ɔːdiəns/

cast (n) ★★★ /kɑːst/

concert (n) ★★ /'kɒnsə(r)t/

drawing (n) ★★★ /'drɔːɪŋ/

gallery (n) ★★ /'gæləri/

landscape (n) ★★ /'læn(d),skeɪp/

lighting (n) ★★ /'laɪtɪŋ/

lyrics (n pl) /'lɪrɪks/

main character (n) /,meɪn 'kærɪktə(r)/

masterpiece (n) ★ /'mɑːstə(r),piːs/

orchestra (n) ★★ /'ɔː(r)kɪstrə/

performance (n) ★★★ /pə(r)'fɔː(r)məns/

play (n) ★★★ /pleɪ/

sculpture (n) ★★ /'skʌlptʃə(r)/

self-portrait (n) /,self 'pɔː(r)trɪt/

sketch (n) ★ /sketʃ/

stage (n) ★★★ /steɪdʒ/

still life (n) /,stɪl 'laɪf/

tune (n) ★★ /tjuːn/

Artists

actor (n) ★★★ /'æktə(r)/

artist (n) ★★★ /'ɑː(r)tɪst/

composer (n) ★★ /kəm'pəʊzə(r)/

conductor (n) ★ /kən'dʌktə(r)/

director (n) ★★★ /daɪ'rektə(r)/

drummer (n) /'drʌmə(r)/

guitarist (n) /gɪ'tɑːrɪst/

musician (n) ★★ /mjʊ'zɪʃ(ə)n/

painter (n) ★★ /'peɪntə(r)/

performer (n) ★ /pə(r)'fɔː(r)mə(r)/

pianist (n) ★ /'piːənɪst/

sculptor (n) /'skʌlptə(r)/

singer-songwriter (n) /,sɪŋə(r) 'sɒŋ,raɪtə(r)/

vocalist (n) /'vəʊkəlɪst/

Adjectives ending in -ing and -ed

amazed (adj) /ə'meɪzd/

amazing (adj) ★★ /ə'meɪzɪŋ/

bored (adj) ★★ /bɔː(r)d/

boring (adj) ★★ /'bɔːrɪŋ/

confused (adj) ★★ /kən'fjuːzd/

confusing (adj) ★ /kən'fjuːzɪŋ/

depressed (adj) ★★ /dɪ'prest/

depressing (adj) ★ /dɪ'presɪŋ/

disappointed (adj) ★ /,dɪsə'pɔɪntɪd/

disappointing (adj) ⋆ /ˌdɪsə'pɔɪntɪŋ/

disgusted (adj) /dɪs'gʌstɪd/

disgusting (adj) ⋆ /dɪs'gʌstɪŋ/

embarrassed (adj) ⋆ /ɪm'bærəst/

embarrassing (adj) ⋆ /ɪm'bærəsɪŋ/

excited (adj) ⋆⋆ /ɪk'saɪtɪd/

exciting (adj) ⋆⋆ /ɪk'saɪtɪŋ/

fascinated (adj) /'fæsɪneɪtɪd/

fascinating (adj) ⋆⋆ /'fæsɪneɪtɪŋ/

frightened (adj) ⋆ /'fraɪt(ə)nd/

frightening (adj) ⋆ /'fraɪt(ə)nɪŋ/

inspired (adj) /ɪn'spaɪə(r)d/

inspiring (adj) /ɪn'spaɪərɪŋ/

interested (adj) ⋆⋆⋆ /'ɪntrəstɪd/

interesting (adj) ⋆⋆⋆ /'ɪntrəstɪŋ/

relaxed (adj) ⋆ /rɪ'lækst/

relaxing (adj) /rɪ'læksɪŋ/

surprised (adj) ⋆⋆⋆ /sə(r)'praɪzd/

surprising (adj) ⋆⋆⋆ /sə(r)'praɪzɪŋ/

tired (adj) ⋆⋆⋆ /'taɪə(r)d/

tiring (adj) /'taɪərɪŋ/

uninspired (adj) /ˌʌnɪn'spaɪə(r)d/

uninspiring (adj) /ˌʌnɪn'spaɪərɪŋ/

worried (adj) ⋆⋆⋆ /'wʌrid/

worrying (adj) ⋆ /'wʌriɪŋ/

Other words and phrases

accurate (adj) ⋆⋆ /'ækjʊrət/

airtight (adj) /'eə(r)ˌtaɪt/

appreciate (v) ⋆⋆ /ə'priːʃiˌeɪt/

autistic (adj) /ɔː'tɪstɪk/

background (n) ⋆⋆⋆ /'bækˌgraʊnd/

brief (adj) ⋆⋆⋆ /briːf/

cancer (n) ⋆⋆⋆ /'kænsə(r)/

canvas (n) ⋆ /'kænvəs/

care (v) ⋆⋆⋆ /keə(r)/

cityscape (n) /'sɪtiˌskeɪp/

comedy (n) ⋆⋆ /'kɒmədi/

common (adj) ⋆⋆⋆ /'kɒmən/

complicated (adj) ⋆⋆ /'kɒmplɪˌkeɪtɪd/

conference (n) ⋆⋆⋆ /'kɒnf(ə)rəns/

context (n) ⋆⋆⋆ /'kɒntekst/

depend on (v phr) /dɪ'pend ɒn/

drama (n) ⋆⋆⋆ /'drɑːmə/

emotional (adj) ⋆⋆⋆ /ɪ'məʊʃ(ə)nəl/

escape (v) ⋆⋆⋆ /ɪ'skeɪp/

expect (v) ⋆⋆⋆ /ɪk'spekt/

explode (v) ⋆⋆ /ɪk'spləʊd/

fantasy (n) ⋆⋆ /'fæntəsi/

gas (n) ⋆⋆⋆ /gæs/

gig (n) ⋆ /gɪg/

graffiti (n) /grə'fiːti/

happy ending (n) /ˌhæpi 'endɪŋ/

horror (n) ⋆⋆ /'hɒrə(r)/

impressionism (n) /ɪm'preʃ(ə)nˌɪz(ə)m/

intense (adj) ⋆⋆ /ɪn'tens/

interpretation (n) ⋆⋆⋆ /ɪnˌtɜː(r)prɪ'teɪʃ(ə)n/

licensed (adj) /'laɪs(ə)nst/

lines (n pl) /laɪnz/

lonely (adj) ⋆⋆ /'ləʊnli/

material (n) ⋆⋆⋆ /mə'tɪəriəl/

meanwhile (adv) ⋆⋆⋆ /'miːnˌwaɪl/

musical (n) ⋆⋆ /'mjuːzɪk(ə)l/

novel (n) ⋆⋆⋆ /'nɒv(ə)l/

optimistic (adj) ⋆⋆ /ˌɒptɪ'mɪstɪk/

panorama (n) /ˌpænə'rɑːmə/

plot (n) ⋆⋆ /plɒt/

publicity (n) ⋆⋆ /pʌb'lɪsəti/

realism (n) ⋆ /'rɪəˌlɪz(ə)m/

record-breaking (n) /'rekɔː(r)d ˌbreɪkɪŋ/

reporter (n) ⋆ /rɪ'pɔː(r)tə(r)/

response (n) ⋆⋆⋆ /rɪ'spɒns/

scene (n) ⋆⋆⋆ /siːn/

science fiction (n) ⋆ /ˌsaɪəns 'fɪkʃ(ə)n/

screenplay (n) /'skriːnˌpleɪ/

series (n) ⋆⋆⋆ /'sɪəriːz/

soundtrack (n) /'saʊn(d)ˌtræk/

subject (n) ⋆⋆⋆ /'sʌbdʒɪkt/

succeed (v) ⋆⋆⋆ /sək'siːd/

symbolic (adj) ⋆⋆ /sɪm'bɒlɪk/

theme (n) ⋆⋆⋆ /θiːm/

thriller (n) ⋆ /'θrɪlə(r)/

tragic (adj) /'trædʒɪk/

version (n) ⋆⋆⋆ /'vɜː(r)ʃ(ə)n/

Gateway to exams: Units 7–8

aim (n) ⋆⋆⋆ /eɪm/

athlete (n) ⋆ /'æθliːt/

checkmate (n) /'tʃekˌmeɪt/

classify (v) ⋆⋆ /'klæsɪfaɪ/

round (n) ⋆⋆⋆ /raʊnd/

Unit 9

Nations

capital city (n) /ˌkæpɪt(ə)l 'sɪti/

currency (n) ⋆⋆⋆ /'kʌrənsi/

flag (n) ⋆⋆ /flæg/

national anthem (n) /ˌnæʃ(ə)nəl 'ænθəm/

prime minister (n) ⋆⋆⋆ /ˌpraɪm 'mɪnɪstə(r)/

president (n) ⋆⋆⋆ /'prezɪdənt/

royal family (n) ⋆ /ˌrɔɪəl 'fæm(ə)li/

king (n) ⋆⋆⋆ /kɪŋ/

queen (n) ⋆⋆⋆ /kwiːn/

prince (n) ⋆⋆ /prɪns/

princess (n) ⋆⋆ /ˌprɪn'ses/

State and politics

campaign (n) ⋆⋆⋆ /kæm'peɪn/

constitutional monarchy (n) /ˌkɒnstɪˌtjuːʃ(ə)nəl 'mɒnə(r)ki/

democracy (n) ⋆⋆⋆ /dɪ'mɒkrəsi/

law (n) ⋆⋆⋆ /lɔː/

member (n) ⋆⋆⋆ /'membə(r)/

monarchy (n) ⋆ /'mɒnə(r)ki/

policy (n) ⋆⋆⋆ /'pɒləsi/

political party (n) /pəˌlɪtɪk(ə)l 'pɑː(r)ti/

republic (n) ⋆⋆⋆ /rɪ'pʌblɪk/

run (v) ⋆⋆⋆ /rʌn/

vote (v) ⋆⋆⋆ /vəʊt/

Noun and adjective suffixes

aristocracy (n) /ˌærɪ'stɒkrəsi/

aristocratic (adj) /ˌærɪstə'krætɪk/

artistic (adj) ⋆⋆ /ɑː(r)'tɪstɪk/

care (n) ⋆⋆⋆ /keə(r)/

careful (adj) ⋆⋆⋆ /'keə(r)f(ə)l/

careless (adj) ⋆ /'keə(r)ləs/

comfort (n) ⋆⋆ /'kʌmfə(r)t/

comfortable (adj) ⋆⋆⋆ /'kʌmftəb(ə)l/

dangerous (adj) ⋆⋆⋆ /'deɪndʒərəs/

enjoyable (adj) ⋆ /ɪn'dʒɔɪəb(ə)l/

fame (n) ⋆⋆ /feɪm/

famous (adj) ⋆⋆⋆ /'feɪməs/

helpful (adj) ⋆⋆ /'helpf(ə)l/

helpless (adj) ⋆ /'helpləs/

hungry (adj) ⋆⋆ /'hʌŋgri/

luck (n) ⋆⋆ /lʌk/

lucky (adj) ⋆⋆⋆ /'lʌki/

mysterious (adj) ⋆⋆ /mɪ'stɪəriəs/

natural (adj) ⋆⋆⋆ /'nætʃ(ə)rəl/

official (adj) ⋆⋆⋆ /ə'fɪʃ(ə)l/

science (n) ⋆⋆⋆ /'saɪəns/

scientific (adj) ⋆⋆⋆ /ˌsaɪən'tɪfɪk/

sensible (adj) ⋆⋆ /'sensəb(ə)l/

terrible (adj) ⋆⋆⋆ /'terəb(ə)l/

terror (n) ⋆⋆ /'terə(r)/

uncomfortable (adj) ⋆⋆ /ʌn'kʌmftəb(ə)l/

useful (adj) ⋆⋆⋆ /'juːsf(ə)l/

useless (adj) ⋆⋆ /'juːsləs/

Other words and phrases

approach (v) ★★★ /əˈprəʊtʃ/
asteroid (n) /ˈæstəˌrɔɪd/
avoid (v) ★★★ /əˈvɔɪd/
bone (n) ★★★ /bəʊn/
bullying (n) /ˈbʊliɪŋ/
cactus (n) /ˈkæktəs/
citizenship (n) ★ /ˈsɪtɪz(ə)nʃɪp/
colony (n) ★★ /ˈkɒləni/
conservative (n) ★★ /kənˈsɜː(r)vətɪv/
conspiracy theory (n) /kənˈspɪrəsi ˌθɪəri/
cross (n) ★★★ /krɒs/
cup (n) ★★★ /kʌp/
curious (adj) ★★ /ˈkjʊəriəs/
curriculum (n) ★★ /kəˈrɪkjʊləm/
divided (adj) /dɪˈvaɪdɪd/
dramatic (adj) ★★★ /drəˈmætɪk/
dress up (v phr) /ˌdres ˈʌp/
explanation (n) ★★★ /ˌekspləˈneɪʃ(ə)n/
fever (n) ★ /ˈfiːvə(r)/
final (n) ★★★ /ˈfaɪn(ə)l/
fine (adj) ★★★ /faɪn/
form (n & v) ★★★ /fɔː(r)m/
government (n) ★★★ /ˈgʌvə(r)nmənt/
hero (n) ★★ /ˈhɪərəʊ/
influence (v) ★★★ /ˈɪnfluəns/
instruction (n) ★★★ /ɪnˈstrʌkʃ(ə)n/
issue (n) ★★★ /ˈɪʃuː/
labour (n) ★★★ /ˈleɪbə(r)/
manifesto (n) /ˌmænɪˈfestəʊ/
minister (n) ★★★ /ˈmɪnɪstə(r)/
nation (n) ★★★ /ˈneɪʃ(ə)n/
nomination (n) ★ /ˌnɒmɪˈneɪʃ(ə)n/
obey (v) ★★ /əˈbeɪ/
pale (adj) ★★★ /peɪl/
poisoned (adj) ★ /ˈpɔɪz(ə)nd/
power (n) ★★★ /ˈpaʊə(r)/
presence (n) ★★★ /ˈprez(ə)ns/
prison (n) ★★★ /ˈprɪz(ə)n/
protect (v) ★★★ /prəˈtekt/
reign (v) ★★ /reɪn/
represent (v) ★★★ /ˌreprɪˈzent/
representative (n) ★★★ /ˌreprɪˈzentətɪv/
residence (n) ★★ /ˈrezɪd(ə)ns/
rugby shirt (n) /ˈrʌgbi ˌʃɜː(r)t/
senior (adj) ★★★ /ˈsiːniə(r)/
significant (adj) ★★★ /sɪgˈnɪfɪkənt/
skin (n) ★★★ /skɪn/
slogan (n) ★ /ˈsləʊgən/
social issue (n) /ˈsəʊʃ(ə)l ˌɪʃuː/

stable (adj) ★★ /ˈsteɪb(ə)l/
tolerance (n) ★ /ˈtɒlərəns/
trailer (n) ★ /ˈtreɪlə(r)/
unite (v) ★★ /juːˈnaɪt/
youth (n) ★★★ /juːθ/

Unit 10

Shops

bakery (n) /ˈbeɪkəri/
bookshop (n) ★ /ˈbʊkˌʃɒp/
butcher's (n) /ˈbʊtʃə(r)z/
chemist's (n) /ˈkemɪsts/
clothes shop (n) /ˈkləʊðz ˌʃɒp/
department store (n) ★★ /dɪˈpɑː(r)tmənt ˌstɔː(r)/
electrical goods shop (n) /ɪˌlektrɪk(ə)l ˈgʊdz ˌʃɒp/
greengrocer's (n) /ˈgriːnˌgrəʊsə(r)z/
jeweller's (n) /ˈdʒuːələ(r)z/
newsagent's (n) /ˈnjuːzˌeɪdʒ(ə)nts/
post office (n) ★★ /ˈpəʊst ˌɒfɪs/
shoe shop (n) /ˈʃuː ˌʃɒp/
sports shop (n) /ˈspɔː(r)ts ˌʃɒp/
stationery shop (n) /ˈsteɪʃ(ə)n(ə)ri ˌʃɒp/
supermarket (n) ★★ /ˈsuːpə(r)ˌmɑː(r)kɪt/

Shopping

afford (v) ★★★ /əˈfɔː(r)d/
bargain (n) ★★ /ˈbɑː(r)gɪn/
cash (n) ★★★ /kæʃ/
cashier (n) /kæˈʃɪə(r)/
changing room (n) /ˈtʃeɪndʒɪŋ ˌruːm/
checkout (n) /ˈtʃekaʊt/
debit card (n) /ˈdebɪt ˌkɑː(r)d/
discount (n) ★★ /ˈdɪsˌkaʊnt/
queue (n) ★ /kjuː/
receipt (n) ★★ /rɪˈsiːt/
refund (n) /ˈriːfʌnd/
trolley (n) ★ /ˈtrɒli/

Collocations with money

borrow (v) ★★ /ˈbɒrəʊ/
donate (v) ★ /dəʊˈneɪt/
earn (v) ★★★ /ɜː(r)n/
lend (v) ★★ /lend/
make (v) ★★★ /meɪk/
owe (v) ★★★ /əʊ/
raise (v) ★★★ /reɪz/
save (v) ★★★ /seɪv/
spend (v) ★★★ /spend/
waste (v) ★★★ /weɪst/
win (v) ★★★ /wɪn/

Other words and phrases

allowance (n) ★★ /əˈlaʊəns/
apply (v) ★★★ /əˈplaɪ/
budget (n) ★★★ /ˈbʌdʒɪt/
busk (v) ★★★ /ˈbɪzi/
charity (n) ★★★ /ˈtʃærəti/
container (n) ★★ /kənˈteɪnə(r)/
deliberately (adv) ★★ /dɪˈlɪb(ə)rətli/
efficient (adj) ★★★ /ɪˈfɪʃ(ə)nt/
faulty (adj) /ˈfɔːlti/
finance (n) ★★★ /ˈfaɪnæns/
fit (v) ★★★ /fɪt/
illegal (adj) ★★ /ɪˈliːg(ə)l/
interest (n) ★★★ /ˈɪntrəst/
item (n) ★★★ /ˈaɪtəm/
list (n) ★★★ /lɪst/
luxury (n) ★ /ˈlʌkʃəri/
packaging (n) ★ /ˈpækɪdʒɪŋ/
pocket money (n) ★ /ˈpɒkɪt ˌmʌni/
position (n) ★★★ /pəˈzɪʃ(ə)n/
rate (n) ★★★ /reɪt/
reasonable (adj) ★★★ /ˈriːz(ə)nəb(ə)l/
reduction (n) ★★★ /rɪˈdʌkʃ(ə)n/
replace (v) ★★★ /rɪˈpleɪs/
resist (v) ★★★ /rɪˈzɪst/
shopping basket (n) /ˈʃɒpɪŋ ˌbɑːskɪt/
size (n) ★★★ /saɪz/
sticker (n) /ˈstɪkə(r)/
tendency (n) ★★ /ˈtendənsi/

Gateway to exams: Units 9–10

boss (n) ★★★ /bɒs/
Caribbean (n) /ˌkærɪˈbiən/
colonise (v) /ˈkɒlənaɪz/
commonwealth country (n) /ˈkɒmənwelθ ˌkʌntri/
custom (n) ★★ /ˈkʌstəm/
democratic (adj) ★★★ /ˌdeməˈkrætɪk/
equal (adj) ★★★ /ˈiːkwəl/
exotic (adj) ★ /ɪgˈzɒtɪk/
explorer (n) /ɪkˈsplɔːrə(r)/
fair (adj) ★★★ /feə(r)/
gain (v) ★★★ /geɪn/
observer (n) ★★ /əbˈzɜː(r)və(r)/
profitable (adj) ★★ /ˈprɒfɪtəb(ə)l/
settle (v) ★★★ /ˈset(ə)l/
shock (n) ★★★ /ʃɒk/
spirit (n) ★★★ /ˈspɪrɪt/
symbol (n) ★★ /ˈsɪmb(ə)l/
trade (n) ★★★ /treɪd/
unity (n) ★★ /ˈjuːnəti/

Unit 1

READING: TRUE/FALSE ACTIVITIES

You decide if statements are true or false depending on the information in the text.

Step 1: Read the text quickly to get a general understanding.

Step 2: Read the sentences that you need to prove true or false.

Step 3: Find the parts of the text where you think the information is. Read them again carefully.

Step 4: If there is no information to say a sentence is true, mark the statement false.

Step 5: When you finish, check that you have an answer for each question. Never leave answers blank in an exam.

LISTENING: MATCHING THE SPEAKER AND INFORMATION

In this type of activity, you match different speakers with what they say.

Before you listen,

- think about the topic of what you are going to listen to. Think of words that could appear.

- read the questions. This can help you to know how many speakers there are and what they may say.

While you listen,

- remember that the speakers may say the same things as in the questions, but using different words or expressions. Thinking of synonyms for the words in the statements can help you to identify the answers.

- don't worry if you don't understand everything the first time you listen. Usually you listen twice. Use the second listening to find the answers you didn't hear the first time.

After you listen,

- check that you have an answer for each question. Never leave answers blank in an exam.

Unit 2

SPEAKING: EXCHANGING INFORMATION

- Make sure you know what the situation is and the specific information that you need to ask for/give. Your mark usually depends on how well you give or find out the information.

- If you don't understand what the examiner or your partner says, ask them in English to repeat or to speak more slowly. Use expressions like: *Sorry, can you say that again?* or *Sorry, could you speak more slowly?*

- Listen to your partner and the examiner. In a conversation we speak *and* listen.

- Show that you're interested in what the other person is saying. Use expressions like: *Really?*, *That's interesting.*, *Do you?*, *Me too.*

- Use *Well*, *Hmm* or *Let me think* to give you time to think.

- Use basic question words like *Who? What? When? Where?* to help you think of more questions to keep the conversation going.

WRITING: CHECKING YOUR WORK

It is normal to make mistakes when you write. That is why it is so important to read your work carefully when you finish. Check for mistakes with:

- punctuation
- capital letters
- spelling
- vocabulary
- word order
- tenses
- missing words
- agreement between the subject and verb

Apart from these mistakes, check that you answer the question and that you include any information that they ask you for. Make sure that the style is appropriate and the content is relevant.

Unit 3

READING: MISSING SENTENCES ACTIVITIES

You have to find the best place to put different sentences taken from a text. The sentences can come from anywhere in the paragraph and there can be more sentences than spaces.

Step 1: Read the text to get a general idea of the overall meaning. To do this type of exercise it is not usually necessary to understand every word, so do not panic if you don't understand everything.

Step 2: Read the missing sentences and identify the key information. What is the sentence about? Do you remember anything connected with this topic when you read the text for the first time? Look again at this part of the text in more detail.

Step 3: Try out each sentence in the most probable space and read again. Is the meaning logical? Do words like *this* or *it* make sense?

Step 4: When you finish, check that you have an answer for each question. Never leave answers blank in an exam.

USE OF ENGLISH: MULTIPLE-CHOICE CLOZE ACTIVITIES

You have to complete a text by choosing the best answer for a space.

Step 1: Read the text to get the overall meaning. Do not worry about the gaps.

Step 2: Read the text more carefully and try to predict which word is missing from each gap.

Step 3: Look at the alternatives. Is one of them the same as the word you predicted?

Step 4: Look carefully at the words which come before and after the space. Do they help you to decide?

Step 5: If you aren't sure which answer is right, eliminate any answers that are definitely wrong.

Step 6: When you finish, check that you have an answer for each question. Never leave answers blank in an exam.

Unit 4

SPEAKING: NEGOTIATING

In negotiating activities, you usually work with another person. The examiner explains a situation where you and the other speaker need to come to a decision.

- There isn't usually a right or wrong answer. However, you should come to a decision by the end of the activity. Above all, the examiner wants to hear you speaking English.

- It is important that neither of you dominates the conversation or is silent. The examiner will usually help you to do this. But remember to take turns and help your partner to speak where possible.

- If you can't think of anything to say, ask your partner a question like *What do you think?* You can also use fillers like *Well*, *Hmm* or *Let me think.*

- Don't be afraid to say something that you think is obvious.

- Remember to give full explanations for your ideas.

- Listen to what your partner or the examiner is saying. In a conversation we speak *and* listen.

- If you don't understand what the examiner or your partner is saying, ask them in English to repeat or to speak more slowly. Use expressions like: *Sorry, can you say that again?* or, *Sorry, could you speak more slowly?*

Unit 4

WRITING: TRANSACTIONAL TASKS

Transactional writing tasks are ones where the instructions tell you who you are writing to and what information to include.

- When a question asks you to put specific information in your text, you lose marks if you do not include the information.
- When you write letters, invitations, messages and notes it is essential to write in the correct style. When you write to a friend, use contractions and informal expressions. When you write a formal or semi-formal letter, don't use contractions or informal language. If your letter is grammatically correct, but not in the correct style, you lose marks.

Unit 5

SPEAKING: GIVING A PRESENTATION

Look at this advice for giving good presentations.

- Make notes with the information you want to give in your presentation and use them when you are giving it; but don't just read your notes aloud.
- Look at your audience. See if they understand you and are interested.
- Don't speak too fast. If you speak too quickly, people won't understand.
- Try to speak for exactly the right amount of time. The more you practise the easier it will become.
- Use intonation to show that you are interested and to make others interested.
- Don't worry excessively about vocabulary. When you don't know a word, explain using simpler words.
- Don't let mistakes stop you from speaking. Correct your own mistakes if possible, or start the sentence again, but don't stop!

WRITING: THINKING ABOUT THE READER

We write in different ways depending on who and how many people we are writing to. Usually in writing exams you will get more marks if you write in an appropriate way for the task. Always read the instructions carefully and check that you know exactly who you are writing to. Write in the correct style (formal, semi-formal or informal) for that reader. Ask yourself if the person reading what you have written will (a) understand it easily (b) find it interesting/informative/useful/exciting.

Unit 6

READING: MATCHING ACTIVITIES

In this type of activity, you have to say which text or part of a text contains a piece of information.

Step 1: Read all the texts quickly to get a general understanding.

Step 2: Read the information that you need to find. Are there are any special words that help you to find the part of the text which contains the information? Remember that in the text the same information may be expressed in different words.

Step 3: Read the specific text or part of the text where you think the information comes again in more detail.

Step 4: If you are not sure that you have found the correct answer, read other sections again in more detail.

Step 5: When you finish, check that you have an answer for each question. Never leave answers blank in an exam.

LISTENING: MULTIPLE-CHOICE ACTIVITIES

In this type of activity, you choose the best answer from three or four different answers. You usually hear the text twice. The questions are usually in the order that you hear them in the recording.

Step 1: Read the different answers before you listen. They can give you ideas about the topic of the text and the vocabulary you are going to hear in it. Remember that sometimes the difference between two answers is just one word.

Step 2: When you listen, remember that you may hear the correct answer, but expressed in different words. You may also hear a word or words that come in one of the possible answers, but this does not mean it is the answer. The word(s) may be there just to distract you.

Step 3: You usually hear the recording twice. Do not panic if you do not understand information the first time. If you don't hear the answer to one question, start listening immediately for the answer to the next question.

Step 4: Use the second listening to find the answers you didn't hear the first time and to check the answers you already have.

Step 5: When you finish, check that you have an answer for each question. Never leave answers blank in an exam.

Unit 7

USE OF ENGLISH: CLOZE ACTIVITIES

In this type of activity, you have a text with gaps. You must fill in each gap by thinking of a word which is grammatically correct and is logical.

Step 1: Read the complete text without thinking about the gaps. This is to get a general understanding of the text.

Step 2: Look again at the gaps and especially the words which come just before and after the gap. Do those words need a special preposition? Is an article or auxiliary verb missing? Think about the type of word you need (noun, verb, pronoun, article, etc.) and the general meaning. The missing words are often prepositions, articles, pronouns, auxiliary verbs, modal verbs, and conjunctions.

Step 3: Fill in the gap with the word that you think is best. Read the sentence again with your answer in the gap. Sometimes there is more than one possible answer, but you only need to put one.

Step 4: When you finish, check that you have one answer for each question. Never leave answers blank in an exam.

LISTENING: TRUE/FALSE ACTIVITIES

In this type of activity you have to listen and decide if answers are true or false. You usually hear the text twice. The questions are usually in the order that you hear them in the recording.

Step 1: Read the questions and answers before you listen. They can give you ideas about the topic of the text and the vocabulary you are going to hear in it.

Step 2: You can usually hear the recording twice. Do not panic if you do not understand information the first time. If you don't hear the answer to one question, start listening immediately for the answer to the next question.

Step 3: Use the second listening to find the answers you didn't hear the first time and to check the answers you already have.

Step 4: When you finish, check that you have an answer for each question. Never leave answers blank in an exam.

Unit 8

SPEAKING: DESCRIBING PAST EVENTS

In some speaking exams you have to talk about something that you did in the past.

Before the exam, make sure you know:

- as many regular and irregular past forms as possible.
- when and how to use the past simple, past continuous and past perfect.
- words and expressions to explain the order of events, e.g. *First, Then, Next, In the end.*

During the exam, make sure you:

understand and answer the question the examiner asks you.

- ask the examiner or your partner in English to repeat or to speak more slowly if they say something that you don't understand. Use expressions like: *Sorry, can you say that again?* or, *Sorry, could you speak more slowly?*
- use fillers like *Well, Hmm* or *Let me think* to give you time to think of what you want to say next.
- use basic question words like *Who? What? When? Where? How? Why?* to help you to think of more things to say.

WRITING: FOLLOWING THE INSTRUCTIONS

In writing exams you must be careful to answer the question and follow the instructions exactly. Before you start writing, check that you know the answers to these questions:

- Who are you writing to or for?
- Is there a word limit? In some exams you may get no marks if you write too many words or not enough words
- Do you know what information is relevant to include? For example, if you only write about the plot of a film, but not your opinion, this is not a film review.
- Is there a paragraph plan to follow? Do you have to write a specific number of paragraphs? Do you have to begin or finish your composition in a specific way?

Unit 9

USE OF ENGLISH: WORD FORMATION CLOZE ACTIVITIES

In this type of activity, you must use the word given in capitals to form a word that fits in the gap in the same line. The words can be any type – noun, adjective, adverb, verb, etc.

Step 1: Read the text once quickly to get a general understanding.

Step 2: Look at the words just before and after the gap. They can help you to decide what type of word is missing. Usually to change the type of word you will need a suffix (e.g. *-ion* to make a noun, *-ly* to make an adverb).

Step 3: Look at the words just before and after the gap and make sure you understand the whole sentence. This will help you to decide if you need to change the meaning of the word, e.g. making it negative. Usually to change the meaning of the word you will need a prefix (e.g. *im-, re-*).

Step 4: Read the completed sentence and check your answer. Check that you have an answer for each question. Never leave answers blank in an exam.

LISTENING: COMPLETING NOTES

- Always read the incomplete notes *before* you listen. This helps you to know what to listen for. Look carefully at the words that come just before or after each space and think about what *type* of word is missing (e.g. noun, verb, adjective, adverb).
- It is not usually necessary to understand every word that you hear. Listen out for the sections which correspond to the information in the notes. Then pay special attention to these sections.
- Read the instructions carefully to know how many words or numbers you can or should write in each space. Be careful with spelling and your handwriting.
- Don't worry if you don't understand everything the first time you listen. Usually you listen twice. Use the second listening to find the answers you didn't hear the first time and to check the answers you already have.

Unit 10

READING: MULTIPLE-CHOICE ACTIVITIES

In this type of activity you choose the best answer from three or four different answers.

Step 1: Read the text quickly to get a general understanding.

Step 2: Read all the answers carefully. Sometimes the difference between two answers is just one word.

Step 3: Find the section of the text where you think each answer comes and read it again slowly, in more detail. You may find the same words in the text and in one of the options but this does not mean it is the correct answer. The correct option will probably express the information in the text using different words. The answers usually come in order in the text.

Step 4: If you aren't 100% sure which answer is best, take away any answers which you know are not correct.

Step 5: When you finish, check that you have an answer for each question. Never leave answers blank in an exam.

SPEAKING: GETTING A GOOD MARK

To get a good mark in a speaking exam, follow this advice.

- Make sure that what you say is relevant to the question(s) that the examiner asks you.
- If you don't understand the examiner's questions or instructions, ask them to repeat.
- Speak! If you are too nervous or shy, the examiner won't be able to give you a good mark. Relax and remember that the examiner is on your side.
- Speak loudly and clearly so that the examiner can hear you.
- Don't write out complete answers before you speak. React to what the examiner or your partner(s) are saying.
- Practise speaking as much as you can before the exam.

Communication activities

Unit 1

DEVELOPING SPEAKING *Using question tags*

Exercise 6, p14

Student A: Read out the first part of these sentences. Check that your partner says the correct question tag.

1 She's American … (isn't she?)
2 They can ski … (can't they?)
3 They don't like football … (do they?)
4 He's got very short hair … (hasn't he?)
5 His grandfather isn't bald … (is he?)

Unit 2

DEVELOPING SPEAKING *Buying a train ticket*

Exercise 6, p26

Student A:

You want to buy a train ticket

Destination: Greenford

Journey – out: Tomorrow afternoon around 5 pm

Journey – return: Saturday

Unit 2

DEVELOPING SPEAKING *Buying a train ticket*

Exercise 6, p26

Student B:

Gateway to exams: Units 9–10

SPEAKING

Exercises 4 and 5, p134

Student A:

Departures

Greenford

Tomorrow: 5.30pm

Change at London St Pancras and Leicester, arrive 8.45 pm

Single fare: £52.60

Return fare: £55.60

Cash or debit card possible

Platform 4

Departures

Greenford

Tomorrow: 4.15 pm

Change at London Victoria, underground from London Victoria to London Paddington, train from London Paddington to Greenford, arrive 6.40 pm

Single fare: £27.30

Return fare: £30

Cash or debit card possible

Platform 14

Departures

Greenford

Tomorrow: 5.25 pm

Change at London Victoria, underground from London Victoria to London Paddington, train from London Paddington to Greenford, arrive 7.50 pm

Single fare: £25.30

Return fare: £28

Cash or debit card possible

Platform 7

Unit 4

DEVELOPING SPEAKING

Exercise 5, p52

Imagine that your school wants to organise a special event for the end of the school year. Which of these five ideas do you think is the best way to celebrate and why?

SCHOOL CONCERT

END OF YEAR CELEBRATION

DAY OUT IN THE COUNTRY

SPECIAL MEAL

SPORTS DAY

THEATRE SHOW

Unit 1

DEVELOPING SPEAKING

Exercise 6, p14

Student B: Read out the first part of these sentences. Check that your partner says the correct question tag.

1   She hasn't got blue eyes … (has she?)
2   That boy is short … (isn't he?)
3   We can't use mobile phones in class … (can we?)
4   They love rock music … (don't they?)
5   Joe doesn't own a pet … (does he?)

Unit 7

LIFE SKILLS

Exercise 4, p89

Things we can change	Things we can't change
1 Smoking – 5	1 Family history of heart problems
2 High blood pressure – 2	2 Gender
3 Being overweight – 1	3 Age
4 Physical inactivity – 3	
5 High blood cholesterol – 4	
6 Stress – 6	

Gateway to exams: Units 9–10

SPEAKING

Exercises 4 and 5, p134

Student B:

Irregular verbs

Infinitive	Past simple	Past participle	Infinitive	Past simple	Past participle
be	was/were	been	let	let	let
beat	beat	beaten	lie	lay	lain
become	became	become	lose	lost	lost
begin	began	begun	make	made	made
break	broke	broken	mean	meant	meant
bring	brought	brought	meet	met	met
build	built	built	pay	paid	paid
burn	burnt	burnt	put	put	put
buy	bought	bought	read	read	read
catch	caught	caught	ride	rode	ridden
choose	chose	chosen	ring	rang	rung
come	came	come	run	ran	run
cost	cost	cost	say	said	said
cut	cut	cut	see	saw	seen
do	did	done	sell	sold	sold
draw	drew	drawn	send	sent	sent
drink	drank	drunk	set up	set up	set up
drive	drove	driven	shine	shone	shone
eat	ate	eaten	shoot	shot	shot
fall	fell	fallen	show	showed	shown
feel	felt	felt	sing	sang	sung
find	found	found	sit	sat	sat
fly	flew	flown	sleep	slept	slept
forget	forgot	forgotten	speak	spoke	spoken
forgive	forgave	forgiven	speed	sped	sped
get	got	got	spell	spelt	spelt
give	gave	given	spend	spent	spent
go	went	gone	split up	split up	split up
grow	grew	grown	stand up	stood up	stood up
hang out	hung out	hung out	steal	stole	stolen
have	had	had	swim	swam	swum
hear	heard	heard	take	took	taken
hide	hid	hidden	teach	taught	taught
hit	hit	hit	tell	told	told
hurt	hurt	hurt	think	thought	thought
keep	kept	kept	understand	understood	understood
know	knew	known	wake up	woke up	woken up
lay	laid	laid	wear	wore	worn
leave	left	left	win	won	won
learn	learned/learnt	learned/learnt	write	wrote	written

Writing bank

Units 1 and 3

AN INFORMAL EMAIL

p15 (Unit 1), p41 (Unit 3)

Style: Use contractions and the short form of words (e.g. *Thanks*, not *Thank you*). Use interjections like *Oh* and *Well*. We can also use exclamation marks and emoticons (e.g. ☺).

Start: *Hi* or *Dear* and the name (not surname) of the person you are writing to.

Useful expressions: To begin, ask questions like *How are you?*, *How are things?*, *Are you doing exams/ on holiday at the moment?*. Use *By the way* or *Anyway* to change the subject.

End: *That's all for now, Write back soon, All the best*.

DESCRIPTIONS

p15 (Unit 1), p41 (Unit 3)

Style: Adjectives are important to make our descriptions interesting.

Useful expressions: In descriptions, we often use the verb *look*. We can use *look* + adjective (e.g. *He looks _____.*), *look like* + noun/pronoun (e.g. *It looks like _____.*), *look like/ as if* + noun/pronoun + verb (e.g. *She looks as if _____.*).

Useful vocabulary: For people, see p6. For places, see p32.

Useful grammar:

1 We use modifying adverbs to make adjectives stronger or softer in order to give more accurate descriptions. For example, we use *very*, *extremely* and *really* to make 'normal' adjectives stronger. We use *totally*, *absolutely*, *really* and *completely* to make 'extreme' adjectives stronger. We use *quite* and *rather* to make 'normal' adjectives a little softer.

2 To make descriptions more interesting, use *so* + adjective or *such* + (adjective) + noun, e.g., *It was so beautiful.*

Unit 2

A BLOG POST

p27

Style: Informal. Use contractions.

Start: Have a name for your blog. Have a title for the blog post.

Useful expressions: To explain the sequence of events when talking about past events, use: *At first, First of all, Then, Next, In the end, Finally.*

To say when things happened, use: *Yesterday, When, Suddenly, A few minutes/hours/days later, The next day.*

Useful grammar: Here are some ways of giving emphasis to what we write, to make our writing more interesting.

1 Use *What* + (adjective) + noun!, e.g., *What a place!, What a beautiful day!*

2 Use *so* + adjective or *such* + (adjective) + noun, e.g., *It was so beautiful., It's such a big building.*

3 Use *do* and *did* in affirmative sentences, e.g., *We do have tickets for the plane., They did come in the end.*

Unit 4

INFORMAL INVITATIONS

p53

Style: Use contractions and the short form of words (e.g. *Thanks*, not *Thank you*). Use exclamation marks.

Start: *Dear* or *Hi.*

Useful expressions: In invitations: *Please come, I'd love to see you there, It'd be great to see you.* In replies: *Thanks for the invitation, Would you like me to bring anything?* or *I'm really sorry, but I/we won't be able to come* (when you can't accept the invitation).

End: In invitations: *Hope to see you there!, Hope you can make it!, Please write back to tell me if you can come o not.* In replies: *I'm really looking forward to it!, All the best, Best wishes.*

Content: In invitations: say what the event is and why you are celebrating it. Say where and when it will take place. Say if people need to bring something or to confirm if they are coming. In replies: make sure you give all the information that the writer asks for. If you can't go, give a reason.

Units 5 and 10

FORMAL LETTERS AND EMAILS

p67 (Unit 5), p131 (Unit 10)

Style: Do not use contractions.

Start: Write *Dear Mr (Smith)* (for a man), *Dear Mrs (Smith)* (for a married woman), or *Dear Ms (Smith)* (when we make no distinction if a woman is married or not). If you don't know the name of the person write *Dear Sir or Madam.*

Useful expressions in applications: Begin *I am writing to apply for …* or *I am writing in response to the advertisement in ...* Use *I believe I would be perfect for this (scholarship/job) because … , I would be grateful to receive the chance to (study/work) in your (university/company).* Use *I believe* (instead of *I think*), *I would be very grateful* (instead of *I'd like*). End *I look forward to receiving your reply*, or *I look forward to hearing from you.*

Useful expressions in letters of complaint: Begin *I am writing to complain about ….* Use *I demand (a refund/replacement/apology), If I do not hear from you (in the next two weeks), I will take my complaint to a Consumer Advice Centre.* Use *I believe* (instead of *I think*), *I would be very grateful* (instead of *I'd like*). End *I look forward to … receiving your reply/hearing from you.*

Useful linkers: Consequence: *Therefore, and so, As a result*. Time and sequence: *Firstly, Next, Then, In the end*. Contrast: *but, although, However, Nevertheless*. Reason: *because, as, since*. Addition: *In addition, What is more, Furthermore*

End: When we know the name of the person we are writing to, use *Yours sincerely*. When we don't know their name, use *Yours faithfully.*

Content in applications: Begin by saying what you are applying for. Explain why you would be good for this position. Mention any experience you have. Give details of some of your strengths that make you a good candidate.

Content in letters of complaint: Begin by explaining why you are writing. Say where and when the problem began. Give details of the complaint. Demand a solution. Say what action you will take if there is no solution.

Unit 6

A FOR-AND-AGAINST ESSAY

p79

Style: Formal. Do not use contractions.

Useful vocabulary: *advantage, disadvantage*

Useful linkers: Introducing and sequencing arguments: *Firstly, Secondly, Finally*. Adding arguments: *Furthermore, What's more, In addition, Moreover*. Making contrasts: *On the one hand … On the other hand …, In contrast, However, but, although, Nevertheless*. Consequence: *Therefore, and so, As a result*. Reason: *because, as, since*. Opinions: *In my opinion, Personally I think … As far as I'm concerned, In my view*. Concluding: *In conclusion, To sum up, All in all*.

Content:

Paragraph 1: State the topic of the composition using general statements

Paragraph 2: Make points for (or against)

Paragraph 3: Make points against (or for)

Paragraph 4: Conclusion – restate the most important arguments and give your own opinion

Unit 7

A MAGAZINE ARTICLE

p93

Style: Magazine articles should not be very formal or informal. They can have titles. It can be very effective to begin with questions to involve the reader, or to use imperatives to create excitement.

Useful linkers: See Unit 6 above.

Content:

Paragraph 1: Introduction saying what your article is about.

Paragraph 2: Main point(s).

Paragraph 3: Additional points

Paragraph 4: Conclusion – restate the most important points and your opinion(s)

Unit 8

A FILM REVIEW

p105

Useful vocabulary: Films: *happy ending, main character, play the role of, plot, scene, screenplay, special effects, the acting, to star*. Positive adjectives to describe films: *amazing, exciting, funny, hilarious, great, inspiring, interesting, spectacular*. Negative adjectives to describe films: *awful, boring, stupid, uninspiring*. Types of film: *action, animated film, comedy, drama, fantasy, horror, musical, science fiction, thriller, war, western*.

Useful expressions: To give your opinion, use *Personally, I think, As far as I'm concerned, In my opinion, I agree/disagree with ...* To explain and justify your opinion, use *This is because, For example*. To give recommendations: *I would/wouldn't recommend you to see this film because …* To give a conclusion, use *To sum up, In conclusion*.

Useful grammar:

1 We use <u>modifying adverbs</u> to make adjectives stronger or softer in order to give more accurate descriptions. For example, we use *very, extremely* and *really* to make 'normal' adjectives (e.g. *good, bad*) stronger. We use *totally, absolutely, really* and *completely* to make 'extreme' adjectives (e.g. *fantastic, awful*) stronger. We use *quite* and *rather* to make 'normal' adjectives a little softer.

2 To make descriptions more interesting, use *so* + adjective or *such* + (adjective) + noun, e.g., *It was so beautiful, He's such a great friend*.

Content: Suggested paragraph plan

Paragraph 1: Basic information about the film

Paragraph 2: A summary of the plot or story

Paragraph 3: Your opinion of the film

Paragraph 4: A recommendation to see the film

Unit 9

A STORY

p119

Useful expressions: To say when things happened, use, for example: *Last weekend, Two weeks ago, On Friday, On Saturday night*.

Useful linkers: To explain the sequence of events, use *At first, First of all, Next, Then, After that, Later, Suddenly, Finally, In the end*.

Useful grammar: Narrative tenses

1 Past simple. We use it to tell the main events and actions in the story.

2 Past continuous. We use it to describe scenes, to say what activity was in progress when another interrupted it.

3 Past perfect. We use it for the background of the story, to talk about actions that happened before other actions in the past.

4 *used to*. We use it to talk about past habits.

5 *must/may/might/can't have*. We use these to make speculations or deductions about what happened.

Content: Suggested paragraph plan:

First paragraph: Explain where and when the story begins. Introduce the characters.

Middle paragraphs: Explain the main events in the story.

Last paragraph: Explain how the story ended and what the consequences were.

CHECKING YOUR WRITING

Check for mistakes with:

- punctuation
- capital letters
- word order
- spelling
- tenses
- vocabulary
- missing words
- agreement between the subject and verb (e.g. *He works* not *He work*.)
- style
- content

Macmillan Education
4 Crinan Street
London N1 9XW
A division of Macmillan Publishers Limited

Companies and representatives throughout the world

ISBN 978-0-230-47093-4

Text © David Spencer 2016
Design and illustration © Macmillan Publishers Limited 2016

The author has asserted his right to be identified as the author of this work in accordance with the Copyright, Designs and Patents Act 1988.

This edition published 2016
First edition published in 2011

Designed by emc design ltd
Illustrated by A Corazón Abierto (Sylvie Poggio Artists Agency) pp 70, 76; Lisa Hunt (The Organisation) pp 25, 46, 98, 129; Javier Joaquin (The Organisation) pp 19, 21, 82.
Cover design by emc design ltd and Macmillan Publishers Ltd
Cover photography by Getty Images/Damir Cudic (teenagers), Getty Images/Tai Power Seeff (castle)
Picture research by Emily Taylor

Author's acknowledgements
I would like to give a big thank you to the whole Macmillan team in the UK for their dedication, hard work, and enthusiasm throughout the writing of this course. Thanks also to all the other Macmillan teams around the world for their help, encouragement and always making me feel welcome. Very special thanks to Colegio Europeo Aristos in Getafe, Spain. The daily contact with my students there continues to be a main source of inspiration and I am sincerely grateful to every one of my students, past and present. Massive thanks, as always, to Gemma, Jamie and Becky for their unending love and support.

This book is dedicated to Emily Rosser.

The publishers would like to thank the staff and pupils at the following schools in Mexico and Spain for helping us so enthusiastically with our research for the course:
Concha Campos, IES Burgo de Las Rozas, Las Rozas, Madrid; Félix Gaspar, IES Las Encinas; Villanueva de la Cañada, Madrid; Cristina Moisen, IES Joaquín Turina, Madrid; Colegio Montessori Cuautitlán; Colegio Conrad Gessner; Colegio Erasmo de Rotterdam; Colegio Kanic, Centro Educativo Erich Fromm; Universidad Franco Mexicana; Centro Pedagógico María Montessori de Ecatepec; Instituto Cultural; Escuela Maestro Manuel Acosta; Liceo Sakbé De México.

The publishers would also like to thank all those who reviewed or piloted the first edition of Gateway:
Benjamin Affolter, Evelyn Andorfer, Anna Ciereszynska, Regina Culver, Anna Dabrowska, Justyna Deja, Ondrej Dosedel, Lisa Durham, Dagmar Eder, Eva Ellederovan, H Fouad, Sabrina Funes, Luiza Gervescu, Isabel González Bueno, Jutta Habringer, Stela Halmageanu, Marta Hilgier, Andrea Hutterer, Nicole Ioakimidis, Mag. Annemarie Kammerhofer, Irina Kondrasheva, Sonja Lengauer, Gabriela Liptakova, Andrea Littlewood, María Cristina Maggi, Silvia Miranda Barbara Nowak, Agnieska Orlińska, Anna Orlowska, María Paula Palou, Marta Piotrowska, N Reda, Katharina Schatz, Roswitha Schwarz, Barbara Ścibor, Katarzyna Sochacka, Joanna Spoz, Monica Srtygner, Marisol Suppan, Stephanie Sutter, Halina Tyliba, Prilipko, Maria Vizgina, Vladyko, Pia Wimmer, Katarzyna Zadrożna-Attia and Katarzyna Zaremba-Jaworska.

The author and publishers would like to thank the following for permission to reproduce their photographs:
Alamy/Age Fotostock pp86, 147, Alamy/Blend Images p38(2.3), Alamy/CandyBox Photography p79(3), Alamy/Chronicle p116(br), Alamy/Cultura p39(tr), Alamy/Ian Dagnall pp40(b), 41, Alamy/DPA Picture Alliance p7(cl), Alamy/Elena Elenaphotos21 p8(bl), Alamy/Gallo Images p116(tl), Alamy/Geogphotos p32(1a), Alamy/Hisham Ibrahim p148(cr), Alamy/Imagebroker p117(cr), Alamy/itravel p18(5d), Alamy/Juice Images p79(1), Alamy/Stuart Kelly p26(tl), Alamy/Lebrecht Music and Arts Photo Library p24(tm), Alamy/MBI pp52(2), 78(2), Alamy/NASA Archive p30(tl), Alamy/The National Trust p67, Alamy/Parker Photography p31, Alamy/Ian Patrick p19(station), Alamy/PhotoAlto p22(3), Alamy/Pixoi Ltd p103, Alamy/Wolfgang Polzer p65, Alamy/Robert Harding World Imagery p32(1b), Alamy/Andres Rodriguez p38(2.5), Alamy/Alex Segre p18(5b), Alamy/Shotshop p38(2.2), Alamy/Spaces Images p18(5a), Alamy/Tetra Images p32(5b), Alamy/Eva Worobiec p18(5e), Alamy/Xinhua p134; Bridgeman Art/Early Sunday Morning, 1930 (oil on canvas) by Hopper, Edward (1882–1967) Whitney Museum of American Art p100(1); Chetwoods Phoenix Towers LNC Image p33(cr); Corbis p114(red brick background), Corbis/2/Rayman/Ocean p104(d), Corbis/Scott Audette/Reuters p64(b), Corbis/Bettmann p90(cl), Corbis/Phil Boorman p78(1), Corbis/Regis Duvignau/Reuters p90(br), Corbis/Stefano Gilera p53, Corbis/Hero Images pp64(c), 66(br), 84(tr), Corbis/Hill Street Studios/Blend Images p148(tl), Corbis/Paul Hilton/EPA p22(1), Corbis/Steve Hix/Somos Images p6(tr), Corbis/Hiya Images p51, Corbis/I Love Images p83, Corbis/Image Source p32(5a), Corbis/Image Source/Ocean p104(b), Corbis/Imaginechina p102(cr), Corbis/Erik Isakson/Tetra Images p148(cm), Corbis/Mitsuaki Iwago/Minden Pictures p13(br), Corbis/G Jackson/Arcaid p32(c), Corbis/JLP/Jose L Pelaez p78(cr), Corbis/Sean Justice p104(a), Corbis/Sebastian Kaulitzki/Science Photo Library p88–89(background), Corbis/K Kreder p117(cl), Corbis/Matilda Lindeblad/The Food Passionates p47, Corbis/Monkey Business Ltd p15(br), Corbis/Mother Image p129(a), Corbis/Moxie Productions/Blend Images p75, Corbis/Reuters p50(1b), Corbis/Stephane Ruet/Sygma p85, Corbis/Sampics p108(tl), Corbis/Bob Strong/Reuters p118(tl), Corbis/Ted Spiegel p72, Corbis/Viosin/Phanie p124, Corbis/Barbara Walton/epa p92, Corbis/Bernd Weissbrod/dpa p97(2), Corbis/Andrew Winning/Reuters p91; Martin Creed/Work No. 8502008 Runners Installation at Tate Britain, London, UK, 2008 Courtesy of Martin Creed/Hauser & Wirth/Photo - Hugo Glendinning p108(cr);

Cy Twombly Foundation/Twombly 2010 Camino Real (II) p100(3); Getty Images/AFP p110(c), Getty Images/Scott Barbour p148(br), Getty Images/Don Bayley pp20, 115(bl), Getty Images/Blend Images pp38(2.1), 89(br), 93, 128, Getty Images/Bloomberg p50(1c), Getty Images/Blue Jean images p10(bl), Getty Images/Brand New Images p79(2), Getty Images/Brand X Pictures p109, Getty Images/ChinaFotoPress p102(tl), Getty Images/Comstock p77, Getty Images/Cultura pp49(tm), 59(bl), 64(a), 110(d), 129(e), Getty Images/Cultura Travel/Richard Seymour p35, Getty Images/Don Bayley p115, Getty Images/Dorling Kindersley p14, Getty Images/Josh Edelson/AFP p45(tmr, cl), Getty Images/Flickr RF p23, 40(a), Getty Images/Fotosearch RF p78(br), Getty Images/Fuse p130, Getty Images/Christopher Futcher p9, Getty Images/Tim Graham p119(br), Getty Images/Jorg Greuel p27(beach), Getty Images/Rosie Hallam p114(bl), Getty Images/iStockphoto p19(sandwich), Getty Images/iStockphoto/Marrakesh p19(coffee), Getty Images/Jack Hill/AFP p111(tl), Getty Images/Hulton Archive p110(f), Getty Images/Chris Jackson pp73, 118(br) Getty Images/Bernard Jaubert p148(bl), Getty Images/Christopher Lee p110(e), Getty Images/Ron Levine p11(3), Getty Images/LOOK p96(cl), Getty Images/Lonely Planet Images pp18(5c), 56, Getty Images/Maodesign p40(c), Getty Images/Maremagnum p112, Getty Images/Tom McGhee p22(2), Getty Images/Moodboard RF p84(cr), Getty Images/John Moore/Banksy, New York 2013 p99, Getty Images/Ethan Myerson p113, Getty Images/PeopleImages.com p38(tl), Getty Images/Purestock pp22(4), 129(b), Getty Images/Quinn Rooney p118(tr), Getty Images/Soundimageplus p19(tr), Getty Images/Stone Sub p104(c), Getty Images/Karwai Tang p6(b), Getty Images/Leanne Temme p52(3), Getty Images/Maria Toutoudaki p126–127(background), Getty Images/Underwood Archives p24(tl), Getty Images/Uppercut p122(bl), Getty Images/Hilal Ustuk/Anadolu Agency p97(1), Getty Images/Abel Mitja Varela p61(br), Getty Images/Ian Walton p6(c), Getty Images/Westend61 p71(cm), Getty Images/Vernon Wiley p7(tm); ImageSource p110(a); Jupiterimages p13(cl); Photodisc p48(tl), PhotoDisc/Digital Vision p13(tl); The Picture Desk/Temple Hill Entertainment p105; Plainpicture/Jim Erickson p148(cl); Rex Features/APA-PictureDesk p7(br), Rex Features/Shutterstock/Page Images p6(a); Scala Images/Lichtenstein Roy Drowning Girl, 1963 © Estate of Roy Lichtenstein/DACS 2015 p100(2); Soylent/Image courtesy of Rob Rhinehart p45(tr); Stephen Ritz/Image courtesy of Stephen Ritz p59(tm, br); Stockbyte p32(d); Thinkstock pp22(background stamps), 36(tm), 48(tablecloth), 70(tm), 74, 88(tr), 126–127(money doodles), Thinkstock/AAA-pictures p76, Thinkstock/Anatoliy Babiy p22(tm), Thinkstock/Matthew Dixon p40(d), Thinkstock/Noel Hendrickson p123(tm), Thinkstock/Getty Images/BananaStock p11(1), Thinkstock/Getty Images/Fuse p64(d), Thinkstock/Getty Images/Hemera pp10(tm), 21, 114(tl), Thinkstock/Hemera Technologies pp10(cl), 38(2.4), Thinkstock/Getty Images/iStockphoto pp6(tm), 10(background), 11(skates, camera, 2), 11(4), 12, 13(cm, tr, bl, tm), 15(tr), 18(tm, 1a, 1b, 1c, 1d), 22(background), 23(bl), 26(br), 27(ryan), 30(tr, tm), 33(tc), 36(background), 44(tr), 44(1a, 1b, 1c), 48–49(background, chef, pepper, fork, steak and chips, salad), 50(1a, 1d), 52(1, 4, 5), 56(tr, tm), 58(tr, tm), 61(tl), 62(mouse), 66(tr), 70(tr, cm, cr), 71(bm, cl, tl), 74(mug, brick, paper balls), 84(tm), 88(tm), 88(br), 96(guitar, paint, book, background), 100–101(background), 100(tm, bottom), 101(frame, paint splashes), 110(tr), 114(tr, cr, b, brick background), 115(poster tl, tr, bl, br), 119(tr), 122(tm), 123(cr), 126(background wood, coins), 129(c, d), 131, Thinkstock/Anthony Harris p114(tl), Thinkstock/Getty Images/iStockphoto/Vasiliy Yakobchuk p62(tr), Thinkstock/Getty Images/Wavebreak Media p62(bl), Thinkstock/Jack Hollingsworth p8(br), Thinkstock/istock/alice-photo p114(bc), Thinkstock/istock/cleanpies p115(tlc), Thinkstock/istock/peshkov pp114–115 (background), Thinkstock/Jupiterimages p48(tr), Thinkstock/Jit Lim p33(tr), Thinkstock/Koosen p114(tr), Thinkstock/Moodboard p44(tm), 122(tr) Thinkstock/Photos.com p111(cm), Thinkstock/Stockbyte pp110(tm), 110(b), Thinkstock/Zoonar RF p48(squares of food).

The author and publishers are grateful for permission to reprint the following copyright material:
Extract from Notes from a Small Island by Bill Bryson (p19). Published by Black Swan. Reprinted by permission of the Random House Group Limited.
Extract from 'Yakutsk: Journey to the coldest city on Earth' by Shaun Walker (p56). Originally published in The Independent on 21 January 2008 © The Independent, 2008. Reprinted with permission. www.theindependent.co.uk
Extract from 'My life in travel: Chris Hadfield' by Laura Holt (p30). Originally published in The Independent on 22 February 2014 © The Independent, 2014. Reprinted with permission. www.theindependent.co.uk
Extract from 'This man thinks he never has to eat again' by Monica Heisey (p45). Originally published in Vice on 13 March 2013 © Vice, 2013.
Extract about Green Bronx Machine © Stephen Ritz, 2015 (p59). Reprinted with permission.
Extract from 'The 2005 Ig Nobel prize winners' © Improbable Research, 2015 (p71). Reprinted with permission.
Extract about 'Coronary Heart Disease' (pp88–89) reproduced under the Open Government Licence v.3.0 www.nhs.uk
Extract from Mo Farah (p91) taken from mofarah.com © mofarah.com
Extract from 'Stephen Wiltshire, the human camera who drew London from memory' by Stephen Adams (p97). Originally published in the Daily Telegraph on 02 April 2008 © Telegraph Group Limited, 2008. Reprinted with permission. www.telegraph.co.uk
Extract from 'Ghosts of the past: 5 haunted royal residences' (p113). Originally published on Visit Britain Blog on 17 May 2013 © Visit Britain, 2015.
Extract about Youth Parliament United Kingdom (p114) © UK Youth Parliament, 2015. Reprinted with permission.
Extract from 'Your Life' by John Foster (p126–127) © John Foster, 2009. Originally published by Collins Educational.
Extract from article on Elizabeth I by Christopher Stevens (p111). Originally published in The Daily Mail on 08 June 2013 © The Daily Mail 2013. Reprinted with permission. www.dailymail.co.uk

These materials may contain links for third party websites. We have no control over, and are not responsible for, the contents of such third party websites. Please use care when accessing them.

Printed and bound in Thailand

2020 2019 2018 2017 2016
10 9 8 7 6 5 4 3 2 1